THIS IS NOT PROPAGANDA

THIS IS NOT PROPAGANDA

ADVENTURES IN THE WAR AGAINST REALITY

Алиса ик
Саша,
Энергии!

PETER POMERANTSEV

PublicAffairs

New York

PublicAffairs
Hachette Book Group
1290 Avenue of the Americas, New York, NY 10104
www.publicaffairsbooks.com
@Public_Affairs

Printed in the United States of America

First Trade Paperback Edition: May 2020
Published by PublicAffairs, an imprint of Perseus Books, LLC, a subsidiary of Hachette Book Group, Inc. The PublicAffairs name and logo is a trademark of the Hachette Book Group.

The Hachette Speakers Bureau provides a wide range of authors for speaking events. To find out more, go to www.hachettespeakersbureau .com or call (866) 376-6591.

The publisher is not responsible for websites (or their content) that are not owned by the publisher.

Print book interior design by Linda Mark.

Library of Congress Cataloging-in-Publication Data
Names: Pomerantsev, Peter, author.
Title: This is not propaganda: adventures in the war against reality / Peter Pomerantsev.
Description: New York, NY: PublicAffairs, [2019] | Includes bibliographical references and index.
Identifiers: LCCN 2019003027| ISBN 9781541762114 (hardcover: alk. paper) | ISBN 9781541762138 (ebook)
Subjects: LCSH: Information society—Political aspects. | Truthfulness and falsehood—Political aspects. | Propaganda. | Pomerantsev, Peter.
Classification: LCC HM851 .P6556 2019 | DDC 303.48/33—dc23
LC record available at https://lccn.loc.gov/2019003027

ISBNs: 978-1-5417-6211-4 (hardcover), 978-1-5417-6213-8 (ebook), 978-1-5417-6212-1 (paperback)

LSC-C

10 9 8 7 6 5 4 3 2 1

CONTENTS

PREFACE: TELEGRAM!

He came out of the sea and was arrested on the beach. Two men in suits standing over his clothes as he returned from his swim. They ordered him to get dressed quickly, pull his trousers over his wet trunks. On the drive, the trunks were still wet, shrinking and turning cold, leaving a damp patch on his trousers and the back seat. He had to keep them on during the interrogation. There he was, trying to keep up a dignified façade, but the dank trunks made him squirm. It struck him they had done it on purpose. They were well-versed in this sort of thing, these mid-ranking KGB men, masters of the small-time humiliation, the micro mind game.

He wondered why they had arrested him here, in Odessa, and not where he lived, in Kiev. Then he realized that they had wanted a few days by the seaside. In between interrogations, they would take him to the beach to go swimming themselves. One would sit with him while the other would bathe. One time an artist took out an easel *and began to paint the three of them. The colonel and major grew nervous. They were KGB, and weren't meant to have their images recorded during an operation.* "Go have a look at what he's drawing," *they ordered their prisoner. He went over and had a look. Now it was his turn to mess with them a little.* "He's not drawn a good likeness of me, but you're coming out very true to life."

He had been detained for "proliferating copies of harmful literature to friends and acquaintances"—books censored for telling the truth about the Soviet Gulag (Solzhenitsyn) or for being written by exiles (Nabokov). His case was reported in the Chronicle of Current Events. The Chronicle was how Soviet dissidents documented suppressed facts about political arrests, interrogations, searches, trials, beatings, and abuses in prison. Information was gathered by word of mouth, or smuggled out of labor camps in tiny self-made polyethylene capsules, which were swallowed and then shat out, typed up, photographed in dark rooms, then passed, person to person, hidden in the pages of books and diplomatic pouches until it could reach the West, handed to human rights groups, broadcast on the BBC World Service, Voice of America, Radio Liberty.

The Chronicle was known for its restrained style. This is how it reported his arrest:

"He was questioned by KGB Colonel V.P. Men'shikov and KGB Major V.N. Mel'gunov. He rejected all charges as baseless and unproven. He refused to give evidence about his friends and acquaintances. For all six days of the interrogation, they were housed in the Hotel New Moscow."

When the colonel would leave, the major would pull out a book of chess puzzles and work on them, chewing the end of a pencil. At first their prisoner wondered if this was some clever mind game. Then he realized the major was just killing time.

After six days, he was permitted to go home to Kiev but the investigation continued. While he was on the way home after work at the library, a black car pulled up and he was taken for more interrogations.

During that time life went on. His fiancée conceived. They married. At the back of the reception hall lurked a KGB photographer.

He moved in with his wife's family, in a flat opposite the Goloseevsky Park, where his father-in-law had put up palaces of cages for his dozens of canaries, an aviary of throbbing feathers darting against the backdrop of the park. Every time the doorbell rang, he would start, afraid that it was the KGB, and begin to burn any private letters and manuscripts that could possibly be used against him. The canaries beat their wings in a panic-stricken flutter. He rose at dawn, gently turned the Spidola radio to ON, pushed the dial to shortwave, wiggled and waved the antenna to dispel the fog of jamming, climbed on chairs and tables to get the best reception, steering the dial in an acoustic slalom between transmissions of East German pop and Soviet military bands, pressed his ear tight to the speaker and, through the hiss and crackle, made his way to the magical words: "This is London," "This is Washington." He was listening for news about arrests. He read the futurist poet Velimir Khlebnikov's 1921 essay "Radio of the Future," in which Khlebnikov predicts that "radio will forge the unbroken chain of the global soul and fuse mankind."

The net closed around his circle. Grisha was taken to the woods and roughed up. Olga was accused of being a prostitute and locked up in a VD clinic with actual prostitutes to make the point. Geli was taken to remand prison and refused treatment for so long that he died.

Everyone prepared for the worst. His mother-in-law taught him a secret code based on sausages: "If I bring sausages sliced right to left, it means we've been able to get out news of your arrest to the West, and it's been broadcast on the radio. If I slice them left to right, it means we failed."

"It sounds like something out of an old joke or a bad film but it's nevertheless true," he would write later. "When the KGB comes at dawn, and you mumble drowsily, 'who's there?' they often shout, 'telegram!' You proceed in semi-sleep, trying not to wake up too much so you can still go back to a snug dream. 'One moment,' you moan, pull on the nearest trousers, dig out some change to pay the messenger, open the door. And the most painful part is not that they have come for you, or that they got you up so early, but that you, like some small boy, fell for the lie about a telegram. You squeeze in your hot palm the suddenly sweaty change, holding back tears of humiliation."

At 8 a.m. on September 30, 1977, in between interrogations, their child was born. My grandmother wanted me to be called Pinhas after her grandfather. My parents wanted Theodore. I ended up named Piotr. One of the first of several renegotiations of my name.

FORTY YEARS HAVE PASSED SINCE MY PARENTS WERE PURSUED BY THE KGB over the simple right to read, write, and listen to what they chose and say what they wanted. Today, the world they hoped for, where censorship would fall like the Berlin Wall, can seem much closer: we live in what some academics call an era of "information abundance." But the assumptions that underlay the struggles for rights and freedoms in the twentieth century—between citizens armed with truth and information, and regimes with their censors and secret police—have been turned upside down. We now have more information than ever before—but it hasn't brought only the benefits we expected.

More information was supposed to mean more freedom to stand up to the powerful. But it also has given the powerful new ways to crush and silence dissent. More information was supposed to mean a more informed debate, but we seem less capable of deliberation than ever. More information was supposed to mean mutual understanding across borders, but it has also made possible new and more subtle forms of conflict and subversion. We live in a world of influence operations run amok, where the means of manipulation have gone forth and multiplied, a world of dark ads, psy-ops, hacks, bots, soft facts, fake news, deep fakes, brainwashing, trolls, ISIS, Putin, Trump.

Forty years after my father's interrogations by the KGB, I find myself following the palest of imprints of my parents' journey, though with none of their courage, risk-taking, or certainty. As I write this—and given the economic turbulence this might not be the case when you read it—I'm working on a program in an institute at a London university that looks at the newer breeds of influence campaigns, what might casually be referred to as "propaganda": a term so fraught and fractured in its interpretation—defined by some as deception, and by others as the neutral activity of propagation—that I avoid using it.

I should add that I'm not an academic and this is not in an academic work (although I quote some academics extensively). I am a lapsed television producer, and though I continue to write articles and sometimes present radio programs, I now often find myself looking at my own media world askance, at what it's wrought and how it can be fixed. I meet Twitter revolutionaries and pop-up populists, trolls, and elves, "behavioral change" salesmen and Infowar charlatans, Jihadi fan-boys, Identitarians, truth cops, and bot herders. Then I bring all I have learned back to the squat, hexagonal, concrete tower where my office has its temporary home, take all the lessons I've learned and shape them into sensible "Conclusions and Recommendations" for neatly formatted PDF reports and PowerPoint presentations, which diagnose and then propose remedies to the flood of disinformation and deception, "fake news," "information war," and the "war on information."

Remedies to heal what, however? The neat little bullet points of the reports I work on assume that there really is a coherent system they can amend, that a few technical recommendations to new information technologies can fix everything. Yet the problems go far deeper. When I present my findings to the representatives of the waning Liberal Democratic Order, the one formed in no little part out of the conflicts of the Cold War, I am struck by how lost-looking they seem. Politicians no longer know what their parties represent; bureaucrats no longer know where power is located; billionaires' foundations advocate for an "open society" they can no longer quite define.

Big Words that once seemed swollen with meaning—democracy and freedom, "the people," Europe, and the West—have been so thoroughly left behind by life that they seem like empty husks, the last warmth and light draining out of them, or like computer files I have forgotten the password to and cannot access. The very language we use to describe ourselves—"left" and "right," "liberal" and "conservative"—has been rendered almost meaningless. And it's not just conflicts or elections that are affected. I see people I have known my whole life slip away from me on social media, reposting conspiracies from sources I have never heard of, some sort of internet undercurrent pulling whole families apart, as if we never really knew each other, as if the algorithms know more about us than we do, as if we are becoming subsets of our own data, which is rearranging our relations and identities with its own logic, or in the cause of someone else's interests we can't even see. The grand vessels of old media—books, television, newspapers, and radio—that had contained and controlled identity and meaning, who we were and how we talked with one another, how we explained the world to our children, talked about our past, defined war and peace, news and opinion, satire and seriousness, right and left, right and wrong, true, false, real, unreal—these vessels have cracked and burst, breaking up the old architecture of what relates to whom, who speaks to whom and how, magnifying, shrinking, distorting all proportions, sending us in disorientating spirals where words lose shared meanings. I hear the same phrases in Odessa, Manila, Mexico City, New Jersey: "There's so much information, disinformation, so much of everything I don't know what's true anymore." Often, I hear the phrase, "I feel the world is moving beneath my feet." I catch myself thinking, "I feel that everything that I thought solid is now unsteady, liquid."

This book explores the wreckage, searches for sparks of sense that can be salvaged from it, rising from the dank corners of the internet where trolls torture their victims, passing through the tussles over the stories that make sense of our societies, and ultimately trying to understand how we define ourselves.

Chapter One takes us from the Philippines to the Gulf of Finland, where we will learn how to break people with new information instruments, in ways subtler than the old ones used by the KGB.

Chapter Two moves from the Western Balkans to Latin America and the European Union, where we will learn how to break resistance movements with new information tactics, in ways subtler than in the twentieth century.

Chapter Three explores how one country can destroy another almost without touching it, blurring the contrast between war and peace, "domestic" and "international"—and how the most dangerous element may be the idea of "information war" itself.

Chapter Four explores how the demand for a factual politics relies on a certain idea of progress and the future, and how the collapse of that idea made mass murder and abuse more possible.

In Chapter Five, I argue that in this flux, politics becomes a struggle over the construction of identity. Everyone from religious extremists to the populists who want to create new versions of "the people"—even in Britain, a country where identity always seemed so fixed—now wants to use the new information system to redefine you.

In Chapter Six, I look for the future—in China and in Chernivtsi.

Throughout the book, I travel, sometimes, but not only, through space. The physical and political maps delineating continents, countries, and oceans, the maps I grew up with, can be less important than the new maps of information flows. These network maps are generated by data scientists. They call the process "surfacing." You take a key word, a message, a narrative, and cast it into the ever-expanding pool of the world's data. The data scientist then "surfaces" the people, media outlets, social media accounts, bots, trolls, and cyborgs pushing or interacting with those key words, narratives, and messages.

These network maps, which look like fields of pin-mold or telescope photographs of distant galaxies, show how outdated our geographic definitions have become, revealing unexpected constellations where anyone from anywhere can influence everyone everywhere. A "rooted cosmopolitan" sitting at home in Scotland guides activists away from police during protests in the Middle East. ISIS supporters disguise campaigns for the Islamic state as iPhone ads.

Russia, with its social media squadrons, haunts these maps. Not because it is the force that can still move earth and heaven as it could in the Cold War, but because the Kremlin's rulers are particularly adept at gaming elements of this new age, or at the very least are good at getting everyone to talk about how good they are, which could be the most important trick of all. As I will explain, this is not entirely accidental: precisely because they had lost the Cold War, Russian spin doctors and media manipulators managed to adapt to the new world quicker than anyone in the entity once known as the "West." Between 2001 and 2010, I lived in Moscow, where I saw close up the same tactics of control and the same pathologies in public opinion that have since sprouted everywhere.

But as this book travels through information flows, across networks and countries, it also looks back in time, to the story of my parents, to the Cold War. This is not a family memoir as such; I am concerned only with how my family's story intersects with my subject. This is in part to see how the ideals of the past have fallen apart in the present, and what, if anything, can still be gleaned from them. When all is swirling, I find myself instinctively looking back, searching for a connection to the past to find a way to think about the future.

But as I researched and wrote these sections of family history, I was struck by something else—the extent to which our private thoughts, creative impulses, and senses of self are shaped by information forces greater than ourselves. If there is one thing I've been impressed with while browsing the shelves of the library of my university, it is that one has to look beyond just news and politics to also consider poetry, schools, and the language of bureaucracy and leisure to understand the formation of attitudes. This process is sometimes more evident in my family, because the dramas and ruptures of our lives make it easier to see where those information forces, like vast weather systems, begin and end.

CHAPTER ONE

CITIES OF TROLLS

Freedom of speech versus censorship was one of the clearer confrontations of the twentieth century. After the Cold War, freedom of speech appeared to have emerged victorious in many places. But what if the powerful can now use "information abundance" to find new ways of stifling you, flipping the meaning of freedom of speech on its head to crush dissent, while always leaving enough anonymity to be able to claim deniability?

THE DISINFORMATION ARCHITECTURE

Consider the Philippines. In 1977, as my parents were experiencing the pleasures of the KGB, the Philippines were ruled by Colonel Ferdinand Marcos, a US-backed military dictator, under whose regime, a quick search of the Amnesty International website informs me, 3,257 political prisoners were killed, thirty-five thousand tortured, and seventy thousand incarcerated. Marcos had a theatrical philosophy of the role torture could play in pacifying society. Instead of being merely "disappeared," 77 percent of those killed were displayed at roadsides as warnings to others. Victims might have their brains removed, for example, and their empty skulls stuffed with their underpants. Or they could be cut into pieces so that one would pass body parts on the way to the market.[1]

Marcos's regime fell in 1986 in the face of mass protests, America relinquishing its support, and parts of the army defecting. Millions came out on the streets. It was meant to be a new day: an end to corruption, an end to the abuse of human rights. Marcos was exiled and lived his last years in Hawaii.

Today, Manila greets you with sudden gusts of rotting fish and popcorn smells, sewage, and deep-fry oil, which leave you retching on the street. Actually, street is the wrong word. There are few in the sense of broad pavements where you can stroll. Instead, there are thin ledges that run along the rims of malls and skyscrapers, where you inch along beside the lava of traffic. Between the malls, the city drops into deep troughs of slums, where at night the homeless sleep wrapped in silver foil, their feet sticking out, flopped over in alleys between bars with midget boxing and karaoke parlors where you can hire troupes of girls, in dresses so tight they cling to their thighs like pincers, to sing Korean pop songs with you.

During the day you negotiate the spaces between mall, slum, and skyscraper along elevated networks of crowded narrow walkways suspended in midair that wind in between the multi-story motorways, where you duck your head to miss the buttresses of flyovers, flinch from the barrage of honks and sirens below, suddenly find yourself at eye level with an oncoming train or eye-to-eye with a woman eating Spam on one of the colossal advertising billboards. The billboards are everywhere, separating slum from skyscraper. Between 1898 and 1946, the Philippines was under US administration; US navy bases have been present ever since, and US military food items have become delicacies. On one poster a happy housewife feeds her handsome husband tuna chunks from a can; elsewhere a picture of a dripping, roasting ham sits over an actual steaming river where street kids swim; behind them an electric sign flashes Jesus Will Save You. This is a Catholic country: three hundred years of Spanish colonialism preceded America's fifty ("We had three hundred years of the church and fifty years of Hollywood," Filipinos joke). The malls have churches with guards to keep out the poor. A city of twenty-two million with almost no notion of common public space. The interiors of the malls are perfumed by overpowering air-conditioners: lavender in the cheaper ones with their fields of fast-food outlets; a lighter lemon scent for the more sophisticated. This makes them smell like toilets, so the smell of the latrine never leaves you, whether it's sewage outside or the malls inside.

Soon you start noticing the selfies. Everyone is at it. The sweaty guy in greasy flip-flops riding the metal canister of a public bus; the Chinese girls waiting for their cocktails in the malls. The Philippines has the world's highest use of selfies. It has the world's highest per capita use of social media. It has the highest use of text messages. Some put it down to the importance of personal and family connections to get by in the face of ineffective government. The selfies aren't necessarily narcissistic: you trust people whose faces you can see.

And with the rise of social media, the Philippines has become a capital for a new breed of digital era manipulation.

I meet with "P" in one of the oases of malls next to sky-blue windowed skyscrapers. He insists that I can't use his name, but you can tell he's torn, desperate for recognition for the campaigns he can't take credit for. He's in his early twenties, dressed like a member of a Korean boy band, and there's almost no change in his always heightened emotions, whether he's talking about getting a president elected or his Instagram account registered with a blue tick (which denotes status).

"There's a happiness to me if I'm able to control the people. Maybe it's a bad thing. It satisfies my ego, something deeper in me . . . it's like becoming a god in the digital side," he exclaims. But it doesn't sound creepy, more like someone playing the role of the baddy in a musical farce.

He began his online career at the age of fifteen, creating an anonymous page that encouraged people to speak about their romantic experiences. "Tell me about your worst break up," he would ask. "What was your hottest date?" He shows me one of the sites: it has more than three million members.

While still at school he created new groups, each one with a different profile: one dedicated to joy, another to mental strength. He was only sixteen when he began to be approached by corporations who would ask him to sneak in mentions of their products. He honed his technique. For a week we would get a community to talk about love, for example, whom they cared about the most. Then he would move the conversation to fear for your loved ones, fear of losing someone. Then he would slide in a product: take this medicine and it will help extend the lives of loved ones.

By the age of twenty, he claims he had fifteen million followers across all the platforms. The modest middle-class boy from the provinces could suddenly afford his own condo in a Manila skyscraper.

After advertising, his next challenge was politics. At that point political PR was all about getting journalists to write what you want. What if you could shape the whole conversation through social media?

He pitched his approach to several parties but the only candidate who would take P on was Rodrigo Duterte, an outsider who looked to social media as a new, cheap route to victory. One of Duterte's main selling points as a candidate was fighting drug crime. He even boasted of driving in a motorcycle and shooting drug dealers when he was mayor of Davao City, in the deep south of the country.

At the time, P was already in college. He was attending lectures on the "little Albert" experiment from the 1920s, in which a toddler was exposed to frightening sounds whenever he saw a white rat and how this led to him being afraid of all furry animals.[2] P says this inspired him to try something similar for Duterte.

First P created a series of Facebook groups in different cities. They were innocuous enough, just discussion boards of what was on in town. The trick was to put them in the local dialect, of which there are hundreds in the Philippines. After six months, each group had in the range of one hundred thousand members. Then his administrators would start posting one local crime story per day, every day, at the same time (peak traffic, early evening). The crime stories were real enough, but then P's people would write comments that connected the crime to drugs: "They say the killer was a drug dealer" or "This one was a victim of a pusher." After a month they dropped in two stories per day, a month later three per day.

Drug crime became a hot topic. Duterte pulled ahead in the polls. This is when, P says, he fell out with the other PR people in the team and quit to join another candidate. This one was running on economic competence rather than fear. P claims he managed to get his rating up by more than five points but it was too late to turn the tide. Duterte was elected president. Now he sees any number of PR people taking the credit for Duterte and it riles him.

The trouble with interviewing anyone who works in this world is that they always tend to amplify their impact. It comes with the profession. Did P create Duterte? Of course not. And there would have been many factors that drove the conversation about drug crime, not least Duterte himself. Nor was busting drug crime Duterte's only selling point: I have talked to supporters of his attracted by the image of a provincial fighting the elites of "Imperial Manila" and the prim Catholic Church establishment. But P's account does echo some academic studies.

In "Architects of Networked Disinformation," Dr. Jonathan Corpus Ong of the University of Massachusetts spent twelve months with his colleague Jason Cabañes interviewing the protagonists of what he called Manila's "disinformation architecture," which was made use of by every party in the country.[3]

At the top were what Ong calls the "chief architects" of the system. They came from advertising and public relations firms, lived in sleek apartments in skyscrapers, and described their work in an almost mythical way, comparing themselves to TV characters from hit HBO fantasy series *Game of Thrones* and video games: "It's game over when you're caught," they would tell Ong. They were proud they had had made it to the top of their profession from modest beginnings. "The disinformation architect," concludes Ong, "denies responsibility or commitment to the broader public by narrating a personal project of self-empowerment instead."

Below the architects came the "influencers," online comedians who, in between posting the latest jokes, make fun of opposing politicians for a fee. Down in the slums of the disinformation architecture were what Ong called the "community level fake account operators." Call centers full of people, paid by the hour, working twenty-four-hour shifts, with one person managing dozens of social media personas. They could be someone who needed a little extra cash (students or nurses, for example), or campaign staff. Ong interviewed one operator, Rina, who had been forced into the work when she joined a mayoral campaign. She had signed on out of idealism. She had been at the top of her class at university. Now she was told to create multiple online personalities—girls clad in bikinis worked best—make online friends, promote her candidate, and smear the opposition. Rina was ashamed: she felt she sabotaged herself, bringing in only twenty Facebook followers whereas her colleagues brought in thousands.

Ong noted that no one, at any level in this business, ever described their activity as "trolling" or producing "fake news." Everyone had their own denial strategies: the architects stressed it was merely a side-hustle to their regular PR work, and thus didn't define them, and anyway they weren't in charge of the whole political campaign; "community level operators" said there was someone else leaving the really nasty, hateful comments. This was the architecture of online influence, which would shift into a more aggressive gear when Duterte came to power.

Duterte had vowed to kill so many drug dealers that their corpses would fatten the fish in Manila Bay; he joked that he would sign a pardon to forgive himself. He boasted of having killed someone over a "look." That the lives of drug dealers meant nothing to him. Now vigilante gangs and cops began to shoot anyone suspected of connections to the drug trade. No one knows exactly how many have been killed in the campaign. Human rights organizations estimate twelve thousand; opposition politicians twenty thousand; the government 4,200. At one point, thirty-three a day were being killed. No one would check if the victims were really guilty. There were frequent reports of drugs planted on the victims after they were dead. Fifty-four children were executed, too. The alleys of Manila's slums filled up with corpses. Men on motorbikes would drive up and just shoot people in the head. The prisons became as crowded as battery chicken farms. One politician, Senator Leila de Lima, who pushed back against the killings, suddenly found herself on trial: imprisoned drug lords were giving testimony that she was involved in their business. Online mobs bayed for her arrest. She was locked away pending a trial that never began; a prisoner of conscience, according to Amnesty International. When the country's archbishop condemned the killings, the mobs turned on him. Next it would be the turn of the media: the so-called presstitutes who dared accuse the president of murders.

And the greatest presstitute the regime would target was Maria Ressa, the head of the news website Rappler. And this was ironic for it was Maria and Rappler who had inadvertently helped bring Duterte into power.

#ARRESTMARIARESSA!

After talking to Maria for a while, I began to notice how uncomfortable she felt at being made the subject of the story. She was far too polite to tell me this herself, but I noticed she was always turning our interview away from herself to the work of her journalists, the dramas of others. In her career, she'd been the one who covers things: first as the head of the CNN bureaus in Southeast Asia, then as the head of news at the Philippines' largest television network, and ultimately as the creator and CEO of Rappler. And now it was not only me interviewing Maria in her office as she tries to swallow a rushed lunch of peanut butter and tinned sardine sandwiches (a Philippine specialty); there was also a documentary crew from the English-language version of the Qatari TV channel Al-Jazeera, who are following Maria around to document her battle with Duterte and disinformation.

The Al-Jazeera crew asked whether they can film me interviewing Maria, and as they crouch in the corner with their huge cameras, I feel increasingly ill at ease. I, too, am used to being the one who observes and edits, and whenever I become the subject of someone else's content, I find myself a little too aware of how I can be recut and re-created later. In my own time as a documentary producer, I learned the skill of making contributors feel significant, meaningful, maybe a touch immortal for a moment while I filmed them, knowing I would have power later in the edit to shape the material. The final story would be accurate, but there's oh-so-often a painful split between a person's self-perception and the way they are portrayed, between the reality reconstructed in the edit and the one that the subject feels is true. That day in Manila, I consoled myself that I would be able to reassert narrative control by writing about the Al-Jazeera crew in the book you are reading now.

So, there we were, one set of journalists filming another interviewing a third. The job of journalists is to report information about where the action is. But, as Maria's own story showed, information itself is now where the action is.

Maria was originally from Manila, but her mother had taken the family to the United States when she was ten, where she was the smallest, brownest girl in Elizabeth, New Jersey, precocious enough to be the first in the family to go to university (Princeton), returning to the Philippines on a Fulbright in 1986 to study political theater, only to find she had landed in the middle of a revolution against Marcos, where the greatest political drama was playing out on the streets. She joined CNN when it was just a tiny US cable operation with grand ideas about becoming the first global news network. At CNN, it was the on-screen reporter who was the most important, who decided which stories to cover, when, and how. Maria wanted that authority. But she didn't like being on camera. Not least because all her life she'd suffered from eczema, which she disguised with all sorts of camera tricks. The camera, however, loved Maria: her lack of pretense and almost puppy-like enthusiasm; the big eyes brimming with curiosity.

Maria became the face of CNN in the region, narrating Southeast Asia's "democratization" in the 1990s, when, after Marcos, one authoritarian regime fell after another. It was tempting to see these changes through the lens of Cold War victory, as a linear tale of ever-expanding freedom, which every new political turn was appearing to confirm. The terror attacks of September 11, 2001, shattered that simplistic story.

Maria was less surprised. Unlike her CNN colleagues, she spoke local dialects fluently, knew how little "democracy" was delivering in the unchangingly poor villages and slums. When she interviewed Al-Qaeda recruits and their families, what struck her was how normal their backgrounds were, how distant fundamentalist purity was for most of them. Bin Laden's trick had been to take the different grievances of different groups and give them the illusion that if they united globally, they would achieve a better world, if only they could get rid of unbelievers. In 2005, Maria moved on from CNN. In retrospect, she realized it was just in time. The network was changing, reporters were being asked to express their feelings rather than just give the facts; making money was becoming a more obsessive motivation. This irked Maria. She wanted to investigate terrorists, not star in some reality-show version of the news.

On June 9, 2008, when she was running the news side of the Philippines' largest television network, Maria was woken early in the morning by her star reporter, Ces Drilon. "Maria, this is all my fault . . . we've been kidnapped. And they want money."[4] Despite Maria's orders to the contrary, Ces had chased an interview with Islamist insurgents and been kidnapped, along with two cameramen, by Al-Qaeda affiliate Abu Sayyaf.

Over the next ten days, Maria worked day and night to help co-ordinate the rescue effort, which ended after Ces's family managed to get enough money to satisfy the kidnappers.

After the hostages had been handed over, Maria began to research the identities of the kidnappers. She found that they were related to Bin Laden through three degrees of association. This fit in with a pattern she had observed since covering the growth of Al-Qaeda from Afghanistan into Southeast Asia. Ideologies spread through networks, and your fealty to them depended on where you stood inside the web. Instead of just studying ideas and socio-economic factors, one had to understand the interconnections between people to see why and how Al-Qaeda's ideology was spreading. The same jumble of personal and social issues could have quite a different expression if it came into contact with a different network. And Maria realized that these physical networks were quickly being replaced with social media.

In 2012, Maria created Rappler, the Philippines' first purely internet-based news site. She wanted to put her insights into networks to good use. Rappler would not merely report on current affairs but engage a greater online community that would help crowdfunding for important causes. It would gather vital information during natural disasters to help victims caught in floods and storms find shelter and assistance. Maria hired twenty-year-olds who knew more about social media than old-school hacks: fashion bloggers, web designers. When you walk into Rappler's orange and glass, open-plan office, you notice how young and how largely female the staff is, with a small band of older journalists overseeing them with a hint of matronly severity. In Manila, they're known as the Rapplers.

When Duterte began his social media–inspired presidential campaign, he and Rappler seemed perfect for each other. The TV networks didn't take him seriously. When Rappler held the Philippines' first Facebook presidential debate, he was the only candidate who bothered to turn up. It was a runaway success. Votes on Rappler's online community showed Duterte was ahead. He only had one message—drug crime—but it was catching on. Rappler reporters found themselves repeating his sound bites about the "war on drugs." Later, when Duterte went on his killing spree, they would regret using the term "war"—it helped to normalize his actions. If this was a "war," then casualties became more acceptable.

The trouble started with a wolf whistle. At a press conference, Duterte whistled at a female reporter from a TV network. The Rappler reporter in the room asked him to apologize. Rappler's online community filled up with comments saying she should be more respectful of the president. "Your mother's a whore," they wrote. The Rapplers were taken aback. This language didn't sound like their community. They put it down to the vestiges of sexism: any time a woman held a man to account, she would be attacked.

Meanwhile, Duterte's language didn't let up in its coarseness.[5] He called the pope and US presidents sons of whores; inquired whether a journalist he didn't like was asking tough questions because his wife's vagina was so smelly; bragged about having two mistresses; joked about how he himself should have raped a good-looking hostage instead of her kidnappers. When officials at the UN and the EU criticized his killing spree, he said their accusations were all vestiges of colonialism, that they were trying to displace the guilt of their historical sins onto him. On TV, Duterte said he wanted to eat the livers of terrorists and season them with salt, that if his troops rape three women each he would take the rape sentences for them.

I learned a little of the linguistic context of these pronouncements when I visited the comedy clubs in Quezon City, the section of Manila where teenage prostitutes and ladyboys congregate by night next to the TV towers of national broadcasters. The comedians pick victims in the audience and roast them, taunting them about the size of their penises, or for their weight, and this right in front of entire families who all laugh along at their relatives' humiliation.

This is the language Duterte partially taps into with his incessant dirty jokes. It's a type of humor he shares with a troupe of male leaders across the world. The Russian president Vladimir Putin made his rhetorical mark by promising to whack terrorists "while they are on the shitter"; the president of the United States, Donald Trump, boasts of grabbing women "by the pussy"; the president of the Czech Republic, Milos Zeman, has called for "pissing on the charred remains of Roma"; the Brazilian president, Jair Bolsonaro, told a female politician she was "too ugly" to rape and that black activists should go "back to the zoo"[6]; while in Britain, the anti-immigration politician Nigel Farage, with his outsized mouth gaping in a braying laugh, pours down pints and belches out rude jokes about "chinkies."[7] This toilet humor is used to show how "anti-establishment" they are, their "anti-elitist" politics expressed through the rejection of established moral and linguistic norms.

When dirty jokes are used by the weak to poke fun at the powerful, they can bring authority figures back down to earth, give the sense that their rules can be suspended.[8] That's why dirty jokes have often been suppressed. In 1938, for example, my paternal great-grandfather went down to the cafeteria of the Kharkiv mega-factory where he worked as an accountant, had a drink, told a wisecrack about the balls of the head of the presidium of the Supreme Soviet, and was speedily reported on and arrested, perishing in a labor camp on the Volga River.

But when such language is used consistently by men with real power to degrade those weaker, this humor becomes menacing: it lays the linguistic path to humiliating victims in other ways as well, to a space where all norms disappear.

As Rappler began to report on Duterte's extrajudicial killings, the online threats became incessant. At one point, there were ninety messages an hour. There were non-stop claims that Rappler was making up the deaths, that they were in the pay of Duterte's enemies, that their stories all were fake news. The messages were like an infestation of insects, swarming into the email in-boxes, descending like a scourge onto their community pages, which Rappler had curated with such care to enable what they had hoped would be the internet's "wisdom of crowds." Sometimes Rappler staff would check to see who was behind a rape threat: maybe it was an automated account? To their disappointment it would turn out to be a real person. People were enjoying this. Rappler journalists were shouted at in the malls: "Hey you—you're fake news!" "Shame on you!" relatives would admonish them.

Maria Ressa bore the brunt of the attacks. Some were so stupid they just bounced off her, like the memes of her dressed in a Nazi uniform.

"Maria you're a waste of sperm, your mother should have aborted you."

Others got under her skin—literally. Her eczema had always been her weak spot. When the attackers started to taunt her for her skin condition, it would flare up without her having time to erect her psychological defenses.

Her first instinct was to blame herself: Had she done something wrong? Misreported something? She checked all Rappler's output over and over but could find nothing. Then the hashtag #ArrestMariaRessa began to trend. Then #UnfollowRappler. The government launched a case against her. One of Rappler's investors had been an American foundation, and the government charged them with following foreign editorial instructions. Some of her board members resigned. Advertising plummeted. She started to walk around town with bail money on her. The first trial against Rappler ended up in the appeals court, where it was settled. And then, when the worst was thought to be over for Rappler, Maria got wind that Duterte's people were preparing another case against them.[9]

During all the attacks on Rappler, Maria's managing editor, Glenda Gloria, seemed to me the most serene person in the room. Perhaps it's because she has seen it all before. Glenda remembered the Marcos years. In the 1980s, she'd been a student journalist covering the regime's torture of opposition figures. Her boyfriend was arrested for running a small, independent printing press and had electrodes connected to his balls.

Back then torture sessions also combined the psychological and the physical; the ultimate aim was not merely to brutalize but to break. Professor William McCoy, of the University of Wisconsin–Madison, who has studied the psychological torture techniques of the CIA and

US client states in the Cold War, relates the story of Father Kangleon, a priest falsely accused of subversion and cooperating with Communists, who was denied sleep and daylight for more than two months. In the denouement of his interrogation, he was blindfolded and led into a new cell and set down on a stool. He could hear people come in. Then different voices taunted him in a pre-planned piece of theater, which, when I read it in 2018, almost anticipates the taunts of anonymous trolls on social media.[10]

"Father, what's the name of the sister you met with at Sacred Heart College? . . . You are fucking her? How does it feel?"

"For me he is not a priest. Yes, your kind is not worthy of respect of a priest."

"OK, take off his shirt. Oh, look at that body. You look sexy. Even the women here think you are macho. You are a homosexual?"

After this, the interrogation became more physical:

"Let's see if you are that macho after one of my punches." (A short jab was delivered below the ribs.)

"Hey, don't lean on the table. Place your arms beside you. That's it." (Another jab.)

"Take the stool away." (He stood up and was hit behind the head, he started to cower, then more blows . . .)

After he agreed to cooperate, Kangleon was taken to a TV station and forced to say on air that he had helped Communist insurgents and to name other clergy supposedly involved in the insurrection.

Under Marcos, remembers Glenda Gloria, the government had agents in every university, every farm, church, and office. They would go around and tell your colleagues, your neighbors, and your friends that you were a Communist—even if you were not—destroying your reputation with a whisper campaign before they came to arrest you. Marcos grouped the media into "proper journalists" and "communists," so every critic was dismissed as a "commie."

"The psychological warfare that Marcos mastered is very similar to what is happening now," Glenda tells me. "The difference is,

Duterte doesn't have to use the military to attack the media. How is it made possible? With technology."

After Marcos was overthrown the new Filipino democracy was far from perfect: human rights abuses continued; journalists' lives, especially in the provinces, were cheap.[11] But unlike most of his predecessors, who tried to obfuscate the abuses under their rule, who at least pretended to abide by some rules, Duterte exults in his extrajudicial killings, celebrates his attacks on journalists.

Now Duterte literally was rehabilitating Marcos. He had his body exhumed and given a military burial with full honors. He formed a political alliance with his son, Bongbong Marcos, who still controlled his father's old stronghold in the country's north. Online a drip of videos appeared, absolving Marcos of his crimes in the 1970s, claiming it was rogue elements in his army who had killed and tortured.

But even as a digital-era trace of the Marcos era returned, Glenda thought there was a difference, too. Back then, you knew what the rules were. If they started to come for you, you had options. You could skip town. Contact a lawyer. Write to a human rights group. You knew who the agents were, who was coming for you, your enemy. There was a predictability to it. A routine.

And now? Where could you hide from social media? It could come for you in a village, in your living room, abroad. And who was it you were really up against? They were invisible, everywhere and nowhere. How can you fight an online mob? You couldn't even tell how many of them were real.

After several months of this onslaught, Maria and the Rapplers dedicated themselves to making sense of the attacks. They could now see a pattern in the chaos. First, their credibility had been attacked; then they had been intimidated. With their reputations undermined, the virtual attacks were turning into real arrest warrants. They wondered whether there was a design lurking behind it all.

The first thing that caught their eye was the Korean pop stars.

They kept appearing in their online community, commenting on how great Bongbong Marcos and Duterte were. How likely was it that Korean pop stars would be interested in Filipino politics? When they checked out the comments the pop stars were making, they matched one another word for word: obviously fake accounts, most likely controlled from the same source.

Now that they had identified clearly fake accounts, they ran a program that could scour the internet to see who else was using the same language. This took two months but they found other accounts repeating the same phrases. These looked more realistic; they claimed to be real Filipinos with real jobs. Maria and the Rapplers began researching each one individually, calling their purported places of employment. No one had heard of them. Altogether they found twenty-six well-disguised but fake accounts repeating the same messages at the same time and reaching an audience of three million.

The Rapplers breathed a collective sigh of psychological relief; here was something to hold onto. Now that they could see the design in the attacks, they could get a sense of firm reality. This wasn't their fault. Somebody was doing it to them.

They began to categorize every narrative the mobs were using to attack them. They listed dozens: that the media are corrupt, that Rappler should be boycotted, that Senator de Lima should be arrested. They looked at the frequency with which each narrative would appear, a sort of heartbeat monitor of mentions. They found they would peak sharply before a political event: mentions of "media corruption" increased massively before the election; calls for de Lima to be arrested right before the police came for her. It was unlikely to have been spontaneous.

They built up what Maria called her "shark tank," a sort of internet attack radar system that warns when fake stories are approaching, when a smear campaign is starting to be built. If the smear is an old one, Rappler can automatically send out ripostes, raising an alarm among their online supporters to defend their cause.

In February 2018, the Rapplers spotted an unusual creature on the Filipino internet. His name was @Ivan226622 and he was reposting articles frenetically: 1,518 pieces about Filipino politics in just one week. The cover photo was unremarkable enough: a Filipino man who claimed to be interested in computing. He had a video lecture pinned permanently to his profile, created by an American university, on the subject of "why can't we trust the media." Except when you looked up the "university" in question, it turned out to be no academic institution but rather a self-awarded accreditation used in videos produced by a right-wing American talk show host.[12]

But what was even more unusual was @Ivan's activity before his appearance in the Philippines. Originally he had been posting frenetically about events in Iran, then Syria. Then he switched his attention to Spain, posting hundreds of articles agitating for the independence of the Catalonia region. The articles he posted were from Spanish-language, Russian state media. A whole cohort of other accounts posted the same articles at the same time.

@Ivan226622's discovery in early 2018 came at a time when there was much talk in the news about perhaps the most infamous troll farm in the world: the Internet Research Agency (IRA) in St. Petersburg, Russia, which gained great notoriety when it was revealed to have tried to influence the US presidential election in favor of Donald Trump. Attribution—knowing who is really behind an account—is always tricky, so these revelations about the IRA led to innocent people who just had interesting internet habits also being accused of being "Russian trolls." @Ivan226622 disappeared soon after Rappler wrote about him, before one could work out who he really was.

But ever since Rodrigo Duterte had met, and gotten along with, President Putin, the Filipino government had started quoting Russian state media. Maria wondered whether @Ivan's appearance was related. It was a little reminder that Rappler's experience was one front of a vast, global phenomenon.

TO CATCH A TROLL

Though it gained global notoriety for its American campaign, the Internet Research Agency focuses on trolling domestic opposition. In St. Petersburg, one young and rather fragile-looking woman, Lyudmila Savchuk, had infiltrated the IRA as early as 2015, with the aim of gathering enough evidence to stop its work. I first bumped into her in Europe, then America, during her long, uphill efforts to stop the troll farm's operations.

Lyudmila reminded me of other activists I'd encountered previously in Russia. Because the state has destroyed most civil society organizations, they often work in various professions—as journalists, small business owners, charity workers—or they move between jobs. When I look up Lyudmila on Google, I notice there's a struggle to define her: she's called by turns an environmentalist, a journalist, an internet activist, a dissident. And in a way, all of these are true.

"Ignore everything you read about me," Lyudmila tells me right away. She's upset about how some journalists defined her as a whistle-blower from inside the troll farm, when she'd set out to go undercover there from the beginning.

"I suppose 'whistleblower' makes for more clicks," she sighs.

Lyudmila had managed to infiltrate the farm by chance. In 2014, she was a TV reporter in the town of Pushkin, covering stories about bureaucrats planning illegal construction projects in conservation areas. Soon she was helping organize protests to stop illegal building projects in parks, then stood for membership in the local council. Increasingly she noticed that activists were being smeared online, accused of being paid stooges, slackers.

There were already rumors of a troll farm in the suburbs of St. Petersburg but no one knew its scale or how it operated, and many were divided as to whether it was worth paying attention to at all. So what if you got trolled? The tougher activists thought it beneath them to respond. Lyudmila felt differently. It riled her when people she respected were attacked.

Then, in January 2015, an old journalist colleague asked Lyudmila if she wanted to join a project for the "good of the motherland." She was putting together a team for "special projects" and needed good writers. Would Lyudmila come for an interview? It dawned on Lyudmila she was referring to the troll farm. Here was a chance to find out how the troll farm really worked. She hatched a plan with journalists from two of Russia's last independent newspapers, Мой Район and Новая Газета. She would infiltrate the troll farm, film and download enough evidence of how it worked, and they would publish it. She hurriedly scrubbed out all her social media accounts. They lent her a smart phone to make the recordings.

The office was in a suburb of St. Petersburg, a four-story new building with square pillars propping up the second floor, its narrow, black-framed windows like long arrow slits. There were no signs on the door. Her friend met Lyudmila at the entrance and took her to see the manager. To Lyudmila's surprise, it was someone she'd heard of: he'd been a columnist at Мой Район. The "farm" wasn't full of secret service guys or PR gurus, but former journalists. One motivation quickly became obvious: she was being offered several times more than a regular media salary and steady work. The manager was uncertain about Lyudmila, however: he knew her investigative background. Lyudmila's old colleague waved it off, saying, "Oh come on, who here hasn't done that sort of work back in the past?"

The farm took up all four floors of the building. The computers were crammed into thin lines of desks, which were manned 24/7 with changing shifts of employees with passes that clocked all arrival and departure times. Even smoking breaks were regulated.

The farm had its own hierarchy. The most looked-down-on were the "commenters," of which the lowest of the low were those who posted in the online comments sections of newspapers; a level up were those who left comments on social media. The more senior editors would instruct the commenters which Russian opposition figures to attack, and they would spend their days accusing them of being CIA stooges, traitors, shills. Some of the commenters had only limited education and their written Russian could be imperfect, so a language teacher would come in to give them grammar lessons.

Lyudmila was on another, more exclusive floor. Her "special project" involved the creation of a mystic healer, "Cantadora," an expert in astrology, parapsychology, and crystals. Cantadora was meant to be read by middle-class housewives who were not normally interested in politics. Lyudmila's job was to drop in the odd bit of current affairs in between blog entries on astrological signs and romance. There were four people working on the profile. Lyudmila liked Stas the most; he seemed utterly depressed by the work and she promised herself that when her mission was over, she would try to get him out of there.

Every day Lyudmila, Stas, and the other writers would be sent Word documents with political news articles and the conclusions they were meant to draw from them: that the EU is just a vassal of the United States, or that Ukraine, which Russia had invaded, was run by fascists. It was up to them to integrate these conclusions into Cantadora's blog. So, Lyudmila wrote, for example, how Cantadora had a sister who lived in Germany and then related a nightmare where she dreamt her sister was in a desert surrounded by deadly snakes and then interpret those snakes as US foreign policy endangering the EU. Some of the farm's work reached a level of granularity that surprised Lyudmila. Two trolls would go on the comments sections of small, provincial newspapers and start chatting about the street they lived on, the weather, then casually recommend a piece about the nefarious West attacking Russia.

As in Manila, no one who worked at the farm described themselves as trolls. Instead they talked about their work in the passive tense ("a piece was written," "a comment was made"). Most treated the farm as if it was just another job, doing the minimum required and then clocking out. Many of them seemed pleasant enough young people to Lyudmila, and yet they didn't blink when asked to insult and humiliate their targets. The ease with which a victim could be smeared, and the scale at which the farm operated, stunned Lyudmila.

She kept herself going with the thought that her research would help stop all this. But it was proving hard to gather the necessary evidence. There were CCTV cameras in every corner, and she would have to flick her long, curly hair over her shoulder so that it covered her hand when she moved it down to put a flash drive into her computer to download documents.

Who gave the farm instructions about what to do? Was it the Kremlin? Or were they churned out inside the IRA? No one discussed this. The farm, other journalists had told her, was owned by one Yevgeny Prigozhin. He relied on the regime for his official business: he provided catering services to the Kremlin. He had known President Putin personally since the 1990s. He had served nine years in prison for robbery.[13] Later it would come out that he also directed mercenaries who fight the Kremlin's covert wars from Ukraine to Syria and beyond.

There were moments when Lyudmila could see that the factory was part of a much larger network. When the opposition politician Boris Nemtsov was murdered in February 2015, shot by a gunman on the bridge underneath the towers of Red Square, the middle management of the factory suddenly started running into every office giving the trolls direct instructions what to post under which articles printed in mainstream Russian publications. The farm was working in concert with the entire regime disinformation complex. No one had time to read the articles, but they knew exactly what to post. The trolls were told to spread confusion about who was behind the murder: was it the Ukrainians, the Chechens, the Americans? The IRA, an agency whose connection to the Kremlin was purposefully blurred, was in turn purposefully blurring the Kremlin's possible connection to a murder.[14]

During the day Lyudmila would see a fake reality being pumped out by the trolls. In the evening she would come home hoping to put the place behind her, only to hear relatives and acquaintances repeat to her lines churned out by the factory. People who considered themselves hardened enough to withstand the barrage of television still seemed susceptible to social media messages, which slithered into and enveloped their most personal online spaces, spinning into the texture of their lives.

Lyudmila spent two and a half months at the farm. Then, as planned, she gave the material to newspapers. They published it as authored by "anonymous." The next day she went back to work to find that the commenters were busy undermining the credibility of her articles. "No troll factories exist," the trolls wrote. "They are all fabrications by journalists paid by the enemies of the motherland." It would only be a matter of time before the senior editors realized that she had been the mole inside the farm: they were already checking video cameras to find the guilty party. But she had played her role so well that no one, at first, could believe it had been her. The woman who had introduced her to the farm defended her the most: "Lyudmila doesn't even own a smart phone!"

Lyudmila quit the farm. She also decided to admit publicly that she was the one who had infiltrated it. She wanted to give interviews about what she had seen there, to campaign to have the place shut down. She couldn't do that as "anonymous." She gave dozens of interviews. She gave talks abroad.

The farm now turned on her. There were articles claiming she was a sexual deviant, a spy, a traitor. There were anonymous phone calls to her relatives saying that people were often killed for what Lyudmila had done. Lyudmila tried to reach out to Stas, the coauthor of the Cantadora blog whom she had liked, but he just sent her bitter messages full of curse words. This saddened her. She knew he hated the farm and thought he might understand her mission. Lyudmila had hoped that by unmasking the workings of the IRA she would cause so much outrage that it would help stop its work, that she would shock people into seeing how they were being manipulated, shame those who work there into resigning. Most of the people she had met there were no monsters. They carried on working at the farm because there was little social stigma linked to its activity.

But instead of an outcry, she found that many people, including fellow activists, just shrugged at the revelations. This horrified her even more. Not only did the lies churned out by the farm become reality, but the very existence of it was seen as normal.

At one point, the death threats and abuse unnerved Lyudmila so much she began to get anxiety attacks and went to see a psychotherapist. The psychotherapist listened to her patiently, nodded, and then asked why she wanted to fight the state this way. Was she some kind of paid-for traitor? Lyudmila, perturbed, visited another doctor, who said the same things. She felt as if the mindset promoted by the troll factory had penetrated the subconscious of the country. She had left the confines of the farm only to find herself enveloped in it.

Then, in early 2018, the US Special Counsel Investigation found that the operations of the troll farm had stretched beyond Russia and deep into the US, creating thousands of fake accounts, groups, and messages, while posing as genuine Americans: right-nationalist, gun-loving Americans who supported the election of Donald Trump; black civil rights campaigners who promoted the idea that his rivals weren't worth voting for. The activity continued after the 2016 election, as the farm tried to make Americans hate each other even more. Over thirty million Americans shared its content among their friends and families.[15]

Certainly, thought Lyudmila, the Americans would punish the troll farm now. She'd always noted how authors at the IRA would write screeds about how awful "the West" was through their troll personas, while fantasizing about holidays in America. Even the most basic threat of a travel ban to the United States, she reckoned, would be enough to put off many from working at the farm and undermine the sense that it was just another normal job.

She would be disappointed. The US Special Counsel opened cases against a few mid-level administrators for technicalities like using fake identities to open bank accounts. Not only did the farm not shut down; it expanded to premises three times larger.

I asked American government lawyers why sanctions couldn't be imposed on trolls. They answered there were several reasons: the primary reason given was that it was hard to define whether the IRA worked directly for the Russian government, and therefore whether their actions constituted the operations of a "hostile state."

Although the IRA's scale of activities was spectacular, it was barely unique. Western PR companies were regularly caught running similar operations with fake online personas for their clients. Starting in 2011 the American military had its own project to run fake online accounts to counter terrorist messaging in the Middle East, called "Earnest Voice." It wasn't just the Russians who used technology this way.[16]

But even more important, I thought to myself, though one might not like what trolls wrote, lies are not illegal. In the marketplace of ideas, better information—the journalistic credo I had been raised with went—is the antidote to lies. After all, isn't freedom of expression exactly what democratic dissidents, such as my parents, had always fought for?

CAMILLE FRANCOIS THOUGHT DIFFERENTLY. SHE WAS A SCHOLAR OF cyber-warfare at Harvard University and later Google, and when she first read about Lyudmila's research and heard about Maria's story, she felt it fit into a greater pattern she had observed across the world: a new version of the old game of power versus dissent, freedom of speech versus censorship that turned the old rules on their head. The previous methods of censorship had become untenable; unlike in the Soviet Union, few regimes can cut people off entirely from receiving or broadcasting information. However, the powerful had adapted. Now social media mobs and cyber militias harassed, smeared, and intimidated dissenting voices into silence or undermined trust in them. But because the connections between states and these campaigns were unclear, a regime could always claim that it had nothing to do with them, that the mobs were made up of private individuals exercising their freedom of expression.

What, thought Francois, if you could establish the connection between states and campaigns? Could you then hold them to account?

Francois had begun her internet career supporting what were known as internet "pirates" in 1990s Paris: hackers who put copyrighted music, books, and software online in the name of sharing all knowledge for free. Francois even advocated that people should give up their computer passwords, so anyone could access each other's knowledge. Two decades later, such idealism had given way to a realization that the internet was an increasingly dangerous place—and she was more preoccupied with questions of security.

In Latin America, she had researched how states hack into the phones and computers of journalists and activists. Now, she got back in touch with those victims and asked whether the hacks had been accompanied by online harassment. Almost everyone said they had.

Martha Roldós, an Ecuadorian politician, who had swarms of online internet accounts accuse her of being a spy, threaten her, accuse her of killing her own parents, put it perhaps most clearly: "In the past I was denied my political rights, I had armed men outside my house pointing a gun at my daughter . . . but not cyber harassment. Since I became a sponsor of investigative journalists, my time of cyber-harassment began."

Over the next three years, between 2015 and 2018, Francois put together a team of twenty researchers who scoured Asia and the Middle East, the Americas, and Europe to categorize what she was beginning to call "state-sponsored trolling." They defined a "troll" as "an online account that deliberately targets an individual with messages of hate and harassment online," and "state-sponsored trolling" as "the use of targeted online hate and harassment campaigns to intimidate and silence individuals critical of the state."

Francois's aim was to create a scale of attribution to tie states to cyber militias and social media mobs. The research, much of which would later be published by the aptly named "Institute for the Future," defined several categories.[17] The most obvious were state-directed campaigns, in which regimes gave instructions about whom to target, how and when, while not necessarily taking an active part in the campaign. This is the case in Venezuela, where the Maduro government has set up closed social media channels where it directs enthusiasts on whom to attack, with what messages and when, but doesn't actually perform the work.

For a modicum of deniability, one could work through a youth movement. In Azerbaijan, for instance, there is IRELI, created "to produce young people who can take an active part in the information war." In practice this means sending online threats to critical journalists like Arzu Geybulla. "I've been called many things: a slut, a dog, a pig—you name it," Geybulla says. "These insults involved my ill mother and deceased father. She was a whore; he was a traitor who slept with an Armenian slut."

Subtler was the situation Francois found in Bahrain, where, during protests in 2011, an internet account suddenly popped up that showed close-up photographs of protesters, along with their home addresses and personal phone numbers. There even was a link to a government hotline to report protesters directly to the regime. Who was behind the account? Nothing was ever proven, but after the government was told about its existence, it did nothing to stop it. Wasn't that enough, thought Francois, to hold them responsible? She classified this as a "state-coordinated" campaign.

Another layer of deniability was to merely fuel attacks but then take no part in their enactment. This is the case in Turkey, where columnists who are members of the ruling party incite mob attacks on anyone who dares criticize President Erdogan.

Such state-incited campaigns have also become a feature in the US. The Institute for the Future report relates instances when the White House social media team, websites that support the president, and indeed the president himself identify journalists, academics, and opposition staffers as "scum," "slime," and "enemies of the people" and target them with hit pieces and social media taunts. The victims then receive vats of online vitriol, phone calls to their place of work demanding they are sacked, and death and rape threats.

"Fake news and aggressive trolling of journalists . . . contributed to a score decline in the United States' otherwise generally free environment," according to Freedom House, a Washington-based organization that rates press freedom, which downgraded the United States' standing in 2017. Freedom House was created in 1941 to fight totalitarian regimes. It advocated for Soviet dissidents in the Cold War. Now it finds itself thinking about abuses of freedom in America. (And not for the first time: in the 1950s, Freedom House opposed the anti-Communist witch hunts of Senator Joseph McCarthy.)

Having established a scale of attribution, Francois began poring over legal documents. States had an obligation, enshrined in their UN commitments, to protect their citizens' fundamental rights. There was certainly nothing that defended a state's "right" to use automated and fake personas to drown out, threaten, and demean its critics.

The issue then stopped being whether state-sponsored trolls had freedom of expression but whether this freedom was being abused to suppress the victims' human rights. This was censorship through noise. "We observe the tactical move by states from an ideology of information scarcity to one of information abundance," writes law professor Tim Wu, "which sees speech itself as a censorial weapon."[18]

It will take a landmark case to establish a precedent where a troll farm and the state that sponsors it are brought to justice. In the meantime Francois has focused her effort on persuading the tech companies themselves: after all it was on their platforms that the abuse was taking place. And to a small extent, she has succeeded. Between 2015 and 2018, social media companies like Facebook and Twitter at least began to admit that coordinated campaigns actually existed and occasionally would take down the offending social media accounts.

In late 2018, I was in Washington, DC, reading Francois' bullet points while experiencing the strange time lapse of jet lag, where the usual logic of day and night was broken, and when, perhaps because time seemed to have lost its hold on me, unnatural exuberance took over. In this hazy time, it seemed to me that Francois' vision was just around the corner. I started imagining a future where all the world's great powers and digital companies would promise to safeguard human rights online. Tech companies would protect dissidents by warning them when a campaign was building to target them, instantly taking down trolls, punishing them so they could never harass anyone again. States would no longer abuse freedom of speech to crush those who speak truth to power; working for a troll farm could no longer be shrugged off as normal . . .

Sauntering down to the cramped lobby of my hotel, I snapped out of my reverie when I encountered Maria Ressa, in town for the same conference. I hadn't seen her for three months and wondered whether the threats against Rappler had subsided. She showed me a text message she'd just received from Glenda. It was a picture of a thick file. A trumped-up tax evasion charge had been brought against Maria that carried a potential prison sentence of ten years. Maria was leaving for the airport on her way back to Manila. She managed to post bail, but a few months later there was another charge, this time accusing her of libel for an article from 2012. I watched a Facebook livestream as she was arrested right in the Rappler offices and then released the next day. Rights groups condemned the charges as politically motivated.[19]

In between interrogations, Maria received the 2018 Knight International Journalism Award, one of the world's most prestigious. "Exponential lies on social media incite hate and stifle free speech," said Maria as she collected her statuette. "We battle impunity from the Philippine government and from Facebook. Why should you care? Our problems are fast becoming your problems. Boundaries around the world collapse and we can begin to see a kind of global playbook."[20]

But despite all the international attention Maria's words mustered, the attacks and cases against her continued, as if someone was trying to say that freedom of speech, in the older sense of being able to shout about your cause to the wider world, was meaningless. You will have to check yourselves whether Rappler's story has a sad, happy, or indeed any ending, and what is going on right now. But it was already clear when writing this in early 2019 that Maria was no longer just a reporter commenting on history but a symptom of how easily it could be undone. That was the paradox of the new media. It was meant to take us further, into the future. Instead it had brought back the past: misogyny we had thought conquered; regimes thought laid to rest. The very form of social media scrambles time, place, proportion: terror attacks sit next to cat videos, the latest jokes surface next to old family photos.

And the result was a sort of flattening, as if past and present were losing their relative perspectives.

CHAPTER TWO

DEMOCRACY AT SEA

Whenever Lina would become stressed her psoriasis would flare up, her skin covered by a red rash. She feared what would happen when the KGB hauled her in for questioning. Would she start itching? How would she keep her composure? What if they threatened to take away her parents' jobs? How could she live with that? And who would feed Petya?

Esfir, her mother, calmed her down. She told her to forget about her parents—they would take care of themselves. She needed to stop worrying about her child—they would find wet nurses. She needed to make sure she didn't break.

"The KGB will interrogate you so long the milk in your breasts will go sour with mastitis. They will swell, the duct will block, burn and cover with abscesses. You will become feverish. So, whenever you feel the need, get up, go to the wall of the interrogation room, and squeeze the milk out

of your breasts onto the walls. Don't be ashamed. Instead make them feel embarrassed."

What shocked Lina was that her own straight-laced lawyer of a mother was describing how to resist the secret police so frankly, seemed to know exactly what to do.

Though they never talked about it, Esfir knew her fair share about arrests.

Back when she was still a student, in 1948, Esfir had been told by the dean of the law faculty to go work as a stenographer at the Kiev courthouse. She had a prodigious memory and there were rather a lot of trials at the time. Except they weren't really trials. They just brought in one person after the next and sentenced them like on an assembly line. It was the time of Stalin's post-war purges of Ukrainian nationalists. After a while Esfir got to know which judge would give how many years: this one was a five-year guy, this one fifteen. If the judge was known as particularly stern, in the seconds before the judgment was read out Esfir would stop typing, and everyone else who worked in the court would stop whatever they were doing, and press their hands hard over their ears. They would see the judge move his mouth to utter the sentence and then the noise would start. A sound like the wind rising to a gale of grief, a wail penetrating every part of you.

"Wooohooooooooooo . . . "

It was the relatives of the sentenced and it was the same every time, and everyone who worked in the courtroom would press their hands to their ears to block the wailing out.

And so, Lina had been raised in a world where everyone did their best to pretend not to hear or speak directly about what was going on. She grew up among silences, everyone speaking in the passive voice and whispers: "X has been taken away." "Y has been disappeared" (when she grew up, she would always feel revulsion at the passive voice and *whispers). Or there was that time the dam holding the water reservoir near the ravine of Babi Yar broke and a whole area of Kiev was flooded so violently buildings and trams were swept away in the torrent. Some say hundreds, others thousands, died. No one knows exactly: all news of the event was stifled by men "from over there." All displays of public mourning barred. Esfir would only say, "the ground had wept." This was a way to describe the unmentionable flood, which in turn invoked another unspoken catastrophe. Babi Yar also was where the Nazis shot tens of thousands of Jews during the war. Evasions were wrapped inside references to silences.*

At university the first banned books began to come her way. Here, finally, the unspoken was expressed. And here, in the little circle around my father-to-be, Igor, were people who said what they thought without whispers, without the passive voice, sharing banned texts that were printed on cheap paper, glued to pieces of card and then packed in shoeboxes.

One evening, a year before Igor's arrest, Lina had come home with a shoebox of Solzhenitsyn's Gulag Archipelago. *Lina had come home with the shoebox-book tucked under her arm, turned to take off her raincoat, glanced in the hall mirror, and in the reflection caught the look of great-grandmother Tsilya in the room opposite, staring at Lina with her one good eye. There must have been something in my mother's look that gave everything away immediately. "Esfir!" great-grandmother screamed, "the child has brought banned literature home." Esfir ran into my mother's room and leaned close over her.*

"You think you're brave? Let me explain what they will do to you. They will take you down a long dark corridor. They will put you in a small cell. They will close the heavy door. And then they will turn the lock."

And here Esfir made a noise with her throat like a great rusty thing turning over and over. It made my mother shrivel. Years afterwards she couldn't work out how Esfir made that sound, what mix of guttural groans and throat movements one needs to communicate metal breaking willpower.

Lina took the shoebox out of the house that night.

"Maybe this is cruel of me, but I can think of no other word but betrayal when I think of those who were adults during my childhood and adolescence," Igor would write later, in an essay called "The Right to Read."

"I felt betrayed by my teachers. Not one spoke a single word of truth about the tragedy of my fatherland.

"I feel as if I betrayed myself. Why did I believe the teachers and newspapers? Why did I take until my twenty-sixth year for my first public outcry in defense of my fellow citizens, mislaid behind bars, behind barbed wire, behind walls of psychiatric hospitals for their ability to think and express their words out loud?

"I felt betrayed by my parents even though I loved them. At least at home they could have, for the sake of their sons, assumed some human dignity and honesty.

"And it was books, only books that never betrayed me.

"I see all genuine literature as anti-Soviet. I feel any good book which acknowledges the human being, individuality, uniqueness is also anti-Soviet because the state dictatorship is directed against the human being as an individual."

Igor had seen his own father mangled by the contradictions of the Soviet experiment. Jacob Israelovich was a Communist true believer who broke with his bourgeois, religious Odessan family thinking he could build a just society free of anti-Semitism. He made editor of the Dnepropetrovsk youth gazette in 1941 and seemed poised for journalistic glory until Stalin began a purge of Jews after the war. Jacob Israelovich was forced to take refuge with relatives in *distant, dead-end Chernivtsi, a Ukrainian provincial town right on the border with Romania, which had been a part of Austria-Hungary until the first world war, then became part of Romania, before final annexation by Stalin in 1944. Even here he worked on the local newspaper—and had his first heart attack after he wrote an article about Yugoslav leader Marshal Tito that was deemed too soft, earning him "a severe party reprimand for intentionally masking the nature of Tito's reactionary regime in Yugoslavia." Jacob Israelovich was so outraged he wrote to* Pravda *in Moscow, violating Party rules, defending his "liberal" editorial. It was the only time Igor ever saw his father "straighten his spine."* Pravda *never replied.*

Jacob Israelovich died after another heart attack when Igor was still a student. On his deathbed, Igor gave his father samizdat texts by Soviet political prisoners. Father and son could at least agree the Soviet Union was institutionally anti-Semitic. By that time Igor had already made his mind up about the regime. His turning point was 1968, when Soviet tanks rolled into Prague in what everyone knew was an invasion but were meant to make believe was "brotherly help."

In his first novella, Reading Faulkner, *written when he was twenty-seven, Igor played on motifs from his own life when his fictional narrator, a young writer, discovers his fictional father's impersonal, official writing and compares it with his own:*

This country has thrown off the chains of Capitalist Slavery! Bourgeois culture was always far from the people! Now it has revealed its true face: the face of the maidservant of monopolistic capital! Welcome the Socialist Sun! Let the Darkness be gone!

and

Just a minute ago you were walking the street, breathing in air and breathing out words, now you have burst through to the page, now it will pour out, like wild berries you'd been carrying inside your jacket. Is there any joy greater than writing in the first person?

The novella is a celebration of the right and joy to define oneself. The narrator, inspired by reading the American modernist William Faulkner's novel, The Sound and the Fury, *tries on different styles to describe his state of mind, Czernowitz, his family. He writes in punctuation-free stream of consciousness and then brusque sentences, returns to a close reading of Faulkner's technique and tries something new again, wonders whether the story of the I starts with personal memories of parents (no), the first questions about ethnic identity (no), the moment when you fall in love and truly notice someone else for the first time (yes).*

I am in a room of music and smoke. My father's taut back. The awfulness of newspaper editorials; what ponderous words father has to juggle; Machine and Tractor Stations, Party Directive. . . . Did Faulkner begin with this? No.

Midday, helmets of cupolas, steep steps, we're in T-shirts, six years old, cool close air of the church. From above, a voice and a pock-marked face grunts: "Out, Jewish runt." Did Faulkner begin like this? No.

A girl, on the shore of you. How high the sky. How deep the kiss. I do not enter—I swim far out into you: past—buoys, past—horizons; glancing back could not see the rim of the shore and was glad. Remember how ten Julys ago you, you went into the breathtaking Black Sea and were a warm current in

it. But does Faulkner have anything to do with this?
He does. He does!

"This admiration you have for William Faulkner?" Colonel Vilen (a shortened form of Vladimir Lenin) asked Igor
in their first interrogation, trying to find a way to get him
to start talking. "You do realize he is a bourgeois writer?"

"Actually, he has been recently republished in the Soviet
Union and announced a Critic of the Bourgeois System,"
Igor countered. The KGB men hadn't done their homework.
The line between acceptable and unacceptable authors was
always shifting depending on the political mood.

Igor's strategy was to refuse to talk about friends,
family, or colleagues, which meant the only thing left to
discuss was books. The interrogations became literary conversations. The KGB would switch between seduction and
intimidation.

"Cooperate with us!" (as in, report on your friends).
"We have lots of writers who we work with. We can help
your career," they would say, smiling, before suddenly
changing the mood and throwing on the table the banned
books he was accused of giving to his friends.

"What criminal depths have you fallen to Igor
Jakovlevich?"

Vilen picked up one of the books. Aptly it was Invitation
to a Beheading by Vladimir Nabokov, the nightmare story
of a man in an unnamed country arrested for an unnamed
crime. Vilen flicked through the book, shaking his head.

"You will get seven and five for this."

The threat wasn't empty. Writers and literary critics in
Kiev were getting the sentence all the time: seven in prison
and five in exile. In Moscow or St. Petersburg, you could
keep Nabokov on the shelves with few repercussions. Here,

where Soviet paranoia about Ukrainian insurrection ran deep, the rules were far stricter.

Igor denied ever having seen the books. "Deny everything" was the time-honored tactic during interrogations, but at the same time it hurt him to say it: books had never betrayed him, but now he had betrayed books. He found his mind wandering to all the other hard-to-find, banned books that must be stored in the KGB cellars. It must be a literary mine!

To keep his mind focused away from fear he tried to humanize his interrogators. What were they like between the crass good-cop/bad-cop routine? In the corridor on the way to an interrogation, he noticed the KGB had their own gazette pinned to the wall. He chuckled; it meant they, too, were forced to write for their company paper, the Dzerzhinetz, *named after Felix Dzerzhinsky, the founder of the original KGB, the Cheka. Did the crossword, Igor wondered, have a professional slant? These men followed some sort of invented professional ethic, which gave them the right to listen in to other people's conversations, record on a magnetic strip someone else's embraces, use those kisses for blackmail, to dictate which books you can and can't read. There seemed no dividing line between the precise, rational logic of their questions and the casual way they would then use violence. He noticed they didn't like being called KGB but preferred the old revolutionary term Chekist, as if that was more romantic, gave them a higher purpose.*

In his poetry of the time, the joyful I is replaced with the third person, as people around him are "disappeared" like pieces of grammar. Sun-dappled days are replaced with cloying nights. Prison barracks loom out of the brown fog and instead of lovers in the moonlight, the secret police become your night companion. In one poem the author, some sort of unidentified animal himself, hides terrified from gangs of alley cats. He likens fear to a hedgehog that first raises its cute muzzle inside his chest then unfolds its spiky spine to rip it to shreds.

The walks home after work were the worst. He listened for every car that drove past and prayed it wouldn't stop, would please keep going. He would pause for an age outside his own door, scared to open it and find out what was on the other side. He knew the KGB was tailing him, methodically calling in everyone he knew for questioning. Which of them would break? Let something incriminating slip? The KGB didn't need much, just for someone to confirm Igor had given them the wrong books to read.

"In October 1977," recorded the Chronicle of Current Events, *"officials of the Kiev UKGB interrogated no less than sixteen acquaintances of POMERANTSEV, in an effort to obtain testimony relating to the charges."* Of those interrogated, only one broke and confessed that *"POMERANTSEV had circulated anti-Soviet fabrications of a defamatory nature, such as that a creative people cannot realize their potential in the USSR."*

The KGB showed Igor the signed confession that had incriminated him. When Igor confronted the snitch, he answered he had no desire to lie, even to the KGB: he was an honest person, wasn't he?

Walking down the street, Esfir bumped into an old friend from law school who now worked "over there": "The case against Igor is fixed. There's nothing you can do."

Igor wrote:

> The deed is done
> and arrest will follow
> in a month or so.
> But in the interval,

even though everything is already determined and
predetermined,
out of habit he thinks,
weighs and calculates,
as if he still had
some kind
of choice.

IN THE 1970S, SMALL BANDS OF DISSIDENTS, NONCONFORMISTS, AND
activists could barely hope to imagine how just a decade later mass
protests would swell across the world, from Moscow to Manila and
Cape Town, authoritarian regimes would be swept away, with millions of ordinary people on the street, pulling down the statues of
dictators, storming the grim, large offices of secret services that had
oppressed them. The old order that Vilen represented seemed gone
forever.

Those images of people-powered revolutions articulated the victory of democracy over oppression, connected to a whole vocabulary
passed down from the struggles of dissidents and civil rights movements. But what if a cleverer sort of ruler could find other ways to undermine the dissidents, rid them of a clear enemy to fight, climb inside
the images, ideas, stories of those great people-power protests, and
suck them dry from the inside, until they were devoid of meaning?
Could they even use the same language and tactics as "the democrats"
but for opposite aims?

WAVES OF DEMOCRATIZATION

Srdja Popovic is halfway through explaining to me how to overthrow a dictator when he gets a call. It's a warning about a hit piece
coming out tomorrow claiming he's connected to the CIA and is
behind revolutions in the Middle East.[1] The piece first appeared in

an Istanbul daily and then reappeared in a minor Serbian-language website that usually serves as a mouthpiece for Russian-baked conspiracies. From there it moved to a site owned by Christian Orthodox patriots and soon would be featured on the front page of one of Serbia's largest tabloids, which, Srdja assumes, is publishing it because conspiracy theories sell rather than because they have it in for him personally.

After all, he makes for a good story. Russian state TV camera crews turned up at his office among the monolithic communist concrete cubes of New Belgrade, where it sits between a hairdressing salon and a pastry shop. They tried to force their way in. If they had hoped to find dozens of CIA operatives, they must have been disappointed. Srdja has a permanent staff of four Serbs, sitting in a neat, grey office that would look like an accountant's were it not for the multiple posters of the clenched fist, which is Srdja's brand. It's here they compile the step-by-step manuals for nonviolent direct-action campaigns that are downloaded in the tens of thousands all across the world (the largest single location is Iran), organize workshops, and schedule courses for Srdja's online training at Harvard that allow activists anywhere to take courses in how to overthrow dictators without firing a shot.

"Look at them widening the battlefield," says Srdja when he gets off the phone. "Copying the same messages even though they're not allies, attacking from different angles—it's as if they've been learning from me. And you know the funny thing? The two places we actually have never worked in are Russia and Turkey."

He's worked pretty much everywhere else, though. As you read this, Srdja might be in Asia or Latin America, Eastern Europe, or the Middle East. Inside a meeting room in an unremarkable chain hotel, studious-looking men and women of all ages, human rights lawyers and teachers, students and small business people, will be sitting in a semi-circle of desks in the middle of which stands Srdja, slim, dressed like a 1990s college kid in a hoodie though he's in his forties, spinning and dipping his knees to rise again as if he is trying to physically lift the mood in the room. He speaks in slightly Americanized English with the deep, rolled Slavic rrrs that give every statement, even the most casual, an extra intensity. Everyone in the room already feels he is their closest comrade and that together they can change history. The students will be taking copious notes, which they keep looking away from as Srdja cracks another joke and they double up with laughter.

Srdja will often start his workshops with something seemingly light like "laughtivism": the use of humorous stunts in revolutionary campaigns. He might mention, for example, how Polish anti-Communist activists in the 1980s would go out on the streets with wheelbarrows filled with televisions during the Soviet news hour to express their rejection of state media.

Laughtivism, explains Srdja, fulfills a double role. The first is psychological: laughter removes the aura of impenetrability around an authoritarian leader. It also forces the regime into what Srdja calls a dilemma situation. If well-armed security services arrest activists for a jape, it can alienate parts of the population. One thing you learn fast in Srdja's workshops: they may promote nonviolence but that doesn't mean they are for the faint-hearted. Srdja's belief in nonviolence doesn't come so much from pacifism as calculation. Regimes have the upper hand when it comes to physical force; what they can't deal with are massive, peaceful crowds out on the street.

The archetypal protest movement Srdja refers back to is the one he led himself,[2] dimming the lights to show videos recorded from the mid-1990s to 2000, when he led the student group Otpor in its attempt to overthrow Slobodan Milosevic, the Yugoslav dictator who led the country into three wars with its neighbors and sponsored warlords who built concentration camps and slaughtered Muslim civilians. Milosevic's media pumped out a version of the world in which Serbia simultaneously was on a centuries-long mission to save Europe while also a benighted victim of the Imperial West. Meanwhile, patriotic gangsters beat up opposition "traitors" in the dark alleys of Belgrade and partied to a local mix of frenetically upbeat techno and folk music.

In the first years of protest, Srdja lived off laughtivism. When Milosevic's domineering wife announced she would rather see the protests end in bloodshed than resign, Otpor set up a blood transfusion station and delivered blood bags to the government: will the Milosevics kindly leave now that they've gotten their blood?

But such pranksterism is just the start. As Srdja's workshop proceeds, the lessons become more strategic. He teaches the need to formulate a vision of the alternative political model you want to see. How to bring very different groups together around a lowest common denominator. How to find the weak spots of the adversary's "pillars of power" and bring them over to your side.

In the last years of Milosevic's Yugoslavia, Popovic and his partners developed a manifesto stating that that real patriotism meant peace with Serbia's neighbors, joining the international community, the West, Europe. The world wasn't a conspiracy against Serbia. The student marches were full of the flags of many nations. This played to many Serbs' senses of self and history. Serbia had fought against the Nazis; had kept its distance from the Soviet Union. Why shouldn't it partner with Western allies? It was a message that could resonate with miners and farmers, not just students.

Otpor was making progress, but when, in 1999, NATO bombed Belgrade to try to halt Milosevic's ethnic cleansing of Kosovo, it only helped reunite the people around the dictator, Srdja believed. The bombs hit Milosevic's television broadcasting complex, nicknamed the Bastille, but by that time its media monopoly was already broken. Srdja had B92, the banned radio station that broadcast from a friend's basement via the internet, a technology the regime was only starting to understand, which mixed punk rock and political discussion and was forming an online network with small independent media throughout the land.

Otpor had begun to win over the bastions of Milosevic's regime, not just students and labor unions but also the police. The organization created street theater that rewarded the "best policeman in Belgrade" with a prize, making the cops feel welcomed by the movement. When they saw polls that showed that most Serbians were now against Milosevic—but would never back urban liberals like Srdja—Otpor activists gritted their teeth and backed a patriotic and almost anonymous academic as a unity candidate in the next election. Milosevic cheated. Protests grew. Belgrade turned into a street party, the students joined by miners and farmers. Milosevic sent the army onto the streets. Girls shone mirrors into their faces so they could see their own reflections and remember their own humanity, put flowers into the barrels of their guns. The army refused to shoot. Milosevic was overthrown and two years later was facing war crimes charges in The Hague.

After 2000, Srdja's fame spread. He got requests from opposition groups in Zimbabwe and Belarus to train them. He realized this could be a job: going around the world, schooling protest movements. Together with another Otpor founder, Slobo Djinovic, he set up CANVAS, the Center for Applied Non-Violent Movements. He trained activists in Georgia, Ukraine, and Iran, who would then take part in what became known as the color revolutions (Rose, Orange, and Green). Then came training for leaders in Egypt, Tunisia, and Syria, who would go on to participate in what became known as the Arab Spring.

Srdja sees these movements as part of a larger historical process: successive waves of democratization, with democracy defined as a mix of multiparty elections, plural media, and independent institutions such as the judiciary. The first recent wave was the overthrow of authoritarian rule in South America, South Asia, and South Africa in the late twentieth century and the end of Soviet power in Eastern Europe: the Velvet Revolution in Czechoslovakia, the fall of the Berlin Wall, the Singing Revolution in the Baltic States, with their unforgettable images of millions pouring peacefully into the streets in one great sea of anti-Soviet sentiment. The color revolutions, argues Srdja, were the next wave, the Arab Spring the one after, swelled by the rise of social media.

Srdja sees himself as the connection between the first and later waves. Yugoslavia was both the last aftershock of the fall of the Soviet system and the first of the new democratizations. He teaches self-empowerment and street protest strategy, based on a simple principle: if people have more power over their lives, democracy will be all the better for it. Democracy's ultimate defenders are the citizens, awake and trained in how to keep their elected representatives accountable.

Over the years Srdja has become a bogeyman for authoritarian leaders. His manuals, he tells me, are required reading at the Russian, Belarus, and Iranian security ministries. All this interest has had a positive side effect for Srdja: the more the leaders in Moscow or Tehran admonish him, the more protest movements want to work with him.

Former Otpor activists who made good in business cover Srdja's office costs and salaries for his four staff. Opposition movements pay for Srdja to train their activists. Greenpeace has paid Srdja to teach courses.

A significant portion of his work comes from partnerships with organizations connected to what one might term the American "democracy assistance complex," which emerged during the Cold War: US Congress–funded foundations like the National Democratic Institute, the International Republican Institute, and Freedom House. Their relationship with Srdja goes back to the final days of the Milosevic regime: it was the NDI that conducted the polling that encouraged the Serbian opposition to unite behind a less urban, liberal leader. Other "democracy assistance" foundations provided the likes of B92 with the technology to set up internet radio channels and helped train 30,000 poll monitors for the 2000 elections, which Milosevic tried to manipulate.

To their enemies, these organizations are just a front for American imperialism and its meddling. To their friends, they represent one of the few decent American initiatives, the funding of pro-democracy groups in places like the Middle East or Central Asia that oppose the dictatorships official American diplomacy makes friends with.

Srdja is irked by the suggestion that he trains activists only in countries that coincide with US foreign policy interests. "President Mubarak of Egypt, who was overthrown by the Arab Spring, was one of the largest recipients of American military and civil aid for decades, and

I helped train activists there during his rule. And you know the only place CANVAS is officially blacklisted? United Arab Emirates, America's close ally. For me there are only two types of societies: places where governments are afraid of the people, which we call 'democracies,' and places where people are afraid of their autocratic governments. I don't care which dictator I'm empowering people to be free of."

But lately Srdja is finding that a new generation of rulers has reinvented their tactics to undermine protest and nullify dissent. If once upon a time one could speak confidently about history's waves of democratization flowing in a single current, now a great storm has broken out and it's hard to tell what's flowing where and in which direction.[3]

SRDJA'S FIRST PRINCIPLE IS TO DEVELOP AN ALTERNATIVE POLITICAL vision and identity to the regime. This used to be pretty straightforward. Autocrat versus democrat, closed versus open. In Serbia it had meant joining the international community instead of isolation.

But today's strongmen are not so rigid. Instead of hanging on to one single ideology, they have learned to speak with different tongues. Early in the Putin era, the Kremlin, for example, mixed paeans to Soviet greatness with Western reality shows and Western consumerism. When a leadership embraces different ideologies so easily, how are opposition forces to find a space to project theirs?

But one doesn't need to go that far from Srdja's original stomping grounds to see how things have changed.

In Serbia, where CANVAS hasn't run any workshops for over a decade, the current president is Milosevic's old information minister, Alexander Vucic. He's begged forgiveness for his "past mistakes." If yesterday he ran a media machine that depicted the West as an implacable enemy encircling Serbia, today he espouses integration with the EU and NATO. "Reforms for all" is one of his slogans.[4]

Vucic has also swapped a dated form of media influence for a more sophisticated one. In 1999, Vucic would call in newspaper editors and threaten them if they didn't toe the line. Today there are dozens of media, including many foreign ones. However, if a newspaper or television station wants to win government advertising, or if its owners want to win government contracts, then it has to toe the government line.[5] It's the same in Erdogan's Turkey or Viktor Orbán's Hungary: market-orientated in form, authoritarian in content. One of the premises of democratization was that a plural media based on free-market rules would help ensure democracy. It was always a tenuous idea. Tycoons with special interests often own the media in democracies, but now it can be utterly hollowed out from the inside.

And the Vucic whom the domestic media portray is somewhat different from the one who meets Western delegations. In the local tabloids he is still a good old Serbian nationalist, tussling with neighbors, lamenting the loss of territory after the war, while simultaneously promising to bring stability to the Balkans when he speaks at summits in Brussels.[6]

All the while Serbia stagnates. At night, wrapped in the shawl of darkness, Belgrade emerges to play at glamour. Tall women and tall men, in tight dresses and black leather, prowl low-lit bars and rows of restaurants at the base of grand squares with ambitious columns stretching toward the moon. Everywhere there's music. From the gypsies on the street. From the boats turned clubs along the river. Only in the morning does the music fade, light returns, and you can see that the tops of the columns, now visible, are crumbling, that the buildings, above the low line of restaurants, are falling apart, that this city that used to rule southeastern Europe feels like a cliff slowly collapsing into the sea.

There are protests all the time. Against corrupt construction projects. Against suspicious election outcomes. But they can never quite connect and build up into a coherent story like Otpor could. If Vucic has a finger in all the alternatives, which one are protesters going to feed off? Pro-European? Vucic has Brussels in his pocket. Pro–free market?

Vucic has incentivized business to stick with him. Anti-business? Perhaps, but that can end up slipping into resentful nationalism—which Vucic is fine with, too.

Meanwhile, media loyal to the government dismiss all protesters as paid stooges of foreign forces. This had been the case in Milosevic's time, too. The difference was that Milosevic believed his own tall tales. During his many wars, Milosevic's media claimed that Otpor consisted of "well-paid, seduced students" directed by the CIA. After the war, Srdja found that Milosevic had sent secret service teams to find Otpor's headquarters in Washington D.C., when all the time it had been based in the living room of Srdja's parents. Vucic uses conspiracies much more subtly, flirting with the West while loyal newspapers publish stories about how "Serbia is surrounded by the CIA," or how MI6 was plotting to murder Vucic. Conspiracy is piled upon conspiracy, a so-called hidden hand behind everything.

Conspiracy theories have long been used to maintain power. The Soviet leadership saw capitalist and counterrevolutionary conspiracies everywhere; the Nazis, Jewish ones. But those conspiracies were used to buttress an ideology, whether class warfare for Communists, or race for Nazis. With today's regimes, which struggle to formulate a single ideology, the idea that one lives in a world full of conspiracies becomes the worldview itself. Conspiracy theory replaces ideology with a mix of self-pity, paranoia, self-importance, and entertainment. Erdogan, Trump, Putin, Orbán, and the rest invoke conspiracies to explain events, often hinting at them without going so far as stating them directly, which only strengthens the sense that what they are establishing is a more general worldview than any single theory. In Russia, this phenomenon is captured by the catchphrase of the country's most important current affairs presenter. "A coincidence—I don't think so!" says Dmitry Kiselev, as he spins between tall tales that dip into history, literature, oil prices, and color revolutions, always returning to the theme that the world has it in for Russia.

And as a worldview it grants those who subscribe to it certain rewards: if all the world is a conspiracy, then your own failures are no longer all your fault. The fact that you achieved less than you hoped for, that your life is a mess—it's all the fault of the conspiracy.

More important, conspiracy is a way to maintain control. In a world where even the most authoritarian regimes struggle to impose censorship, one has to surround audiences with so much cynicism about anyone's motives, persuade them that behind every seemingly benign motivation is a nefarious, if impossible-to-prove plot, so that they lose faith in the possibility of an alternative, a tactic the renowned Russian media analyst Vasily Gatov calls "white jamming."

And the net effect of all these endless pileups of conspiracies is that you, the little guy, can never change anything. For if you are living in a world where shadowy forces control everything, then what chance do you have to turn it around? In this murk, it becomes best to rely on a strong hand to guide you. "Trump is our last chance to save America," is the message of his media hounds. "Only Putin can raise Russia from its knees," say Trump's Moscow counterparts.

"The problem we are facing today is less oppression but lack of identity, apathy, division, no trust," sighs Srdja. "There are more tools to change things than before, but there's less will to do so."

PERMANENT REVOLUTION

I saw for myself how hard it was becoming to use the logic of previous protests when I had the privilege of attending one of Srdja's workshops in Mexico, where activists, journalists, academics, and political strategists gathered, in a bland conference room in a chain hotel, to discuss how to plan an anti-corruption movement.

Mexico had its great moment of democratization in 2000; seventy years of single-party rule by the Institutional Revolutionary Party (PRI) had ended and the country had become "democratic." Now the problem wasn't dictatorship—the country had real elections—but every new regime seemed just as corrupt, just as in league with the narco-barons as the previous one, oligarch-controlled media working closely with the government.

Some of those at the workshop, especially those jaded by decades of working in Mexican politics, had little faith that anything could ever change. Mexicans had a hundred years of disappointment in revolutionary change. In the nineteenth century, Mexico fought a war of independence from Spain only to be subjugated by its own dictators. At the start of the twentieth century, Mexico was a hotbed of socialist and utopian dreams, projected onto the walls of Mexico City in mind-bending murals by revolutionary artists that depicted a new society. But these hopes ended up in seventy years of single-party rule under the PRI.

When I left Srdja's workshop to meet those struggling to create protest movements in Mexico, I began to see how his ideas were being played out in a new, digital dimension.

WHEN I FIRST MEET ALBERTO ESCORCIA, HE LOOKS TOO TIRED EVEN to be frightened. Someone's been ringing his doorbell then running away so he can't sleep at night, shining green laser beams into his bedroom, sending online death threats with his name spelled out in bullets, thousands of death threats every day so that his phone vibrates with alerts 24/7, like some sort of psychological torture implement.

But there's no way Alberto can go offline. It's his livelihood. More than that, it's sort of his religion. "I see the internet in metaphysical terms, a war between love and fear that I can calculate through the algorithms." There's something a little otherworldly about Alberto. He can spend months analyzing linguistic patterns in thousands of social media posts to find connections. The sort of things others use machines to do, he does himself.

But somehow talking about the divinity of data doesn't seem so unusual when you are in Mexico City, where religious drama is interwoven into everything, where the cocktail of mountain air and exhaust fumes makes the thin light shimmer and refract like through stained glass, and where millions of pilgrims every year climb a hill above the city, past rows of roses and limbless beggars to pray in the massive basilica of Our Lady of Guadalupe. Here the icons of Jesus are decorated with real hair and the priests command vast congregations to not follow the more popular cult of Our Lady of Holy Death, the Lady of Shadows, Santa Muerte, the patron saint of the narcos, who carries a scythe and a globe at her great festival on the Day of the Dead, when all of the city dresses up as skeletons.

Alberto is a great admirer of Srdja Popovic. He's never been to any of the workshops, but he and his friends would pore over Srdja's manuals as they planned their own protests, all united in their hatred of routine police beatings, drug-related shootings, stuffed ballot boxes, and rigged deals, and the chasm between the black glass-fronted boutiques and the security fences in the posh Polanco district and the toothless, impoverished Indians sleeping in piles in the baroque squares, a difference not so much between rich and poor as between different epochs.

Alberto and his friends began with actions that raised awareness of police brutality. After students were beaten by police, they went on silent marches and staged lie-ins where they stretched out supine on the street, blocking traffic. Protesting began as something personal for Alberto. In 2009, his family, along with other workers, had gone on a hunger strike to save the Central Light and Power Company in his hometown of Necaxa. Alberto, already a well-known blogger, helped amplify the protest to the nation. The workers won.

In the second decade of the twenty-first century, protest has become a way to connect to a greater world. While he was helping his hometown, Alberto was also constantly in touch with activists in movements in Spain and the United States, who were in turn talking to others in Turkey and the Middle East.

Dr. Marcos Bastos, a Brazilian academic at London's City University, analyzed twenty million tweets from these movements between 2009 and 2013. He describes them as powered by "rooted cosmopolitans"—for example, a young woman unable to leave her home in Scotland as she had to look after aging relatives would watch livestreams of protests in the Middle East and guide protesters on how to avoid armed police. Discrete interests were pooled into something broader. A Swedish "serial activist" told Bastos, "I don't fight for class struggle, feminism, ecology, or anarchism. My political reference is my mother. I need to persuade her. I'm fighting to reach out to the 99 percent: public values like justice and freedom instead of private values."[7]

But Alberto found himself frustrated with the hit and miss nature of rooted-cosmopolitan protests. Some caught on; others were a waste of time. At meetings his co-organizers would blame failures on the weather, the government. Their approach, which mirrors Srdja's, was to gather different groups, establish the lowest common denominator of mutual interests then spread the message to those whom they hoped would be the right people. But how would they know which themes to choose? The way they approached it seemed unscientific. And Alberto sensed that rational political interests were only part of what was needed to make a protest work. People wanted to be part of something emotionally powerful. That's why they came to some protests and not to others. He sensed this instinctively, but he wanted to use data to turn his hunch into something practical.

Alberto started looking at Google searches in the periods leading up to protests. He found that interest in certain topics (gas prices, police shootings) would become visible online months before they became articulated as reasons for protest. That meant that one could also anticipate the issues that would unite people.

Then Alberto began to look at how social media messages travelled among people in successful protests. Protests grew as the communication among users increased online, forming a dense lattice of interconnections, what computer scientists call "capillarity." Alberto read tens of thousands of messages that generated the most connections. He went through every line individually, a painstaking process that took months. He found that every wave of protests involved a certain amount of words that made the lattice of communication grow thicker, words that worked almost like magical magnets powering capillarity. It was these increasing interconnections that Alberto described with the word "love."

He realized that if he knew in advance which subjects brought people together, and which words strengthened the interconnections, he would be able to inspire protests.

To show me, he opened up a laptop. In the center of the screen was a vibrating ball of dots with lines in between, with new lines joining in between the dots all the time, the whole thing quivering, growing, thickening. This was a real-time representation of online conversation among protesters during Mexico's biggest-ever demonstrations in 2014, when hundreds of thousands came onto the streets after forty-nine students were murdered by narcos and the government did nothing to investigate. Each dot was a person. Each line a conversation between persons, and the links grew with the mention of the words powering the movement.

As Alberto showed me the graphic representation, an actual march went by outside the café we were sitting in. This is how I'd always seen protests: images of passionate people, slogans, speeches, stories, history. Alberto saw them differently, as something more abstract: little throbbing lines and dots, individual words emanating power outside the linear logic of full sentences.

From the top of the screen something new emerged: many little darting, bat-like shapes. These did not connect with each other; instead they descended separately on the ball, pecked away at it, pulling it apart. "These," says Alberto, "are the bots and cyborgs."

The protesters weren't the only tech-savvy actors around. During the 2012 elections, Mexico became famous in computer science circles for the automated social media personas, basically computer programs pretending to be people, used by the eventual winner, Enrique Peña Nieto. Known as peñabots, these were Twitter accounts that could be produced by the thousands and then programmed to push out pro-Peña messages. Bots usually were pretty stupid: they just repeated the same message over and over. Cyborgs were a step up. Bots would push the original line, but when someone took the bait and interacted with it, a real human operator would step in and guide the conversation.[8]

One time a cyborg came to see Alberto. PR companies close to the government would pay "bot herders" like her, a student, to run more than a hundred fake personalities on social media. She said she felt guilty. But the pay was good.

With the protests swelling, government bots and cyborgs were now repurposed to undermine them. Protesters suddenly found themselves being smeared as being paid by the opposition, as anti-patriotic. Instinctively protesters started to respond, defending themselves online against their accusers. On Alberto's screen you could see the consequences. As the little bat-shaped bots pecked at the ball, the little nodes representing protesters would stop interacting with each other and instead turn outwards to engage with the attackers, and as they did so the thick lattice became thinner, the ball started to break apart, becoming a quivering, shapeless thing.

At this moment of crisis for the protests, Alberto had an idea. He knew the words that thickened the links between protesters. What if he could flood the internet with these words? He created a YouTube video. It was just a girl talking to the camera, listing the reasons the protests were important. But every word she said had been carefully scripted by Alberto, each one selected as a linguistic potion.

When the video went viral, protesters stopped being distracted by the cyborgs and began talking to each other again, repeating the words that brought them together. Alberto could see the quivering ball coalesce, the little bats pecking in vain.

"That's what I mean when I say the internet is a great battle between love, interconnectedness, on the one side, and fear, hate, disjointedness, on the other," he explains.

After the cyborgs came the sock puppets, social media accounts that embed themselves within the protesters' online community and then manipulate it from the inside.

In 2017, when there were protests against a hike in gas prices, the sock puppets acted. Activists had been guiding protesters to move around the city safely, avoiding the police and being beaten up. Now the sock puppets gave fake directions and pushed the protesters into the arms of the police. They spread fake stories that there had been violence and looting, posting photos of supermarkets with their windows broken. The photos were of riots in other countries and relabeled as if they were in Mexico. Criminals began to join the protests, which gave the police an excuse for violence.

And after the sock puppets came the online death threats, the green laser beam shone into Alberto's apartment, his doorbell buzzing.

One takes such threats seriously in Mexico. During my visit Alberto asked me to meet him at the annual gathering of Article 19, an international NGO that helps protect journalists, and which derives part of its funding from Freedom House and the US State Department and European Foreign Ministries. At the Article 19 event, the faces of murdered journalists were flashed on the walls: eleven had been killed in the last year, with 99.75 percent impunity. The event was held in one of those colonial, russet-colored palaces in Mexico City that usher you into a cool courtyard of columns, arches, and cloisters so tall and graceful it somehow served to rub in the sad context of the gathering.

As canapés were handed around, one of the directors of Article 19, Ricardo Gonzales, told me the story of a journalist from Reynosa, a city in the Northeast.

In Reynosa, the narcos controlled the local newspapers, which, like Soviet-era publications, only talked about how clean, peaceful, and prosperous the city was when the reality was drug shootouts, with locals getting caught in the crossfire of gun battles that officially did not happen. Then social media came and changed everything. A Twitter channel, Reynosa Follow, would give live updates on shootings. Reynosans warned each other about dangers: "Two gunmen on the corner of Third and Fifth, take an alternative route . . . " Everyone who contributed to the project did so anonymously. As Ricardo explained, the narcos were offering money to anyone who would reveal the identity of those behind Reynosa Follow. They were particularly pissed off with an account named La Felina, who had a picture of

Cat Woman as her avatar, and who would even post photos of local
narcos with demands for their arrest.

Then, one hot August day, a narco gang in Reynosa was caught
in a shootout and one of their men was hit and wounded. The narcos rushed to the local hospital. Three doctors, two male and one
female, were assigned to him. Nervous at being in a hospital too long,
they kidnapped the doctors and took them to a safe house to treat
their wounded colleague: a common practice. They took the doctors'
phones. When they checked the woman's, it opened up on La Felina's Twitter. It turned out this plump, fifty-something medic treating
the wounded narco was the person they had been looking for. A few
hours later La Felina tweeted:

> FRIENDS AND FAMILY, MY REAL NAME IS MARÍA DEL ROSARIO FUEN-
> TES RUBIO. I AM A PHYSICIAN. TODAY MY LIFE HAS COME TO AN END.
>   DON'T MAKE THE SAME MISTAKE AS I DID, YOU WON'T GET ANY-
> THING OUT OF THIS. I REALISED THAT I FOUND DEATH IN EXCHANGE
> FOR NOTHING. THEY ARE CLOSER TO US THAN YOU THINK.

Her last two messages were photos: one of her looking directly
into the camera, the next of her lying on the floor with her face blown
off. They had live-tweeted her execution. Then they replaced her Cat
Woman avatar with Maria's blown-off head.

The narcos like to show that information technology can't be
used to undermine them. One gang took a corpse and dressed him
up as a carnival figure made up of computer parts: a keyboard to
replace his mouth, CD-ROMs instead of eyes. The narcos were good
at symbolism.

Given this context, Alberto decided it would be wiser to spend
some time outside Mexico.

In the 2017 general election, the PRI lost to Andrés Manuel Lopéz
"Louis" Obrador, otherwise known as AMLO. Obrador promised
to clean up corruption but in his own way, top-down. He spoke

the language of old-school state socialism and nationalism. Alberto knew some of Obrador's team and he felt it was safe enough to return home. He liked the promises, but he was also wary. He felt that the new government had capitalized on the hard work of protesters—but would it listen to them when in power?

"Obrador also used bots in his campaign. I will be watching him."

With the PRI out of power, Alberto wanted to learn more about his adversaries. He'd heard about a campaign manager called Chochos, who was reputed to direct an army of online trolls, bots, and cyborgs. On Chochos's Facebook page was a grinning clown face.[9]

Chochos agreed to talk to Alberto over Skype but refused to show his face.

Though they were on opposing sides of the digital barricades, Alberto and Chochos spoke like two mutually respectful professionals swapping notes. When my translator transcribed their conversation, she kept getting confused about who was who.

Alberto asked about the fake pictures of looted supermarkets that had been spread during the gas protests, which encouraged them to turn violent.

Chochos said he knew exactly who was behind those. It was a nineteen-year-old member of a social media group called the Scientific Sect. Whenever one of their fakes would go viral, they would celebrate. Media might talk about "organized cyber criminals," and "psychological warfare," but the Scientific Sect was just a bunch of teenagers who wanted attention.

Alberto told him how people had started coming around his flat, ringing his bell.

Chochos shrugged it off. The kids created avatars for themselves that were intimidating on social media. Now they were getting the online world confused with the real, pushing their avatars into reality. It was still all a game. The thing with Twitter is you can be whoever you want to be, a woman, a troll, an activist. You can play both sides of an argument and no one will know. They weren't, he insisted, actually violent.

"It's like a nightclub," said Alberto. "As soon as the lights go out you can be whoever you want."

Alberto saw a greater problem up ahead. He still believed that the internet could reveal a society's true needs and desires, demands for change lurking in the fluctuations of search engines and algorithms. The tragedy of digital manipulation was not just that individuals were harassed and abused but that they once again were being divided from their own reality. Mexico had seventy years of "truth" being dictated by a one-party state. People had accepted the reality the regime imposed on them as normal. Today bots, trolls, and cyborgs could simulate a climate of opinion, of support or hate, that was more insidious, more all-enveloping than the old broadcast media. And this simulation then would be reinforced as people modified their behavior to fall in line with what they thought was reality. An Oxford University analysis of bots calls this process "manufacturing consensus."[10] It is not that one online account changes someone's mind; it's that en masse they create an ersatz normality.

Over the decades there have been many studies that show how people modify their behavior to fit into what they think is the majority point of view. In 1974, Elisabeth Noelle-Neumann, a German political scientist and pollster, demonstrated how people will go along with the majority opinion to fit in.[11] The need to belong is one of the deepest human inclinations, Noelle-Neumann argued, and people are motivated by fear of isolation. That is why exile, expulsion from the group, is one of the oldest forms of punishment.[12]

In the age of mass communication, media become the gauge through which people decide what the dominant public opinion is. Noelle-Neumann, rather prettily, describes the dynamic as a "spiral of silence." On one side are interpersonal connections, which push alternative opinions up the spiral, on the other are mass media, which push them down. At the bottom of the spiral lies the silence.

Noelle-Neumann defined two types of persons who fight against the silence. The first are what she termed the "hardcore," who feel so rejected by society they don't care what anyone thinks of them and revel in a lost, invented past.[13] The other are the "avant-garde," activists who do want people to listen to them despite all setbacks: "Those who belong to the avant-garde are committed to the future and thus by necessity, are also isolated; but their conviction that they are ahead of their time enables them to endure."

It seemed a good way to describe Lyudmila, Alberto, Srdja, and the other activists I had met.

"Dark days are coming, Peter," Alberto told me when I was back in London. "A new generation of bots and trolls are pushing us further and further into a world of pure simulation."

PARODYING PROTEST

Although regimes have become adept at disrupting and diverting protests, the real challenge is to co-opt the tactics of Srdja Popovic for authoritarian aims, to reverse engineer "how to bring down a dictator" to strengthen one.

The Kremlin had started thinking about how to create its own variation on the color revolutions. As early as 2004, the then-chairman of the Duma foreign affairs committee Konstantin Kosachev, declared: "[Russia] cannot explain the purpose of its presence in the former Soviet Union. . . . The West is doing this under the banner of democratization, and one gets the impression we are doing it only for the sake of ourselves. . . . Our activity is following too openly Russian interests. This is patriotic but not competitive."[14]

Inside Russia the Kremlin created Nashi, a "patriotic youth movement," one of whose stated aims was to stop any Srdja-style, color revolutions from ever taking hold in Russia. In their "near-abroad" the Kremlin developed its own "banners": networks of Russian cultural centers among diaspora populations in former Soviet republics. In 2007, in Estonia, the world saw what a Russian version of a "color" protest might look like.

"THIS ONE WAS SHOT, THIS ONE WAS DISAPPEARED—APPARENTLY killed—this one was deported." Toomas Ilves, then president of Estonia, walked me down a long corridor in his Tallinn residence, pointing out portraits of the men who led the country during the country's first period of independence—between the fall of the Russian empire in 1917 and the Soviet occupation of Estonia during the Second World War, an occupation that continued until the fall of the USSR in 1991.

Ilves was dressed in his trademark tweeds and bow tie, a counterpoint to his mission to make Estonia the most digitally progressive country in Europe. Under his presidency, the government declared internet access a human right; citizens can vote, get medical prescriptions, deal with taxes, bank electronically, and pay for parking with a mobile phone. A new school program required all pupils to learn to code from the age of seven. This e-Estonia project is practical—it represents a search for an economic niche—but also symbolic, a way to tear the country away from its Soviet-era image as Moscow's backward province. This was meant to have been sealed in 2004 with Estonia's accession to the EU and NATO. But this smooth sense of a historical journey, from liberation out from the Kremlin, through internet-powered reforms and into the security of NATO and joining the club of liberal democracies in the EU, soon would be undermined.

Since Soviet times, every year on May 9, known as Victory in World War Two Day, Russian nationalists and war veterans living in Estonia gather to celebrate in the center of Tallinn, at a statue known as the Bronze Soldier[15]—a large, Aryan-looking hunk meant to commemorate the Soviet victory over the Nazis. Around a third of Estonians are Russian, or at least primarily Russophone; the vast majority of these are descendants of Russians who were relocated from the Soviet Union after the Second World War while thousands of Estonians were being deported to the gulag: between 1945 and 1991, the number of Russians in Estonia rose from twenty-three thousand to 475,000. After 1991, some felt like second-class citizens in the new, independent Estonia: Why weren't prescriptions available in Russian? Why couldn't Russophone towns have street signs in Russian? Why did you have to take a language test to gain citizenship if you had been born in Soviet-occupied Estonia? More than 70 percent watched the Russian state media easily available in Estonia, which claimed that the Soviet Union had never invaded Estonia in the first place, that Estonian Communist forces had invited them (in reality these had been Soviet agents). Russian politicians would suggest that Estonia was not a real country. Russian historical TV dramas featured Estonian fascists as the go-to baddy.[16]

When Russian nationalists and Soviet nostalgists would gather at the Bronze Soldier to sing Soviet songs and drape the statue with flags, Estonian right-nationalists began to organize counter-marches at the same spot. In 2006, one Estonian writer threatened to blow the statue up. In March 2007, the Estonian parliament voted to move the statue to a military cemetery—officially, for reasons of keeping the peace. But Russian politicians and media responded furiously. "Estonian leaders collaborate with fascism!" said the mayor of Moscow; "The situation is despicable," said the foreign minister. The Russian media nicknamed the country "eSStonia." A vigilante group calling itself the Night Watch camped around the Bronze Soldier to protect it from removal.

On the night of April 26, 2007, as the statue was about to be removed, ethnic Russian crowds started throwing bricks and bottles at Estonian police. Riots broke out. There was mass looting. One man died. Russian media reported that he was killed by police (he was not), that Russians had been beaten to death at the ferry port (they had not), that Russians were tortured and fed psychotropic substances during interrogation (they were not).

The next day, employees of the Estonian government, newspapers, and banks arrived at work to find their computer systems down, crippled by a cyberattack known as distributed denial of service, or DDoS, in which so many requests are sent to an internet address that it crashes. e-Estonia was taken offline. The whole country was paralyzed by a combination of propaganda, cyberattacks, and street riots.[17]

Who was behind the attack? The Estonian security services claimed to have observed meetings between the Night Watch vigilantes and the staff at the Russian embassy. But ascertaining that the unrest had been coordinated by the Kremlin was a different matter. The Russian patriotic youth group, Nashi, took credit for the cyberattack but claimed they had done it on their own; the government had nothing to do with it. It was early patriotic trolling, with the victim being an entire country.

For Ilves and his national security team, the precise aim behind the riots was something of a riddle. "When Russian politicians make threats about being able to conquer Estonia, does that mean they would actually invade?" Iivi Masso, the Estonian president's security advisor, wondered when I asked her about this. "Are they just trying to demoralize us? Or do they want Western journalists to quote them, which will send a signal to the markets that we're unsafe, and thus send our investment climate plummeting? Sometimes we wonder whether the point of the attacks is only to make us sound paranoid and unreliable to our allies." What the attacks definitely signaled was that despite entry into NATO, Estonia could not easily get away from its former colonial master. The NATO alliance is predicated on a single phrase, contained in Article 5 of the treaty, which holds that a military attack on one member is an attack on all. For all the invocations of the idea of the West, its practical, geopolitical expression is Article 5, a sentence, a promise. But what if that sentence was rendered meaningless? Russia could not risk a military war with NATO, but what if the attack was non-military and non-attributable?

After he completed his two terms as president of Estonia in 2016, Ilves moved to Palo Alto, California, where he was offered a fellowship at Stanford University. Dressed as ever in his tweeds and his bow tie, he visited the technology companies with their trays of jelly beans, where everyone wore sneakers and rode around the brightly painted corridors on bicycles. These precocious computer science geniuses didn't understand the first thing about politics or history or their role in either.

He increasingly was thinking that the digital age meant redefining alliances. NATO had made sense when aggression was physical; it was called the North Atlantic Treaty Organization for a reason. But now that you could have interference anywhere, did geography make sense as a main principle of unity? And what did NATO stand for? It contained countries like Turkey that were not really democratic. Could the world's actual democracies combine for some sort of cyber NATO?

In Estonia, Ilves had made the idea of the internet synonymous with post-Soviet progress. Now that he was among the social media companies he was disenchanted: they were empowering the very forces he had tried to free Estonia from, but they didn't seem willing to recognize or accept responsibility. He wrote an essay for Facebook about how it could be exploited by undemocratic powers, but they took so long to publish it that by the time it came out events had made it obsolete: social media companies were being forced to investigate and disclose how the Kremlin used a mix of hacks and fake online accounts to covertly try to influence the US presidential election to help Donald Trump, and fuel ethnic hatreds and social divides. Ilves rolled his eyes when he saw how the political and media classes in the United States reacted as if nothing like this had ever been seen before: a digital 9/11 some called it, an online Pearl Harbor, said others. How narcissistic, thought Ilves. The attacks on the United States were mild compared to what had happened to Estonia nearly a decade earlier.

After the 2016 elections, academics and experts debated how to measure the effect of the Kremlin's information operations in the US. There were at least two separate ones to consider. One was the hack and subsequent leak of emails of senior staff in the Democratic Party, which one could argue were influential as they became a major talking point in the election. The troll farm activities were much harder to make sense of. They were tiny compared to the overt and covert online political campaigning in the US. So should one ignore the effects of such a relatively small foreign campaign and focus on the impact of the larger, US-produced mass? Or should one focus on the foreign operation, as that could have tipped the scales in a tight race?

Or, I wondered, could one think about the impact of the Russian campaigns in another way: as eating away at the set of associations between events and images that had defined democratization?

Estonia had been one of the places where the mass nonviolent protests that helped bring down the Soviet Union first took hold. The Singing Revolution began with ordinary people belting out patriotic songs in the main square of Tallinn in 1987, and culminated in 1991 with singing protesters facing down Soviet tanks. It was a constant reference point for advocates of nonviolent revolutions such as Srdja Popovic. Now, the Kremlin was working to undermine the association between people out in the streets demonstrating in Eastern Europe and the greater story of waves of democratization. When authoritarians create their own versions of protests, the effect is almost satirical, taunting and undermining the original. Two could play at people protests, Moscow seemed to be saying.

In the United States, one of the tricks of the St. Petersburg troll farm was to take on the personas of American civil liberties campaigns, Black Lives Matter for example, and then use them to encourage votes for the pro-Russian candidate, Donald J. Trump, or depress them for his rivals. The troll farm even organized protests in US cities, both for and against Trump. One protest in particular reminded me of a really bad imitation of Srdja's political street theater: a troll posing as a Donald Trump supporter in a fake Facebook group called Being Patriotic convinced a woman in Florida to hire an actor to wear a rubber Hillary Clinton mask, who then was locked in a makeshift jail cell and wheeled about like in a carnival procession.[18]

But it's when the Kremlin's efforts are unveiled that they have perhaps their most significant effect. When one hears so many stories of fake accounts that seemed to be supporting freedom and civil rights but that in fact turn out to be fronts of foreign governments like Russia, one starts doing a double take at everything one encounters online: Is that American civil rights poster over there actually from St. Petersburg? Is anything what it says it means? When the Kremlin crawls inside protest movements online, the very notion of genuine protest starts to be eroded, making it easier for the Kremlin to argue that all protests everywhere are just covert foreign influence operations. This reinforces the larger narrative the Kremlin (and

Iranian and Chinese) media are trying to reinforce, that movements such as the color revolutions and the Arab Spring are not genuine but US-engineered regime-change plots, that there is no such thing as truly bottom-up, people-powered protest, a message that is only reinforced when the American government gets caught trying to use social media to covertly stir up anti-government sentiment abroad, as it has in Cuba.[19]

When exactly did the Kremlin begin to think about how to crawl into digital pro-democracy movements to subvert them? After the troll farm's interference in the US was discovered, Dr. Marcos Bastos, the Brazilian London-based professor who had collected twenty million tweets from years of protests by rooted cosmopolitans, became curious: what had all those internet personas been doing previously?

Bastos went back to his database. He looked back to 2012 to analyze protests in Brazil, Venezuela, and Spain, and he found the Kremlin's masked accounts had been there all the time, from the peak of the "third wave of democratization." Even as the first protests had rolled through Brazil, Venezuela, and Spain, the Kremlin already was experimenting with the possibilities of penetrating and exploiting them. In 2012, the Kremlin sock-puppet accounts didn't do anything spectacular. They just embedded themselves, building capillarity, impersonating their way into the digital networks of the revolutionaries. When he dug deeper, Bastos found some accounts had even been created back in 2009, though whether those were created by the troll farm, or had been compromised by them later, is another matter.

Bastos recalled a lecture he had given in 2013 at the Higher Economics School in St. Petersburg. It was about how influence in digital protest movements was not achieved through having a few powerful influencers with many followers but many small ones communicating incessantly. Usually his audience consisted of fidgety academics or wealthy hipster students barely paying attention. This time there was someone else: two late-middle-aged men, in suits, staring at him, taking in every word like recording automatons, carefully writing notes.

MEANWHILE, IN BELGRADE, SRDJA WATCHES HIS OWN TACTICS BEING used against his own ideals like in some distorted hall of mirrors.

When genuine protests broke out against prime minister of Macedonia and Putin ally Nikola Gruevski in 2015 and 2016, demonstrators poured red paint into the fountains near where Gruevski's bodyguard had murdered a student. They threw paint balls against the buildings of corrupt state institutions that had wiretapped journalists and opposition parties, so that the city center began to look like a huge Jackson Pollock painting. They held night rallies bearing torches and wearing white masks, to symbolize how the regime wore a false face. So far, so Srdja.

But every time the opposition would protest, the regime would bring in its own counter-protests. They wore the same masks and bore the same torches, matching the original protests symbol for symbol. Gruevski would eventually be voted out but the counter-protests showed how easily color revolution tactics could be co-opted.

This phenomenon would reach a different pitch the next year in Montenegro, where a Montenegrin oligarch who made his money in Russia, Russian oligarchs, and the Kremlin's secret services tried to disrupt the Montenegrin government that brought the country into NATO.

First, they united an utterly fractious opposition around a lowest common denominator, government corruption, relates Srdja, talking about the creation of a Montenegrin opposition movement that brought together Serbian Nationalists, Orthodox Christians, and Communists.

Then they widened the battlefield by bringing international players, with Russian money; then they prepared to claim electoral victory, and when they lost, they launched street protests.

"What happened in Macedonia and Montenegro is right out of my book, but reversed, and missing the most important parts," argues Srdja, as he sits in front of the huge clenched fist that has become synonymous with all the protests he has inspired, scrawled on walls from Cairo to Caracas. "They think that popular will does not matter, that you don't need to win elections, for example, while we make it the basis of our strategy. And they think you can use violence to make up for the lack of popularity, while we know that nonviolent movements are the more successful."

Throughout all this topsy-turviness, where the direction of the waves of democratization is under question, Srdja remains indefatigable. Anyone who is lucky enough to attend one of his workshops will experience the sense that change is possible. Though with time, some of the lessons have changed. Sometimes Srdja finds he is teaching his students not so much how to overturn authoritarian regimes, but how to defend democracies.

"What is the lowest common denominator among your institutions? Which are the ones you can gather a coalition to protect? Is it the courts? The media?" he asks.

While we speak, there is only one moment when he becomes frustrated—when I describe what he does as a technology, or a model.

"This is not a model," he says. "This is not a technology. We give people skills. We teach them how to play the guitar, not what to play. That's the great difference between us and them. That's why their protest movements never succeed. They think you can use people like puppets. We train people to take power themselves."

But what, I can't help wondering, if the people who want to take power do so to crush other people?

THE DISCORD CHANNEL

A Discord channel is a closed internet site usually used by computer game fanatics but which has become increasingly popular among far-right groups to meet online and plan digital influence campaigns. To gain access to the Infokrieg group, for example, you might want to first create an avatar that expresses interest in the philosophy of Friedrich Nietzsche and maybe spend some time developing an online alter-ego that regularly reposts articles about migration and cultural cohesion. Once inside Infokrieg, you will be able to download an Information War Manual in which you will find you have been given a status based on how many followers you have: twenty-five to one hundred is a Baron; more than ten thousand makes one an Ubermensch Influencer. You will then read up on different campaign tactics—how to coordinate "sniper missions" against journalists; post malicious comments to the Facebook pages of politicians; plan "dislike" campaigns on YouTube, where you vote down videos of your opponents. If you get into an online dogfight with the enemy, a debate you can't win for example, the Infokrieg Information War Manual tells you to post the hashtag Air Support and other Infokrieg members will come to your aid, spamming the conversation with their taunts.

Infokrieg also has its own meme factory, where activists are provided with existing pictures, and they deface them with their own words in order to change their meaning. One meme created by Infokrieg, for example, showed a highly saturated drawing of a happy American family right out of a 1950s ad, with the words "Right Wing Extremists" printed beneath it, indicating that traditional ways of life are being marginalized.

But what caught my eye on Infokrieg was the language used by some of the participants: "Don't use any National Socialist memes. Focus on lowest-common-denominator themes: mass migration, Islamification, Identity, Freedom, Tradition." "Lowest common denominator" was a concept right out of Srdja's playbook.

Infokrieg was created by members of the Generation Identitaire movement. Martin Sellner, leader of the Identitarian Movement of Austria, is perhaps the most prominent figure and intellectual leader of the movement. Sellner advocates for a culturally homogeneous Europe and the "remigration" of Muslims: a sort of soft, peaceful path to achieve aims that sound not dissimilar to the ethnic cleansings Milosevic supported in Yugoslavia.

Sellner is perhaps best known for a stunt he had pulled called "Defend Europe," when he chartered a ship to sail out into the Mediterranean and stop humanitarian organizations that help migrants making the dangerous crossing to Europe across the sea from North Africa. He has been banned from entering the UK on the grounds of "not being conducive to the public good."[20]

When I talked to Sellner over video he told me that Srdja Popovic's writing had a massive influence on him. He sounded genuinely impressed when I told him I knew Srdja.

Sellner, with black-rimmed glasses looking more like a philosophy student than a skinhead, proudly and enthusiastically told me about two Srdja-inspired stunts he'd pulled. Sellner claims that we are ruled by a "soft authoritarianism" that makes discussion of migration taboo—an accusation that seemed absurd to me sitting in London, where the biggest-selling newspapers run on a diet of anti-immigration fearmongering.

One could analyze Sellner's work through the prism of CANVAS's strategies. He has clearly articulated the change he wants to see—a culturally homogenous Europe. In migration, he has found the lowest common denominator that can unite disparate interests. When Julia Ebner and Jacob Davey,[21] two researchers of the digital growth of right-nationalist movements, analyzed the motivations of the different groups that supported Sellner's Defend Europe escapade, they found anti-Muslim and anti-leftist attitudes, worries about terrorism, and fears about whites being displaced from Europe. Sellner's supporters also included general anti-establishment groups and conspiracy theorists. Sellner has "widened the battle field," as Srdja puts it, coordinating an international network of forces. He has built alliances with British anti-Muslim activists, makes regular appearances on Russian state broadcasters, and has registered his group in Hungary. His girlfriend, Brittany Pettibone, is a leading US alt-right personality. Almost half of the online support for Defend Europe came from the United States. And finally, Sellner has an electoral strategy: Infokrieg campaigned for the Alternative für Deutschland Party in Germany, which in 2017 dominated social media to Twitter-storm its way into the German parliament for the first time.

After our video call, Sellner sent me a message: "Greetings to Popovic."

CHAPTER THREE

THE GREATEST INFORMATION BLITZKRIEG IN HISTORY

Esfir pinned her most precious diamond earrings to Lina's lobes and then someone, Lina could barely register who, took a cigarette, tapped the ash on their fingers and smeared the ash on the earrings to hide the shine; "If the customs officials ask, say they're just glass."

We were at the airport. A crowd had come to say goodbye forever. As far as anyone knew we would never see parents and sisters, brothers and best friends or anything ever previously known as home ever again. All my parents could fit in their canvas bags were kilograms of reusable diapers (they knew of no disposable ones in the USSR). They had US $180 in cash and that was it. Soviet citizenship was revoked. We were stateless. At the border we were strip searched. My mother had held me so tight that when she took off her shirt there was an imprint of my face on her chest.

"In November 1977, Major MEL'GUNOV gave a formal warning to POMERANTSEV. The protocol listed circulating defamatory fabrications, regular listening to hostile broadcasts and contacts with foreigners. In the same month KGB Major A.L. IZORGIN advised POMERANTSEV to emigrate."

In many ways Igor was lucky. He had the semblance of choice. The major had made it clear that if he stayed, he would have the full seven years in prison and five in exile to face. If he had been a Ukrainian language poet, he would have probably been locked up immediately. Repression in Ukraine focused on exterminating any signs of independent Ukrainian culture outside the cultural crèche of state-sanctioned Soviet "Ukrainianness." But Igor wrote in Russian, the language of the colonizer. He had been published in the Moscow-based cultural journal Smena, which had more than a million readers. If he were put away there was a chance that someone in Moscow would kick up a fuss and then it would be all over the Western media, raised at international conferences. The charges against him didn't even lead to arrest anymore in Moscow, where rules were laxer due, in part, to the presence of Western journalists able to make stars and saints out of dissidents (or at least write a column about them).

The Soviet Union was still going through the motions of posing as utopia, so elevating minor poets to prisoners of conscience for reading books was a bad look. In 1977, for example, the most famous Soviet dissident, the physicist Andrei Sakharov, could write a letter in support of other political prisoners to American president Carter and have it published in the New York Times:

"Dear Mr. Carter, it's very important to defend those who suffer because of their nonviolent struggle, for openness, for justice, for destroyed rights . . . our and your duty is to fight for them. I think a great deal depends on this

struggle—*trust between the people, trust in high promises and the final result—international security."*[1]

Sakharov provided a list of names he wanted Carter to raise with his Soviet counterparts. These weren't empty appeals. Ever since 1974, when the Soviet Union signed the Helsinki Accords promising to respect human rights and fundamental freedoms, American leaders would raise the issue of political prisoners at summits. Sometimes they even managed to get someone released. At the very least it embarrassed the Soviet Union and made the Americans look superior.

From the mid-1970s, the Politburo had decided that emigration was often an easier way to get rid of troublesome dissidents than arresting them. It also was more profitable.

Igor and Lina saw themselves facing frightening choices about freedom, family, literature. But our fates were also decided by warheads and wheat. Technically we were being allowed to leave on a "Jewish visa," the provision of which would fluctuate depending on the amount of grain the USSR was allowed to export to the US. In 1976, fourteen thousand Jewish visas had been issued. In 1978, as the US and USSR negotiated the SALT nuclear arms reduction treaty, which included easier grain exports, the number rose to twenty-nine thousand. We were three of those twenty-nine thousand.[2]

The visa allowed you to travel to Vienna, where you had to choose between a final destination of the United States or Israel. My parents had no desire for either. They wanted to stay in Europe.

"Dear Mark,

"You were there to say goodbye to us at the airport and said goodbye at customs. I want to tell you what happened next. At customs we were strip searched. I carried all our huge canvas bags as Lina had Petka in her arms. I was soon sweating and wanted a drink. On the second floor there was a sparkling mineral water dispenser but I didn't have one Soviet kopek on me to put in the slot. Mark, if you ever emigrate, take some small Soviet change. It's illegal to take any Soviet money with you but you will get away with this.

"You then saw my hand waving to you from the window of the bus, but you didn't see I was crying. We found seats in the tail of the plane. In front of us sat two quiet, smiling Japanese. When the plane took off, the stewardesses started to bring breakfast. We were treated like foreigners. They even served us wine. But in half an hour the plane began to shake like an autumn leaf: we had flown into a thunderstorm. Water sprayed on our cheeks. Snow fell through the cabin. There was an announcement in English that we would be making an emergency landing in Minsk, Soviet Belarus. Just to have something to say I told Lina to fasten her seat belt. 'I'm nervous,' she told me. Petr was asleep on her knees. It was hailing from all sides, and from below and above. I put one hand over my head and the other around my son's face. The wheels collided with the Minsk landing strip and with a great crunch buckled, the airplane skidding on its belly another 328 feet, knocking down cabins and flags.

"In the airport, we were guided to the 'mother and baby' waiting room. Lina was crying and didn't want to go. I pushed her forward with my elbow and it came out rough so she cried even more. We were separated from the other passengers. 'Main thing is not to worry,' I told myself. 'We have foreign visas. We've been stripped of Soviet citizenship. We're foreigners now and that's it.' There was a man in a suit with his back to us when we walked into the room. For some reason I exclaimed 'Good day!' to him *in English. He paid no attention and began making calls. I could hear him say the names of our KGB interrogators from Kiev, Villen Pavlovich and Valeriy Nikoaevich. Then he mentioned the Belarussian town of Bobruysk. They took us away in the evening. We walked towards the van, I with my wet shirt, Lina with her face smeared and puffy with weeping, the sleeping boy in her arms. 'At least I don't have to carry the bags,' I thought. So, they will take us to Bobruysk. They will be there already. Villen will have taken off with some woman. Valeriy will be working on chess puzzles, checkmate in four moves, knocking the pen against his lower teeth yellow with nicotine, squinting . . .*

"*Our van rattled on the rough roads; we were squashed in the back into one wet, salty mound.*

"*We arrived in Bobruysk at night. In Bobruysk they executed us by firing squad.*
—*Igor*"

Igor wrote this nightmare scenario a few weeks after arriving in Vienna as a way of communicating the fear he felt during the flight. All through their first months in the West, Igor instinctively still would listen for the click of the KGB eavesdropping on the phone line, for the knock on the door.

It was the colors that struck Lina when they first landed: she was almost blinded with the searing yellow of bananas in the grocery stores. As Vienna came into focus around her, she regained a sense of order. The architecture, with its art nouveau twirls was comfortingly reminiscent of Czernowitz and Kiev. Then she found herself thrown again by the sight of so many handicapped people in the streets: old people in wheel chairs, groups of children with Down syndrome. She struggled for an explanation: "Is this some sort of punishment for what they did in the war?" she blurted out to Igor, even as she realized how nonsensical this idea was. Then she *understood: in the utopia of the Soviet Union, the disabled were locked away, hidden in horrible homes far from the city or trapped in apartments. Censored.*

We rented rooms in the dormitory of the Vienna conservatory, so all these first impressions of bananas and children with Down syndrome and art nouveau stucco swirls were bound together inside the sound of strings and trumpets and pianos tuning up and practicing scales in a din of dissonance that would sometimes suddenly combine in harmony. Into this cacophony pulled up a large, bright blue Mercedes, out of which stepped a tall woman with a familiar face. It was Anneliese and she was here to guide us (she had even paid for the dorm in the conservatory).

Anneliese had visited Kiev in the mid-1970s, where she had gotten to know Igor and Lina. She had come to the USSR as a curious tourist and left determined to help the dissident friends she made there. She was a Studienrat, a teacher and civil servant, at a grammar school in a small German town, and she had a plan to get us from Austria to Germany. She and Harold, one of her last-year pupils, had spent days researching the thick forest on the border and mapped the quickest way to cross it by foot: they had it down to a brisk half-hour walk.

They drove the blue Mercedes to the border and Anneliese led us into the woods while Harold drove on to meet us on the other side. Lina shushed me. I stayed abnormally still. There was no path and soon everyone's feet were drenched and what was meant to take a half hour was taking more than sixty minutes. Every snapping twig made them start with fear. Anneliese had lost her way, but both Igor and Lina kept up the pretense that she knew what she was doing. She was the one taking the mad risk, not us. Anneliese was a civil servant. If she were to be caught smuggling us across the border she would, at the very least, lose her job. But she knew how badly Igor wanted to stay in Europe, closer to Kiev, Odessa, and Chernivtsi, which he saw as part of a greater Europe.

Then, just as their strength was fading, they emerged at the other side by the autobahn, and the blue Mercedes drove us farther into West Germany, past villages, across dark forests, and along the castles on the broad, curving Rhine to Anneliese's home village of Lahnstein, where she took Igor into the police station and he requested political asylum. If the policeman were to ask how we had made it into Germany, then Anneliese could have been in trouble. The policeman looked my father up and down, looked at Anneliese, and never asked the question. In 1978, West Germans were delighted to welcome political refugees from the Eastern bloc, proof that their system was superior to East Germany's communism. The application for asylum would take a year but in the meantime, we would be given an apartment on Adolfstrasse.

As part of the asylum application, Igor was "invited" to the regional capital, to be screened by the German and French secret services. They meant to check if he was a spy. Two young, polite, and smiling officials asked him what he did, where he had studied, what he wrote. He answered and then waited for them to begin a more thorough vetting. When none was forthcoming, he became worried: the Europeans were so naive, the KGB would waltz past them. Why hadn't they tried to interrogate him properly?

Then the Americans asked him in for a chat as well. This time there was more intrigue. He had to go to a nondescript office with no sign, where two men with crew cuts were waiting for him. The Americans tried to catch Igor out: How many stairwells were there at your work? How many floors? What could you see out of the window? Igor was relieved. At least someone was investigating him *properly. It even sounded like they had people in Kiev who could double-check what he had told them. Maybe there was hope for the West after all. The men with crew cuts asked him if he could tell them about his army service—the size and location of the unit. He told them he had taken a military oath of honor not to divulge such secrets. The Americans were from the security services themselves and nodded respectfully at this sentiment.*

In Lahnstein, for the first time in his adult life, he found he couldn't write poetry. He couldn't stop thinking about the friends he'd left behind. Some were now locked up in the USSR's last camps for political prisoners in Mordovia and the Perm region. He picketed outside the Soviet Embassy in Bonn with placards demanding their release. He wrote essays that tried to evoke the world he left behind, the dramas of Ukraine so often ignored by Western readers who knew only about Moscow and St. Petersburg. "I have a motherland," he wrote, "and it remains within me forever. We are as inseparable as an eye and a tear."

He described how they all felt revulsion at the Soviet invasion of Prague in 1968, how each of them could remember where they were that day. He wrote about the literary critic jailed for seven years and who, in those seven years, has seen his wife exactly seven times yet still wrote to her without a note of bitterness, merely asking she send on new copies of Bakhtin. Igor wrote about the friends who woke up, read the morning newspaper, and discovered that they were this morning's story and had committed some awful crime. The composer who discovered he had "beaten up a construction worker in front of many witnesses right in the middle of Kiev." Though the worker didn't exist, the sentence was very real. The Jewish activist who was informed that he had viciously beaten up a female nursery teacher. He discovered that he went so far as to break her leg while she was walking home, carrying a cake. When his friends searched through every nursery in Kiev, they never found a teacher with a broken leg.

Igor's angriest writing was saved for the cynicism he encountered in the West. The German journalist who told him that "the truth must be somewhere in between the Gulag Archipelago and official Soviet statements." Or the response of the newspaper editor whom Igor was trying to persuade to write about his friend Peter Vince, who faced another charge while still inside the gulag: "This theme is old and boring, does the Russian want money?" Did the editor not realize that one article in his newspaper could change a prison sentence? Did the journalist not realize that there was no middle between truth and lies?

"No one needs you dissidents here," an older Russian exile told Igor, meaning that no one in the West actually cares about all this business with rights—so why does he even bother? "He who was a conformist at home is a conformist here," wrote Igor. "I'm sure the man who told me this lived in the USSR as if he didn't know or care about the thousands imprisoned inside political camps in Mordovia or Perm. His words were just an excuse, a lie. There are people here who care." In 1980, Igor opened the Chronicle of Current Events to find that someone had been arrested in the Soviet Union for possession of this essay. He was now the "harmful literature" the KGB seized people for.

The Cold War had a cultural front and Igor was rapidly finding himself drawn into it. His essays were published in small literary magazines with tiny circulations, but which were, so the theory went, influential as they targeted a cultural elite. There was, for instance, Partisan Review, where Igor's essay on the "Right to Read" appeared squeezed between Amos Oz and Joyce Carol Oates. Decades later, it would emerge that the CIA helped the magazine survive by *buying up copies when sales were low. There was* Encounter, *whose own CIA-funding scandal had already passed back in 1967.*[3]

Meanwhile, Igor's essays were gaining a little attention. In 1980, he was invited to London for a job interview at the Russian Service of the BBC. Igor's interview, like all such others, would be vetted by a member of MI5. Britain's intelligence service never requested the vetting process; it was the BBC itself that asked MI5 to do it. (If the British government ever was to complain that the BBC was in any way disloyal to the country, the corporation would be able to say that all its employees had been vetted before their hiring. The vetting was not just for foreigners, many staff at the corporation went through it.[4]

There was also a security consideration. In 1978, a member of the Bulgarian BBC Service, Georgi Markov, was walking to the office across Waterloo Bridge when he felt a twinge in his hamstring. He turned around to see a man passing by with an umbrella. A day later, as he lay dying from ricin poisoning, he would realize that the poison had been injected into him via the umbrella. Later it would emerge that the assassination had been carried out by the Bulgarian KGB, with poison provided by the KGB poison factory near Moscow.[5]

Igor passed his writing test and the vetting. We moved to London, part of a tiny quota of Soviet refugees allowed in—the British granted few entry visas to immigrants beyond their former empire. But we were being recruited for a Cold War effort.

TODAY, TALK OF COLD WAR HAS BEEN REPLACED BY INFORMATION war. My office is stacked with thick reports and papers on the "Kremlin's Firehose of Falsehood," the "Digital Maginot Line." I have written about the "Weaponization of Information" and "How to Win the Information War," analyzing the Kremlin's use of media in neighboring countries.

During my research, I came across a Russian manual called *Information-Psychological War Operations: A Short Encyclopedia and Reference Guide* (the 2011 edition, credited to Veprintsev et al., and published in Moscow by Hotline-Telecom, can be purchased online at the sale price of 348 rubles). The book is designed for "students, political technologists, state security services and civil servants"—a kind of user's manual for junior information warriors. The deployment of information weapons, it suggests, "acts like an invisible radiation" upon its targets: "The population doesn't even feel it is being acted upon. So, the state doesn't switch on its self-defense mechanisms."

The encyclopedia seemed to take the idea of information war beyond just cyber and media campaigns, as I had taken it to mean, and to hint at something more expansive. And the more I delved into the Russian literature on information war, the more it seemed to be more than a foreign policy tool but almost a quasi-ideology, a worldview. How is it different from the Cold War—and how does one win, or lose, at it?

OPERATION PERESTROIKA

In the late 1990s and the first decade of the twenty-first century, the idea of information war began to obsess a certain breed of security agency–connected Russian geopolitical analyst looking to explain historical changes and the failure of the Soviet Union in particular. Secret service agents turned academics assert the Soviet Empire[6] collapsed not because of its poor economic policies, human rights violations, and lies but because of "information viruses" planted by Western security services through Trojan horse ideas such as freedom of speech (Operation Glasnost) and economic reform (Operation Perestroika). Alleged secret agents in the Soviet establishment who posed as so-called modernizers, allied with a US-dictated fifth column of anti-Soviet dissidents, oversaw the dissemination of these "viruses."

For a long time, such theories were not mainstream. But as the Kremlin searched for ways to explain uprisings against dictators and the growth of discontent at home, which erupted in hundreds of thousands protesting Vladimir Putin's rule in 2011 and 2012, this pervasive information-war philosophy increasingly was amplified by TV spokespeople and spin doctors. Today, runs the argument, the West wages information war against Russia with the conniving use of the BBC and human rights NGOs, fact-checking organizations, and anti-corruption investigations.

One of the most outspoken public promoters of the information war is Igor Ashmanov,[7] a frequent guest on TV talk shows and radio. But Ashmanov is no crusty spook. He is one of the fathers of the Russian internet, the former head of the country's second-largest search engine. When I once visited his high-tech office in Moscow, where there were piles of fresh fruit, dates, and nuts on the table, I could just as easily have been in Palo Alto or Berlin. Ashmanov, in his sports clothes and wire-rimmed glasses, could fit in at any tech gathering.

"The fall of the Soviet Union, Yugoslavia, Iraq. We've lived through many information wars,"[8] Igor Ashmanov said in one of his many interviews. He's also told Russian lawmakers that Google, Facebook, and Twitter are ideological weapons aimed at Russia, and that profit is only a secondary necessity for them. He explained that American secret service operations, such as Google, need to be economically self-sufficient.[9]

Ashmanov's big idea is "information sovereignty," government control over what information reaches the population, which China is well on the way to achieving, and which the West, he claims, tries to disguise with talk about freedom of speech. Information sovereignty can't be achieved, he argues, without an ideology to defend your rationale for letting some streams of information through and others not.[10]

"If your ideology is imported, as with liberalism, then you are always playing to foreign rules, which are always being changed by someone else. You can always be called guilty, breaking the rules of democracy. Ideology should be created inside a country, like operational systems, rockets, insulin and grain. Supported and defended by information sovereignty."[11]

Information, in this worldview, precedes essence. First, you have an information warfare aim and then you create an ideology to fit it. Whether the ideology is right or wrong is irrelevant; it just needs to serve a tactical function. Instead of clashing ideas leading to a Cold War, here information war necessitates the creation of ideologies. America, this argument goes, has cynically used democracy as an information weapon to undermine other countries while ignoring much worse behavior in allies.

Indeed, it's not hard to find many instances where America acted, to put it mildly, hypocritically when it came to support for freedom and human rights, supporting their promotion in adversaries and ignoring their violation in allies. In the sly words of diplomats, values and interests don't always align. But as long as they kept up the façade of believing in something when promoting their image abroad, they would have to at least sometimes do something about it.

As the Oxford professor Rosemary Foot relates,[12] you can trace the roots of the American freedom narrative back to President Franklin Delano Roosevelt's 1941 "Four Freedoms" speech, which called for freedom of speech and religion, and freedom from fear and want, as the basis for a democratic world. As early as 1949, the "Negro question" had been highlighted by the US Embassy in Moscow as a "principal Soviet propaganda theme" that had to be battled at home for the sake of US foreign policy. During the civil rights movement, the US Justice Department could argue that desegregation was important as it would help promote America's international image as a bastion of freedom.

In the early 1970s, in the aftermath of the Vietnam War, American support for coups in Chile, and US intervention in the Dominican

Republic, Congress held hearings on human rights abuses in those countries. The resulting report established a human rights bureau within the State Department, meant to make rhetoric about freedom and human rights closer to actual policy.

Even the USSR's utopian declarations could, on occasion, act as the tiniest of checks on small parts of its behavior: "Obey your own laws" was the clarion call of the dissident movement to the regime.

These were tiny victories in the grand scale of the horrors of the Cold War—but the notion of information war as an idea of history demolishes even these achievements, replaces hypocrisy not with something better but with a world where there are no a priori higher values. In this vision all information becomes, as it is for military thinkers, merely a means to undermine an enemy, as a tool to disrupt, delay, confuse, subvert. There is no room for values or ideas.

But that raises a tricky question. In his book *Don't Think of an Elephant!*, the cognitive linguist George Lakoff defines winning and losing in politics as being about framing issues in a way conducive to your aims. Defining the argument means winning it. If you tell someone not to think of an elephant, they will end up thinking of an elephant. "When we negate a frame, we evoke the frame . . . when you are arguing against the other side, do not use their language. Their language picks out a frame—and it won't be the frame you want."

I had already seen this in the Philippines, where the Rapplers had indulged Duterte's rhetoric of a war on drugs, thus making it easier for him to start his actual killing. The directors of Russia's international broadcasters, RT and Sputnik, indulge in the language of information war; they even receive military medals for their services to the government.[13] Western journalists and analysts, myself included, then call them out for being information war organs. But by describing them as such, is one actually lending them a hand, framing them in the ways they need to secure more funding from a regime that wants to view everything through the lens of information war?

The long-term implications go deeper. If all information is seen as part of a war, out go any dreams of a global information space where ideas flow freely, bolstering deliberative democracy. Instead, the best future one can hope for is an "information peace" in which each side respects the other's information sovereignty: a favored concept of both Beijing and Moscow, and essentially a cover for censorship.

But to merely ignore the Kremlin's influence operations would be foolish. The disabling of Estonia with a mix of information and hacking in 2007 had been a foretaste of what that might be like.

At endless panels in think tanks in Washington, London, and Brussels, military theorists, journalists, and officials have tried to make sense of the Russian approach to war and international conflict. Some call it full-spectrum warfare, others nonlinear war, yet others ambiguous and gray zone warfare.[14] In Eastern Europe, "hybrid war" state research centers have sprung up, where "hybrid" seems to be a diplomatic way of not saying "Russian."

There are some things that at least a few experts can agree on. First, that the Russian approach blurs the line between war and peace, resulting in a state of permanent conflict that is neither on nor off. And in this conflict, information campaigns play an important role. Summarizing the aims of Russian "Next Generation Warfare," Janis Berzins of the Latvian Military Academy describes a shift from direct annihilation of the opponent to its inner decay; from a war with conventional forces to irregular groupings; from direct clash to contactless war; from the physical environment to human consciousness; from war in a defined period of time to a state of permanent war as the natural condition in national life.[15]

This leaves us with a paradox. It is necessary to recognize and reveal the way the Kremlin uses information with a military mindset to confuse, dismay, divide, and delay. However, there is a risk of reinforcing the Kremlin's worldview in the very act of responding to it.

It is in Ukraine where this paradox plays out at its most intense. This is where the Kremlin's "next-generation" warfare is being tried out, but also where they are trying to spread an all-encompassing worldview of information war.

So how can one fight an information war where the most dangerous part could be the idea of information war itself?

THE GREATEST INFORMATION BLITZKRIEG IN HISTORY

Of all the things one might think Tetyana could be, a soldier is not one of them. But in early 2014, at the height of Ukraine's revolution against a pro-Moscow president, Tetyana suddenly found herself able to command life and death. Sitting in her father's apartment, in her pajamas, with her hand over a keyboard, knowing that if she pressed one key, she might send many very real people to very real deaths, and if she pressed another, the revolution and all that she, her friends, and thousands of others had fought for might be lost.

Tetyana ran the Facebook page of Hromadske Sektor (the Civic Sector), one of the main opposition groups in the Ukrainian revolution against President Yanukovych and his backers in the Kremlin. She posted photos and videos right out of Srdja's philosophy of nonviolent action: a protester playing a piano in the streets facing a row of riot police; photos of protesters holding mirrors up to the security forces; a drawing of a cop dueling with a protester, with the cop holding a gun and the protester "shooting" with a Facebook sign. Online digital activists could organize everything from medical help to legal aid, coordinating million-strong protests and raising funds for food and shelter from Ukrainians abroad.

She had kept up the click-beat over many months of protests. Hromadske Sektor had forty-five thousand followers and one hundred fifty thousand visitors attended their protests—people who didn't trust politicians but believed in volunteers like Tetyana.

She had joined Hromadske because she wanted to be part of a historical moment: something to tell her future children about. The uprising was nicknamed the Revolution of Dignity. It had begun when

President Yanukovych very suddenly dropped a long-standing pledge to sign an Association Agreement with the European Union in favor of a $16 billion loan from the Kremlin. After Yanukovych's police beat protesting students, it had grown to symbolize for many the desire for a government that was less corrupt, for a different sort of society bound up in the word "Europe": "Euro-Maidan" was the revolution's other nickname.

Tetyana would post on the site as she filed stories for her real job as a financial journalist. She told herself she would somehow stay above the fray; she was for democracy and human rights, sure, but she wouldn't get dragged into disinformation.

Tetyana's shift was in the morning. She was usually based in Kiev but one day she happened to be in her hometown of Luhansk, one of the capitals in the far east of the country known as the Donbas, where most people watched state or Russian TV, which portrayed the revolution—referred to as the Maidan, the name taken from the square where protesters gathered—as a neo-fascist, US-orchestrated conspiracy. In Luhansk, Tetyana never mentioned her work for Hromadske Sektor.

She woke at 9 a.m. and switched the computer to the live feed coming from Kiev. At first, she thought she had tuned into some action movie by mistake—snipers were mowing people down, and there was blood on the streets. Then her phone rang: it was activists at the center of the action. She could hear guns going off and after a brief time lapse heard them crackle on the livestream, too.

"Get people to come to Maidan. We need everyone here."

But Tetyana could also see posts popping up on her Facebook feed from people on the square warning everyone to flee and save themselves. She kept getting calls from the Maidan, asking that she tell people to come.

"But there are people being killed," she said.

"The snipers will stop shooting if more people come."

"And what if they don't?"

"It's your decision."

It wasn't the first time she'd found her journalistic instinct to remain above the fray clashing with her revolutionary loyalties. A few weeks previously, the pagan-nationalist, balaclava-clad Pravy Sektor (the Right Sector) had started hurling burning Molotov cocktails through the snowstorms at the riot police. Few people had heard of Pravy Sektor until then. There were only a few hundred of them, but all the publicity around their violence greatly raised their profile. Kids looking for a little ultra-violence were now signing up to join them.

Tetyana didn't approve of Pravy Sektor's violence or ideology. The Maidan was full of different sectors, everything from neo-Cossacks to neo-anarchists and neo-fascists, all able to organize with the help of the internet. My parents' friends who had been put through the wringer of the KGB were there, too. They could see in the Maidan a distant echo of their own struggles, though now raised to a level of mass protest one couldn't dream of in 1978.

Hromadske Sektor decided to ignore Pravy Sektor, but Tetyana couldn't ignore the massacre on Maidan Square that morning. What was her role? Was she, ultimately, a propagandist? A journalist? Was she reporting on the war or was she a soldier in it? Every time you post or tweet, or just repost or retweet, you become a little propaganda machine. In this new information flux, everyone has to find their own boundaries. Tetyana had reached hers. She refused to encourage crowds to come to the Maidan. She simply reported on what was going on and let people make up their own minds.

One hundred and three protesters died in those few days. But the crowds didn't stop coming. They kept pushing, storming the Presidential Palace, while in the regions, local council after local council was stormed by protesters, many of them now armed. President Yanukovych fled to Russia.

Then the Kremlin began exacting its revenge. Russian TV was filled with invented stories about how Pravy Sektor was coming to slaughter ethnic Russians in Crimea, where most of the population are ethnic Russians. In Sevastopol, the Crimean city, Cossack groups, separatist parties, and Orthodox priests (all funded by the Kremlin) led crowds begging Putin to rescue them. He obliged and annexed the peninsula.

Russian TV broadcast scare stories about Pravy Sektor coming to murder Russians in East Ukraine, too. The internet, the medium through which the revolution had been empowered, was flooded with Kremlin content pumped out of the troll factory in the St. Petersburg suburbs. Young people working in Lyudmila's old organization were paid to post pictures, comments, and videos, sowing confusion, enmity, and panic in East Ukraine.[16]

The Kremlin's information campaign was the prelude to action: irregular forces, local proxies of the Kremlin, seized cities in East Ukraine. Donetsk. Tetyana's home town of Luhansk. These parodied the same visual language as the Maidan, with flag-waving crowds (sometimes bussed in from across the border) and piles of burning tires, which had become the symbol of events in Kiev. It was labelled the Russian Spring by Kremlin media, tapping into the language of the Czechoslovak rebellion against the Soviet Union in 1968. The Kremlin was trying to satirize the Maidan into insignificance. At the same time, Russia was desperately trying to reconfigure the Maidan uprising into a greater story of Ukrainians manipulated by covert American forces, all part of American regime change, which had brought catastrophe to Iraq and Libya. Igor Ashmanov and Russian state media honchos pronounced the Ukrainian uprising was, of course, a product of information war.

One motif to the Kremlin storytelling was this: that the desire for freedom didn't lead to peace and prosperity but to war and devastation (a message, first and foremost, meant for its own people so they didn't become overenthusiastic about the idea). To make this narrative real meant ensuring that Ukraine could never achieve peace. The country had to bleed.

When the Ukrainian military would attack the separatist strongholds, the Kremlin would send in tanks and defeat the Ukrainian army, then retreat and claim they had never been there in the first place. Over the next years, indeed to the time of this writing, the conflict flowed here and there, not quite a full-blown war but never becoming peace, either. Towns in the Donbas are taken and then lost again. Shells go off either side of the lines. When the Russian army held mass exercises on the border with Ukraine, mass panics would break out throughout the country. The violence also has had unintended consequences. In July 2014, when a Russian high-tech anti-aircraft gun shot down a Malaysian Airways passenger airliner full of Dutch tourists, killing 298, over territory controlled by Kremlin proxies, the information operation went into absurd overdrive: the plane had been shot down by Ukrainians who thought it was Putin's private jet; dead bodies had been put on the plane in advance and the whole thing was staged; Ukrainian fighter jets had taken the plane down.[17]

NATO's Supreme Allied Commander had called the Russian campaign to take Crimea "the most amazing information warfare blitzkrieg" in history. But it was ordinary Ukrainians, often abandoned by a shoddy government, who had to find ways to make sure the information blitzkrieg wouldn't spread to the rest of the country, too.[18]

"THE WORST THING ABOUT ALL OF THIS," BABAR ALIEV TOLD ME AS we sat, on a burning summer's day in 2015, in a Severodonetsk café blaring painfully loud techno overlaid with high-pitched Russian female vocals, "is that I have to carry a weapon again. Ten years ago, I promised never to carry a gun. But I regretted that promise when the separatists came. Next time I will be ready."

In early 2014, Babar woke to find fifty new Twitter trolls on his trail. Severodonetsk is in eastern Ukraine, close to the Russian border, where Russian troops were massing in what seemed to many the preparation for an invasion. A rumor had just swept through Severodonetsk's internet portals about how Right Sector were on their way to haul down the town's Lenin statue, a symbol of pro-Russian leanings.

Local groups—Russian Cossacks, and Russian wrestling, laser-tag, and literary clubs—gathered to defend it. The rumor was false; someone was trying to get the pro-Russians fired up. This wouldn't be too hard. Severodonetsk is not a town that feels much historic loyalty to the Ukrainian state. It was built in the 1950s, a perfect grid of Soviet modernist white rectangles designed around sixteen science colleges and four chemical plants. As in much of eastern Ukraine, the inhabitants came from across the USSR.

After World War II, it was one of the few places you could go with no papers, a bureaucratic trick to get criminals and vagabonds to come work in heavy industry. After the end of the Soviet Union, the town went to pot: the plants are stripped carcasses, the neat modernist rectangles cracked and peeling, the potholes in the roads so bad you drive in weird swerves. The writer Owen Matthews once compared parts of the former Soviet Union to an experiment abandoned by its scientists, the people lab rats left to rot and eat each other. In Severodonetsk, with its mix of symmetry and dilapidation, this seemed particularly apt. For many, Russia represents a better place.

Babar, a thirty-something web designer (of mixed ethnicity from across the former USSR), noticed that the pro-Russian clubs started to proliferate after 2012, just as Vladimir Putin was facing mass protests against his rule in Moscow. Since the start of the Maidan, more clubs had appeared. At the time he thought nothing of it—Ukraine was a democracy, after all. Now he suspected someone had been planning something for a while. During the day, the pro-Russians would gather at rallies on the main square, where Orthodox priests (from the Moscow patriarchate) and Communist Party leaders were holding daily rallies calling for unification with Russia, claiming the Maidan had been led by fascists and fed by drugs.

"If we let them pass, then the country rolls backwards," Babar thought to himself. He had been in Kiev during the Maidan and had felt that the revolution was some sort of historical leap into something new. He had been disgusted when he saw the riot police beating up students in Kiev. Over the last few years, he had seen how Yanukovych's party was raiding businesses and pillaging the country; government run as a protection racket, propped up by Putin. Now, in a Severodonetsk abandoned by the government, he felt it was up to him to fight an information war all by himself, hoping that he could galvanize others. Maybe he was motivated by the feeling that what was happening recalled a part of his own past that he didn't want to return.

As a teen in the mid-1990s, Arif was a gang leader. His specialty was planning and executing complex burglaries. (He always looked down on mere protection rackets: where was the art in that?) Then he moved on to stripping the local chemical plants of precious metals, gold and platinum. (He had read up on the periodic table.) He dropped the thug life after he was finally caught. (He had studied law and knew how to bribe his way out.) But even now, when he has long been a web designer and minor internet PR guy, he has the swagger, shell-suits and quick eyes of the smart hoodlum (as well as the sudden, ecstatic grin of a toddler). In Severodonetsk, many still find it hard to believe that Arif, as he likes to put it, has "developed an aversion to slicing people up."

During his time in the Maidan, Babar had developed a Facebook following among pro-Ukrainians in Severodonetsk and now he used it to fight the separatists online, to "nightmare them," as the Russian phrase goes. Babar put out a story that separatists had beaten up some gay activists and now a battalion of gay fascists was coming from Holland to take revenge. The story was ridiculous but some of the separatists fell for it and started to get alarmed, which made them look like idiots. Babar also put out a story that two hundred Right Sector undercover agents had holed up in flats in Severodonetsk; that they rode the trams listening to people's conversations; that when they heard pro-separatist talk the agents would take people off the tram and they were never seen again; that they recorded the names of taxi drivers who wanted Severodonetsk annexed. The separatists' portals were in a panic and Babar felt he was winning the disinformation war. He wanted them to doubt everything and lose their bearings, to do to them what the Kremlin was doing to Ukraine.

Now he needed to build a coalition that would take to the streets. But how would he motivate them when there was no overall idea of Ukraine they related to, and when each tribe in the city lived in its own little information bubble?

Babar went to the organized crime bosses, known as Vor v Zakone (Thieves-in-Law), who lived according to a strict prison code. Some of them had been in Arif's first gang before he straightened out. "How can you be on the same side as the cops?" Arif asked them, slipping into Fenya, the prison jargon that Vor v Zakone communicate in. The cops were with the separatists—shouldn't that make the Vori for Ukraine? "You used to be an honest prisoner (someone who lives by the prison code), now you're a goat and you've got horns on your head" (in prison jargon a goat is a turncoat, the lowest of the low).

The Vor v Zakone and Babar calculated the costs to their business interests if the Kremlin invaded. It was better for them to remain Ukrainian. They offered Babar men and guns.

Babar also went to see the hoodlums who ran the protection rackets. Did they really want to have Russian gangsters come here? They would take away their territory. And although the local gangs had the Ukrainian police sewed up, Russian police might have other ideas. The gangs told Babar they would back him.

Then Babar went to the businessmen. "You guys have been to Europe," Babar said. "You know how much easier it is to do business there, no hassle from bureaucrats wanting bribes or gangs wanting protection money. Well, the Maidan is all about us having European rules. Don't you want that?" The business men came on board, too.

Now that he had his coalition, Babar reached out to Kiev Maidan activists who had connections to the new government for backup. Just a few special forces would be enough. Throughout the spring of 2014, town after town in the East was being taken by separatists backed by Russian special forces, raising the flag of the independent Donetsk and Luhansk "People's Republics." Babar kept on waiting for a sign from Kiev but none came. He began to suspect the Donbas had been traded for some deal with Moscow. He kept on calling his contacts, explaining to them that he'd done all the preparatory work, the disinformation campaign, built up the alliance of different groups.

In May, the separatists took power in Severodonetsk. The local administration welcomed them, taking down the Ukrainian flag and replacing it with the tricolor of the Luhansk People's Republic. The thing that hurt Babar the most was that when the separatists came for him, they sent only three men. When he had been arrested back in the 1990s, the cops had sent three vans with SWAT teams in flak jackets. Now there were just three guys with guns who put him on a train to Kiev. His attempt to fight his own version of a one-man information war had failed. He had tried to reverse engineer the Russian approach, first spreading disinformation to confuse the enemy, then using irregular forces, gangsters and mercenaries, to hold a town. But the Ukrainians were still too slow to cotton on.

A few months later the Ukrainian military finally arrived, now reinforced by patriotic and ultra-nationalist volunteer battalions, including the Right Sector. The army surrounded Severodonetsk and lobbed it with heavy artillery. The separatists hoped the Russian military would intervene but no one seemed to care enough about holding "Sever"; they pulled back to the heartlands of their new republics, the areas around the cities of Donetsk and Luhansk. Babar returned. But when I met up with him at the Severodonetsk restaurant blaring out the high-hat beats of a Russian girl-band, he showed little sense of victory. The same politicians and cops who had backed the separatists were still running the town. Some of the Ukrainian soldiers and volunteer battalions had alienated the locals. There had been a shooting during a bar brawl; one of the volunteer battalions had decided to enforce its authority over the local mafia by forcing a gangster to swim across a river and then shooting him in the head when he was halfway across. This wasn't how you built coalitions.

I asked what his plans were for the future. He told me that the financial crash that came with the war meant his old website development orders had disappeared. He wanted to set up media literacy classes for local people, but for the moment would do anything, even hauling crates, to get by. I asked him what the media literacy classes would involve. He explained they would teach people how to check whether a piece of news online is real, check it for the reliability of sources, use a reverse image search to verify pictures were from where they claimed to be from, discern information and disinformation.

Hadn't he used disinformation himself when he nightmared the separatists with his fake rumors? How did he square that with promoting media literacy campaigns?

"I believe in disinformation for the other side and media literacy for my side," Babar said, smiling.

UKRAINE WAS FILLING WITH INFORMATION VIGILANTE GROUPS, AND I wanted to know what it was like to be on the receiving end of their campaigns.

"R u still alive you separatist? I wonder how long for?" said the SMS text on Andrey Shtal's pre-smart-phone-era mobile. "As always there's no number to trace it back to," said Andrey. He seemed used to the messages and was more worried that patriotic Ukrainian activists from a civic information war group had put him on a list of "traitors" but listed an old address. "What if they go around and beat up the person living there now, someone totally unrelated to any of this?" he wondered.

Shtal was from Kramatorsk, just south of Severodonetsk. Like Sever, it had first been taken by Russian proxies and then retaken by Ukrainian forces. Andrey worked at the Kramatorsk municipal gazette. When the proxies took Kramatorsk and declared it to be part of the Donetsk People's Republic, most of the staff fled. Andrey stayed on as editor. His paper published information about sewers and roadworks and schools, nothing political, and he never strayed into anything that was off topic. This saved him when the Ukrainian army took the town back. He was arrested by a pro-Ukrainian volunteer battalion in Dnepropetrovsk. They beat him, and held him for three days with a bag over his head, but eventually he was released.

It's Andrey's poetry, rather than his journalism, that got him in trouble with the patriotic activists.

"In poetry I can be myself. The head of the Donetsk People's Republic likes my poetry, and he improvises verses back over Facebook."

We walked across Kramatorsk's tidy city park and down a grand, neoclassical Soviet avenue to a local café with Wi-Fi so we could look up his poetry. In the distance you could see the sun shining off the hills of the Donbas.

There were dozens of pages of Andrey's lyrics on local poetry portals. We clicked through to his most recent work. It started with satires on the Maidan, in the style of a Soviet children's poem.

> *They will create hell here and horrid night,*
> *And turn you, my hero, into a sodomite.*

"I was against the Maidan," Shtal tells me. "I sensed straight away it would lead to war. I get premonitions of the future sometimes." He had grown up with the young men who joined the proxy Russian forces in Kramatorsk. In his poetry he conveys the careless, chaotic way they decided to take up arms. "They were local druggies and gangsters, the kids of policemen and officials. How could I hate them? No one can hear the Donbas."

"No one can hear the Donbas": I heard that phrase often in the East, a catchphrase expressing the sense that politicians in Kiev didn't understand local needs.

As the conflict spread eastward, Shtal's verses became grimmer:

> *I used to be a musician and artist,*
> *But now I woke up as a separatist . . .*
> *I live in Rus, Rus isn't dead yet!*
> *What I wish for is a bullet in the Prime Minister's head!*[19]

Much of Shtal's poetry evokes Soviet motifs and songs. He is haunted by a memory from his teens, when he was on a school trip to Lithuania in 1991 and witnessed the crowds trying to pull down the statue of Lenin. On the long train journey back to Donetsk he wrote his first poem, an allegory of the Soviet Union as a train that has become too old, and of a country falling into civil war.

"Lenins were falling then and they are falling again now," he sighs. "Back then I already had a bad feeling about the future."

When we met in Kramatorsk, the government in Kiev had just passed laws forbidding Soviet street names and symbols. The Lenin statue on the central square had been pulled down, leaving an empty plinth with a Ukrainian flag tacked on. It was argued the street name changes and statue demolitions were a necessary part of the information war with the Kremlin, with its non-stop diet of Soviet movies and social media campaigns that reframe the present as an endless World War II against eternally returning fascists. But the laws could also play into the Kremlin's game, shifting the focus of the Maidan from the search for a better future into the battle over the past, which could only be divisive.

"The Communists built everything here. Anyone who achieved anything was from the party—why should we forget them?" complained Shtal. "There are a lot of people here who can't show what they think openly. They live online instead and it's important for them not to be lonely. I can formulate what they feel."

By embracing and parroting back the language of the Kremlin, Ukrainian information warriors risked playing into Moscow's game. You were either on this or that side of an information conflict, either a traitor or a patriot. And this was just the sense of division that the Kremlin needed to foster its very real war. How could society be able to hold together?

I started to get even more of a sense of the consequences in Odessa, the scene of my father's arrest, where the full-spectrum, nonlinear, hybrid, next-generation war had one of its most deadly moments.

WHEN IGOR WAS ARRESTED IN ODESSA IN 1976, THE MEDIA IN THE city was strictly censored. Today Odessa boasts fourteen local TV cable channels alone, not to mention the dozens of Ukrainian and the hundreds of international ones available in most free-to-air packages. Online there are dozens of local news sites and masses of social media groups.

Odessa has always been a port city, populated by Jews, Greeks, Romanians, Russians, Ukrainians, and Bulgarians. Today, the port is a major international thoroughfare for goods legal and illicit coming into Europe. Many goods are traded at the Seventh Kilometer, a vast outdoor market, with acres of shipping containers stacked onto each other in a multilayered maze, each one transformed into a shop where Nigerians sell fake Nikes, fake stereos, and fake Gucci; Vietnamese trade money; Indians hang out silks and muslins. They say you can buy weapons here, too, if you know whom and how to ask. Not just guns but anti-aircraft missiles.

It was Odessa's delicate ethnic balance that the Kremlin tried to tip into civil war. In May 2014, just as Kremlin proxies were taking town after town in the Donbas, pro-Ukrainians fought with pro-Russians holed up in Odessa's Palace of all Trade Unions. A fire broke out, and even as the flames were still engulfing the building and the dead were still being counted, rumors and lies already were fanning through the media. The first YouTube videos were blurry and horrific. Hundreds of pro-Russian activists had been holed up in the building. Pro-Ukrainians threw Molotov cocktails and shot at them. The fire broke out. People began falling out of the windows, and so quickly it looked like they were pushed to their deaths. Some of the Ukrainians cheered.[20]

The first photos from inside showed dozens of corpses in twisted poses. One was of a pregnant woman. Interviews appeared online with eyewitnesses who claimed Right Sector death squads had been hiding in the building. The unnamed witnesses claimed the Right Sector had been prepared; they wore gas masks and executed people on the spot. The initial death toll put the number of victims at around forty but stories spread that there actually were hundreds.

The story went international. Pro-Kremlin activists in Belgium and Italy campaigned to have a European square named after the "Odessa Martyrs."

In the days following the fire, the people of Odessa, citizens of a city of ceaseless chatter, a city famous for its humor, stopped talking to each other. No one trusted anyone. The rumors began to turn the city against itself. Opinion polls showed an even split between those who wanted the city to be part of Russia and those who wanted it to be part of Ukraine. Pro-Russian bloggers began to ask Putin to save the city from chaos and invade. Later recordings would emerge of Russian politicians talking on cell phones with gangs of thugs in Odessa, giving them orders on when to provoke more fights.

A group of Odessans, both pro-Russian and pro-Ukrainian, decided to take it on themselves to launch a public investigation. They felt Odessa needed to know what happened in the fire if the city was to be whole again. It was clear that no official investigation would be forthcoming; too many bureaucrats would have to take too much blame for all the casualties.

The civic investigation pieced together the events of the day from video and multiple witness statements, autopsies, and photographs. The trouble had started earlier in the day. The investigators found that both sides threw Molotovs and fired shots. That the barricades around the building had lit up accidentally. That autopsies showed thirty-four deaths, all from asphyxiation, none from execution. The "pregnant" woman had been over fifty and had died from the fumes, falling back into a position that made her stomach look swollen. The eight people who had fallen to their deaths had lost consciousness and tumbled out; none had been pushed.

The public investigation managed to establish the essential truth about what happened at the fire. But when the findings were presented, few were interested. "There's no unity here," Tatyana Gerasimova, one of the instigators of the public investigation, told me as we sat in a café by the opera house. "Everyone lives in their own reality, everyone has their own truth, there is no reconciliation. We created the investigation to show that there is a difference between truth and lies. In that sense we failed."

I would hear similar sentiments from students at the university where I was giving a lecture about, inevitably, information war. The students' friends and relatives just chose the story of the fire that better fit their worldviews. As they discussed the fire in their social media groups, pro-Ukrainians saw it one way, pro-Russians another. Faced with wildly conflicting versions of reality, people selected the one that suited them.

But despite this fracturing of shared reality, Odessa hadn't toppled into civil war. The week I visited, summer was in full swing. The bars and discotheques were full. The opera was sold out. "The city needs to feel alive again after it looked death in the face," said Gerasimova.

But this hadn't been achieved purely spontaneously. Zoya Kazamzhy worked on local government information campaigns when the threat of civil war was at its highest. She felt she knew something about their hometown Putin didn't. Yes, Odessa is as fractured as any globalized city, but its different communities had something deeper in common. Apart from a few fanatics, most saw Odessa as a wealthy, open trading port, a city of markets and merchants. They would go with the force that could guarantee their security, whether Russian or Ukrainian, the EU or NATO. So, instead of playing on ethnic tensions as the Kremlin might have wanted, instead of looking to divide the city further between patriots and traitors, they decided to target what all sides had in common. They put up posters across Odessa with pictures of the wrecked cities of the neighboring Donbas, where separatism had led to a destructive war. No one in Odessa wanted that sort of future, despite their differences. No one wanted physical destruction. The most potent maneuver in the information war was to jettison the language of information war altogether, and to show what real war lead to.

But as I headed into the zone of fighting proper, I would soon find that even if the shooting and shelling were real enough, at the same time every action, including military action, was perceived by all sides with its impact on the information war in mind.

HOW TO FIGHT A WAR THAT MIGHT NOT EXIST

Dzerzhinsk is a mining town at the very edge of the territory held by Ukrainian forces; separatist positions are a just a short distance away. There was a summer storm brewing when I arrived, thunder mixing with the sound of heavy artillery. A few days earlier a shell had hit the local lake. Fish had flown out onto the cracked paths or floated dead to the surface. The people of Dzerzhinsk ate some of the fish, but a few were dying on the paths and many more were floating belly-up in the lake. The smell was strong.

I travelled with a small crew from an internet TV station from Kiev, one of the few Ukrainian media organizations not in the pocket of an oligarch. Driving through town, we passed along roads with coffin-sized craters; empty factories with their walls ripped out. A young boy leading his drunk mother down the lanes; local men with scabs on their faces. I stopped to photograph a concrete coal store with a gaping hole in its walls. I assumed it had been shelled but it turned out it had been taken apart long before the war by locals looking for scrap metal.

Dzerzhinsk is named after Felix Dzerzhinsky, the man responsible for the first Soviet secret police, the notorious Cheka. When I asked a local teenage girl whether she knew who he was, she told me she'd "heard of him at school but couldn't remember." This wasn't unusual: a few weeks earlier, a TV channel had broadcast a report about how young people in Dzerzhinsk had no idea whom the town was named after. Later that year, it was renamed Toretsk, in accordance with the laws against Soviet names. There were no great protests.

The local administration of Dzerzhinsk has weathered every revolution. In April 2014, they welcomed the separatists with open arms. The newspapers supported the Donetsk People's Republic. When the

Ukrainian army retook the town a few months later, they shelled the town hall. The administration quickly cut a deal with them. But though the town was now officially in Ukrainian territory, it was still hard to get Ukrainian TV unless you had a cable package. Russian and DPR TV were still available everywhere—Dzerzhinsk may be in Ukrainian territory, but it still is under the Kremlin's informational sovereignty.

The pro-Ukrainian activists were jumpy. There was Oleg, an older man with a grey moustache and a cap. He had been one of the miners who helped bring down the Soviet Union in the great strike of 1989, blocking the roads with broken glass to stop the Kremlin's tanks. Volodya was younger, with big arms and a boy-band fringe. He was a miner, too, but had worked in Sweden for several years. He knew things didn't have to be this way.

Volodya and Oleg were sure the administration wanted the activists, with their annoying anti-corruption rallies, out of town. They were worried they'd bribed someone high up in Kiev to stay in power. That Kiev was ready to abandon them.

"If there's no mention of us on TV, then it won't be a big deal if the town is lost," said Volodya. "We're being erased." In the front of his van was a stack of leaflets.

Seven to twelve years punishment for everyday separatism: call this number if you spot an everyday separatist!
How to spot an everyday separatist?
—Calls for Russia to invade
—Insults Ukrainian values
—Spreads lies
—Plants defeatist feelings

I asked Volodya where he had obtained the leaflets. He told me with no little pride that he had made them himself. I asked whether that was such a good idea.

"The telephone numbers on them aren't even real," he said. "They're just to intimidate people. We're all alone here. We need to do something."

We arrived at a Soviet block of flats, rising above an area of wooden shacks, several of which had been blown apart. The Ukrainian army base was about seventeen hundred feet away and this area was frequently hit. Oleg showed us the shrapnel holes in the metal door of the apartment block. Some women sat on a bench outside the front door. They were angry that the Ukrainians had put their base near here. There had been no fighting when the town had been part of the DPR. The Ukrainian army had brought the war with them. One woman told me how a shell had exploded through her balcony.

Oleg got angry. "Our mayor is a separatist. That's why the army is here. He should be in prison."

"I worked all my life for pennies and what's my reward?" said a woman in a sunflower-patterned dress. "Bombs!"

"They came from over there—those are Ukrainian positions! That's not DPR!" shouted one of the women. Later she showed me a crater in the ground. A tree had collapsed into it. "Look," she said. "It's clear it came from the Ukrainian position."

It didn't seem clear at all. I thought it unlikely that the Ukrainians could shell themselves from seventeen hundred feet away. But this wasn't about piecing together evidence. Journalists who had travelled the region had warned me about this phenomenon: people would rearrange the evidence to fit what they saw on television, however little sense it made.

"The Ukrainians are bombing each other!" said someone else. "The Pravy Sektor wants to march on Kiev and they're fighting each other."

"It's the Americans. They've come here to take our gas. I heard there are wounded American soldiers in the local hospitals."

Oleg was becoming increasingly irate, shouting at the women that they were traitors. They started shooing him away. He took off his shirt and showed them a bullet wound. The Russians, he said, had shot at him when he delivered food to the front lines. He said Putin was in Ukraine because he was afraid that Russia would fall apart. The women said Putin wasn't afraid of anything.

Oleg went to the car and came back with the leaflets and started handing them out.

"Ha—you think we're afraid of this?" The women laughed and threw the papers in the bin.

Then they turned to the cameraman and me and started shouting at us.

"You'll re-edit what we say anyway. Why should we trust you? Nobody wants to hear the Donbas!"

Nobody hears the Donbas. It reminded me of a mantra, a prayer, a religious lamentation for a lost God, the recurring theme of the Psalms of crying out to a vanished God; the Yom Kippur prayers that beg God to hear the people.

"O God who answered Abraham, Jacob and Isaac, O God who answered us in Sinai, Hear, Hear, Hear the Donbas!"

I WOKE UP IN THE BILLIARDS ROOM. IT WAS STILL DARK AND I nearly collided with some soldiers who were slumped, fully clothed, on sofas. One soldier was sleeping with his head on the floor, propping up his fat torso; he was so exhausted that he didn't notice he was sleeping in a half-headstand. Outside, the rose garden and tennis court were just becoming visible in the dawn light. The roses were wilted and the tennis net was missing. I could hear rhythmic splashing: a soldier was doing the breaststroke in the outdoor pool. The light was coming on fast, revealing summer houses and garages; high-security fences; the hills beyond and the dark green, almost black, pine forests of the Luhansk. We were northeast of Dzerzhinsk, on the edge of the territory held by Ukraine bordering the Luhansk People's Republic.

We were bivouacked on the country estate of a deposed local minigarch, formerly a senior judge in the territory now held by the separatists. He now was lying low in Kiev, waiting to see which side would win. There was a hyperrealist portrait of his wife in the billiards room, a plump, grinning blonde lying in a summer field with a garland of red poppies over her head.

In a cottage near the pool, an officer was making breakfast: chopped cabbage and corned-beef meatballs. The TV was bursting with war propaganda. The Ukrainian president, dressed in military fatigues, was inspecting well-equipped troops. There were slow-motion clips of proud wives waving soldiers off to war or meeting them by the train with tears of joy. It was the sort of war propaganda that was used to build national morale and spur mobilization everywhere throughout the twentieth century.

But there was something strange: for all the war visuals, what was happening was not being called a war. On TV, the president spoke of an "anti-terrorist operation," an "ATO." "What the hell is an ATO?" cursed the officer as he chopped more cabbage. One of the clever twists of the Kremlin's approach was that it waged war without ever openly declaring it, undermining the narrative of fighting a clearly identified enemy.

Later, the soldiers took us to the front line. Every vehicle was a different make. I sat in the back of a small Nissan jeep and was told to look out the window to watch for separatist snipers. The window had been shattered in a previous gunfight and was held together with scotch tape. You couldn't see a single thing through it.

We stopped on the edge of a bluff opposite the separatist positions on the other side of the river. You could just about see them with the naked eye. "If they start shooting, jump away from the cars," said the commander, known as the ComBrig. "They will aim for them."

The ComBrig ordered heavy artillery to spread out along the bluff in a show of strength. Then he timed how long it took the separatists to get their people in position, a ruse to get the other side to reveal where they had hidden their forces on the far side of the bluff. The story was that new Russian units had recently arrived.

From there, we drove to the village of Lobachevo, a collection of single-story wooden houses set at skewed angles. A cow stood in the road, staring at an outhouse. Three elderly men in dusty string vests, flip-flops on dirty feet, sat drinking and smoking on some logs out-side. One of them, known as Uncle Kolya, had no teeth. He claimed a separatist had knocked them out after he refused to sing the Luhansk National Republic anthem. The soldiers suspected he had concocted the story just for them and that the second their backs were turned he would curse Ukraine. "We spent a long time winning their trust," said the ComBrig. "At first they thought we were all Pravy Sektor monsters from the Russian propaganda machine."

Across the riverbank, you could see the separatists with rifles slung over their shoulders, pacing up and down by the old ferry station. The ferry had been blown up during the fighting. Families who lived on different sides of the river had been split. The school was on one side, and the shops were on the other. Local women crossed in a tiny rowboat with a tiny motor. They complained that if they carried more than one bag of potatoes, they could be arrested for smuggling con-traband. They didn't care about Ukraine, Russia, or the Luhansk Na-tional Republic. They cared about their village, and their potatoes.

We drove out from Lobachevo, past abandoned churches and blown-up bridges that had collapsed into the green river, past women walking with goats. There was no obvious profit to be made from any of this land. Kiev had done nothing to develop it in twenty years of independence but the Kremlin had little need for it, either. If you looked closely, both sides were prepared to lose Luhansk: the Kremlin wanted to hand it back to Ukraine while maintaining covert political control; Kiev made noises about "unity," but many people, from top brass to academics, argued that the best outcome was a frozen terri-tory that the Kremlin would have to fund and feed.

War used to be about capturing territory and planting flags, but something different was at play out here. Moscow needed to create a narrative about how pro-democracy revolutions like the Maidan lead to chaos and civil war. Kiev needed to show that separatism leads to misery. What actually happened on the ground was almost irrelevant—the two governments just needed enough footage to back their respective stories. Propaganda has always accompanied war, usually as a handmaiden to the actual fighting. But the information age means that this equation has been flipped: military operations are now handmaidens to the more important information effect. It would be like a vastly scripted reality TV show if it weren't for the very real deaths: a few months after my visit, on November 3, 2015, the Kharkiv 92nd Mechanized Brigade would be caught up in a fire-fight near Lobachevo. The ComBrig was wounded but survived.

Our vehicles stopped by a bend in the river. The soldiers took off their donated uniforms, grabbed a Tarzan swing that drooped from a tree on the bank and leapt into the water, whooping. Some tried backflips and others belly flopped: this was a daily ritual to help them wind down after the patrol.

The ComBrig was in the river when his phone went off. It was an emergency: shelling had started again over no-man's-land. On the previous day the 92nd agreed to a cease-fire with the separatists so that electricians could come into the firing zone and fix some cables. Now the separatists were shelling overhead. If the 92nd fired back it would look like they were firing on civilians. "Whatever you do, don't react," said the ComBrig, hurriedly pulling fatigues over wet boxer shorts. "It's a provocation for the cameras."

In the evening, we drank moonshine cognac from a plastic bottle and looked up at the stars, as thick as grapes, listening for the sound of shells and following traces of missiles in the sky. We were looking for signs of our military fate like medieval men had looked at comets in search of meaning. Some of the "stars" moved: drones, spying on us. I felt as though I was inside a modern icon, the information war had broken so much of my sense of scale. The activists behind their laptops seemed as big as ministries; mythological fiends from Twitter as real as tanks. The borders between Russia and Ukraine, between past and present, between soldier and civilian, rumor and evidence, actor and audience had buckled, and with that the whole rational, ordered sense of perspective suddenly gave way to thinking that was magical and mystical, in which reality was unknowable and seemed to be decided somewhere up on high by divine conspiracies. The layers of spheres and angels had been replaced with endlessly reflecting media stories; information was no longer simply the recording of actions but the point of it. We were all caught up in the recordings, revolving and refracting in the information heavens.

A drone paused up above us.

"Smile," said the ComBrig. "It's taking your photo."

CHAPTER FOUR

SOFT FACTS

I had my first fact-check in my first year of primary school. I was three when I arrived in London. Playing football was my only way of communicating when I went to school, watching football on TV was my way into the language; football commentary, which matches words to action, was a way to learn vocabulary. I learned to read English from children's football magazines.

Between ages four and seven I spoke semi-English. I only half-understood people around me and could only partly communicate. I spent a lot of time in my head. I would compose football games in my mind, commentating on them in my handicapped English. I invented teams. I described the players' lives and moods in detail in the commentary. The players got older and had problems. They changed teams and were reinvigorated. I made up leagues. I, too, was a player in this imagined world, and after many setbacks I made it into the England side. But I used myself sparingly, often as a substitute. I preferred commentating on the others.

Once at school I blurted out that I was off to Montevideo to play in a tournament (I had just discovered Uruguay on a map). My teacher, Mrs. Stern, called my parents and asked if I needed time off school for my trip to Uruguay. They told her there was no trip. The next day she asked me to stay behind after class. I'd never been held after class before and I knew it was important. "So, it turns out everything you told us about going to Uruguay, about you playing football, was a fib," Mrs. Stern said. From her tone I could tell I had done something wrong but the problem was I didn't know what "fib" meant. Back home I looked it up. It didn't seem right. I hadn't thought of my imaginary world as a lie, just a parallel reality, and the one reality had spilled into the other.

By that time, I was seven; it was 1984, and my English was improving. I had developed it in the linguistic playing fields of my invented football universe. With the word "fib," everything seemed to fall into place: I now had two words for the same thing (lie and fib) and it felt as if I had crossed a border into knowing English. The shock of people thinking I'd lied snapped me out of living so intensely in my imagination.

We were all getting used to our new country in different ways.

After arriving Lina got a job teaching Russian at London University. The other academics told her that, "of course you were opposed to the Soviet regime. It was because you were dissidents! You can't be objective about it."

No, she would try to explain, it's because of the objective nature of the regime we became dissidents. No one is born a dissident. It's a series of choices, then labels that are applied to you by the KGB. You can have copies of Nabokov and Solzhenitsyn in Kiev and end up a dissident and have the same books in Moscow and be fine. They seemed bemused by this. They were nice but they weren't sure she was unbiased.

Lina was finding her own language, and concepts were being challenged, too. In the Soviet Union, the regime had captured the language of socialism, associating it with oppression. In London, many of her friends thought themselves socialists but were appalled by the Soviet Union.

Igor now worked for the BBC, one of the foreign media he had listened to in secret in Soviet Ukraine. During holidays, he took me with him to that tall island in the middle of the Strand known as Bush House, home of the BBC World Service. In 1929, when it was being built, Bush House was the most expensive building in the world, the Corinthian columns at its entrance crowned with six-foot statues in recessed portico inside a dome cut above mighty iron doors worthy of a great cathedral.

It was a wondrous island for a child. As soon as my father was locked in the aquarium-like glass case of the broadcasting studio I was free to roam every floor. Down the wide stairs I went, around me every color and ethnicity the world knows, all speaking, shouting English but with different accents. All typing, smoking, sprinting, between slamming doors to break the latest news. Every section of the vast building was another country or even continent. From one floor to the next, I travelled from Greece to the Middle East, up the lifts to Poland. Sometimes I would find myself lost in Latin America, stranded in Africa, with only the gloomy London light in the windows constant. Every other journalist seemed a great exiled poet or minister-in-waiting. When my father was too busy, I would play football in vast, purple-lit, marble corridors with Egon from the

Czech Service. He would later be a deputy prime minister, but when I was eight, I beat him at penalties.

Igor's favorite shift was night watchman. After 9 p.m., with the office empty, he'd make his way down to the BBC members' bar, one of the few places in London where alcohol was served past 11 in the evening, acquire a bottle of Bordeaux Black Prince, uncork it, place it in a plastic bag, pick up some roast beef from the canteen, go back up to the office, put his feet on the desk opposite the ticker tape of news to check that no great crisis was breaking, pour a glass, and consider his new place of work.

"There's a kind of gas in this building," Igor's boss, the editor in chief of the Russian Service, a former military translator, Barry Holland, liked to say, "invisible, but very much present. It's an atmosphere, if you like, the ethos of a balanced view." It was a gas that would drive Igor's more politicized colleagues up the wall, frustrated at the amount of time the World Service would give to spokespeople of dictatorial regimes. "If you had the chance to interview Christ you would give the devil equal time as well," one of Igor's colleagues lambasted Holland. "Certainly," Holland answered. "But I would give Christ the chance to say the final word."

The gas was a means of gaining credibility. Trust. To project the image of Britain as the sort of place that you could rely on for the BBC trinity of "accuracy, impartiality, and fairness," which in turn was meant to promote what the founder of the BBC, Lord Reith, had called the British values of "reasonableness, democracy, and debate," which, in turn, was meant to make Britain more admired globally. Unlike the rest of the BBC, the World Service was funded with a grant from Her Majesty's Foreign Office. It existed to "serve the national interest" (which was not, every editor would insist, the same as the government interest).

When he arrived Igor's first assignments were to trans-
late lectures on classic English writers; how Christmas is
celebrated in England. Maybe this was meant to be in the
national interest as it "built bridges" with Russian audiences. But, why, thought Igor, when the Soviet Union censored so much, were they broadcasting something every
Soviet school child knew? He wasn't alone in his frus-
tration. In the early 1980s, a new generation of editors
emerged who launched their own small cultural revolution
at the Service.

Igor put on works never broadcast in the Soviet Union:
the love letters of James Joyce, full of sexual references un-
imaginable on late Soviet-era broadcasting; Samuel Beckett's
Krapp's Last Tape (about a man who obsessively records
himself and then repeatedly listens to and comments on his
own recordings); Audience by Václav Havel (about a dissident who is persuaded to spy upon himself, and Igor's version
of which Havel listened to on the BBC Russian service while
serving his prison sentence in Czechoslovakia. In 1978 Havel
had called on people to stop repeating official language; it
was the the repetition of things you didn't believe that helped
to break you. He had been jailed for subversion soon after).

At first, Igor had looked down on radio from the heights
of literature. Now he was finding himself drawn in by it.

"Most listeners use radio as a source of information,"
he would write later, "but what kind of information? And
how does it differ from what you find in newspapers or on
television?"

Around Igor were the reel-to-reels, magnetic tapes with
voice recordings. Editing tape was the work of an artisan:
like a glass-blower blew glass, he was molding sound.

"It is my belief that the meaning of radio is in the magic
of the voice, the magic of sound. And in this sense poetry
and radio share the same element—air. A free element."

Russia and Ukraine were cut off physically from the rest of the world and books were censored. The rare phone calls he had with home took hours to arrange through a dispatcher, and every word was eavesdropped on by secret services. But barriers and homesickness fell away when Igor entered the BBC radio studio, where he felt like a pilot breaking through censorship.

"The hermetically sealed and soundproofed booths, the control panels, the lack of outside windows make radio studios like spaceships. And your voice alone is capable of unlocking this closed space. I am convinced that, as they sit by the radio, many listeners are on a voyage round the world, no, into outer space, more like. I, too, am a travel maniac; I jump from wave to wave."

There was a generation of recent émigrés who felt they knew their audience better than the English, and a generation of editors who agreed. Zinovy Zinik made programs about punks in east London for a Soviet audience whose idea of the city was stuck in Edwardian literature. Seva Novgorodtsev's music program intermingled satire of Soviet language with heavy metal references, mimicking the pathos of official bulletins: "Our metallurgists produce various metals for the people: from the graceful effervescent bronze to the stunning pig iron . . . "

It became a hit. The World Service received an unheard of amount of letters from fans inside the USSR, one of the few ways the BBC could gauge its popularity beyond the Iron Curtain: listeners were ready to risk KGB censors or sent them via foreign students who smuggled them out. Soviet newspapers ran attack pieces on how Seva was corrupting Soviet youth. This came to the attention of World Service leadership. A panel was convened to judge whether Seva was "impartial." All the playful humor was lost in the translation *of his transcripts, and they came out anti-Soviet diatribes. The World Services' senior management were displeased. The new head of the Russian service, also a reformer, said he would do something about it. And then, after the hubbub passed, he quietly let Seva get on with his heavy metal Soviet satire; it was drawing Soviet listeners to the current affairs content.*

The BBC's combination of "accuracy" and absurdist theater, heavy metal and "balance" was up against Soviet broadcasting—which was about to experience its first tremors.

In the corner of the BBC newsroom was a telefax, which every few hours would chug and squeal with fresh reports from a country house near Reading. This is where BBC Monitoring was based and where eighty monitors, all fluent linguists, would spend all day and night listening to all the output of Soviet media in forty-two languages, which they broadcast no less intently than the BBC. Radio Moscow's typical style was so stiff it made the BBC seem informal. It would reel off statistics from Communist Party plenums about the supposed success of the Soviet economy, the "onward march of socialism" across the world, the inevitable "objective, scientific progress of history." Even when it peddled what the KGB called "active measures," disinformation campaigns that claimed, for example, that the United States had invented AIDS as a weapon, it would do so with po-faced seriousness, broadcasting interviews with fake scientists, providing fake evidence, all intended to keep up a façade of factuality.

In 1983, Monitoring noticed something most unusual:[1] a host on Radio Moscow's English Service began to call Soviet soldiers who had invaded Afghanistan "occupiers" instead of using the official language of "limited contingent" of "internationalist warriors" bringing help to the "fraternal people of Afghanistan."

What the radio host, a previously unassuming man named Vladimir Danchev, was doing was unheard of. He was soon suspended and sent to a psychiatric ward in Uzbekistan. Later he would say he had made the first reference to "occupiers" by accident, but once he started he just couldn't stop himself from saying what he thought.

In retrospect, the Danchev episode seemed a first crack in the Soviet firmament. Lies were becoming intolerable. Soon listeners would be turning to the BBC in droves.

Like a radio transistor, a Geiger counter is attuned to pick up invisible signals pulsating through the atmosphere. It measures radioactive emissions, gamma rays and particles, and when they increase, the Geiger counter starts to make a clicking, ripping sound.

On April 26, 1986, scientists and amateur observers of radiation levels began to see unusually high counts on their Geiger counters. They spotted a radiation cloud of unrecorded magnitude moving toward Europe from Soviet Ukraine. The BBC and other news outlets began reporting on it. Soviet state media's one brief report said that there had been a small, negligible accident at the nuclear reactor in Chernobyl. They didn't report on it again. In Moscow and Kiev, May Day parades, with their vast columns of soldiers and warheads symbolizing Soviet might, went on as usual.

Although Soviet media were silent, the BBC and other Western media continued reporting the radiation levels. In Kiev rumors were rife that Communist Party elites were evacuating their children from the city. A pilot who had been chartered to fly a plane full of nomenklatura children grounded the plane, disgusted by the injustice. Another rumor recommended drinking sweet wine to treat radiation poisoning. Everyone started drinking. The came the counter-rumor: red wine only made the poisoning worse! No one had any idea what to do.

The BBC broadcast programs with scientists and medical experts on radiation poisoning. Tuning in became necessary for sanity and survival. It would take another two weeks before the Soviet leadership made any serious announcement, by which point any remaining faith in them was shot.

In 1987, the new general secretary of the Soviet Union Mikhail Gorbachev admitted that the lack of truth surrounding Chernobyl had been a disaster.[2] He argued that it showed the USSR needed to change. Without self-criticism and self-expression there could be no progress. He promised to give new freedom to Soviet media. He opened up restrictions on foreign books, films, video cassettes. He called the policy glasnost, meaning "giving voice." Glasnost had been initiated in 1986 but it was only after Chernobyl that it began to be enacted in earnest.

In 1988, the Soviet Union ceased jamming the BBC. The World Service was jubilant. For Igor, it felt like the artist, activist, and journalist in him were flowing into one: freedom to access information and creative freedom, individual rights and the right to be utterly individualistic. In Igor's own novellas and poems from the 1980s, politics and current affairs are usually conspicuous by their absence, but were latent in everything in their celebration of liberation from constraint. He wrote in stream-of-consciousness swirls of impressionism, crossing the borders between realism and fantasy, poetry and prose. He recreated Bush House as populated by animals, hedgehogs and foxes, with some sort of nameless animal gripped by panic as a blue, sticky fog bursts the windows on every floor. He reinvented himself as a boy who wakes up with a fever, takes a thermometer, places it in his armpit only to discover it is now an abyss as he falls into it. He visited Ticino and crossed the Italian and Swiss borders, reveling in the freedom to cross all barriers.

In one of his poems he had written, "If I were a red Indian, my nickname would be Barrier-Crosser." Now all the barriers would be coming down. Could the regime, which seemed immortal, permanent, immovable, actually be changing? Or even be finished? Could Russia, and Ukraine, become something else?

That year, Prime Minister Margaret Thatcher, wearing a checked jacket and pearl necklace, conducted a live phone-in with Soviet listeners on the BBC Russian Service. Nothing of the kind had been attempted previously.[3] Soviet citizens rarely got to talk to their own leaders, let alone engage a foreign one, and a woman, too, in live conversation. To a question from Kaunas, Lithuania, about whether the changes in the Soviet Union (glasnost as well as the economic and political reforms of perestroika) were reversible if someone other than Gorbachev took charge, Thatcher answered:

"I think that once you have tasted the increasing freedom of speech and discussion, the liveliness of debate that you are having now, then I think that it would be very difficult to reverse that.

"But I do not think that they would go forward with anything like the same momentum if Mr. Gorbachev were not there. I recognize someone who has a vision for the future. In a way, I felt like that myself when I became prime minister of my country."[4] At the end of the program, Thatcher was heard to say: "Oh, was that all, we could have done with more time on air."

DURING GLASNOST, IT SEEMED THAT THE TRUTH WOULD SET EVERY-body free. Facts seemed possessed of power, dictators seemed so afraid of facts that they suppressed them. But something has gone drastically wrong: we have access to more information and evidence than ever, but facts seem to have lost their power. There is nothing new about politicians lying, but what seems novel is their acting as if they don't care whether what they say is true or false.

When Vladimir Putin went on international television during his army's annexation of Crimea, and asserted, with a smirk, that there are no Russian soldiers in Crimea when everyone knew there were, and then just as casually later admitted that they had been there, and even publicly awarded medals to the soldiers whom he had earlier said hadn't been there, he wasn't so much lying in the sense of trying to replace one reality with another as saying that facts don't matter. Similarly, Donald J. Trump is famous for having no discernible notion of what is true and factual. Yet this has not in any way been a barrier to his success. According to the fact-checking agency Politifact, 76 percent of his checked statements in the 2016 presidential election were rated "mostly false" or downright untrue, compared to 27 percent for his rival. He still won.[5]

Why has this happened? Is technology to blame? The media? And what are the consequences in a world where the powerful are no longer afraid of facts? Does that mean one can commit crimes in full view of all? And then just shrug them off?

OBJECTIVITY IS A MYTH IMPOSED ON US

Forty years later, my office is opposite the old Bush House. The BBC World Service long since has abandoned it. First, it was mooted that Bush House would be sold to Japanese property developers and converted into luxury apartments. This plan failed when the UK property market started sagging in the wake of the 2008 financial crash. As of this writing, it is home to a university department.

All of the BBC, World Service and Domestic, news and entertainment, TV, radio, and "multimedia," is squeezed into a building on Regents Street that is curved like a compressed accordion, with people sitting far too closely together because the architects forgot to factor in the right amount of desk space in their design.

When I talk to BBC editors and managers, the architectural dispro-portion seems to mirror a media one: the world has changed and the old values of the BBC, of accuracy, impartiality, and fairness leading to democracy, reasonableness, and debate, have been upended.

During the Cold War, the BBC defined "impartial" as balance be-tween left-wing and right-wing opinions. Left and right were clearly de-fined political positions represented by political parties and newspapers.

In the 1990s and 2000s, things got more complicated. There was no clear left or right wing anymore. Economic interests did not nec-essarily equal party affiliations. In the late 2010s, audiences have bro-ken down into mini-values that they cling to and that define them.

"Even as affiliation to political parties has weakened, the impor-tance of values people identify with such as religion, the monarchy or minority rights have become stronger," James Harding, the former director of BBC News told me. "And so, with it, perceptions of bias and how people understand impartiality have changed, well beyond traditional ideas of left and right."

The BBC used to determine what to be impartial about by following the agendas set by political parties and, to a much lesser extent, news-papers. These were meant to be representatives of greater interests. But what happens when newspapers are no longer read and parties are so fractured that they no longer represent anything coherent? When I was a child in Britain, we lived in a series of sublimations, our sense of self squeezed into the vessels of media, politicians who represented us and whom we identified with almost like football teams, sucked through the cathode-ray tube of the TV to join a greater whole. For better or worse, those vessels have burst. And as a consequence, the concepts with which the BBC used to negotiate reality have been scattered. Even at the best of times the BBC struggled to get balance right,[6] but what does it mean to be impartial in such a fractured world?

But something more fundamental has changed, too. Impartiality and fairness always were slippery terms. Back in the 1980s, Marga-ret Thatcher's government was fighting a war against the domestic BBC, accusing it of being biased for attacking Conservative politicians, of being disloyal for broadcasting Irish terrorists. There were even threats to close down the BBC: why should one have a publicly funded broadcaster if Thatcher believed in market freedom?

But now the attacks are aimed not only at the BBC's impartiality but at the very idea that there is such a thing as impartiality.

Kremlin media figures insist that broadcasters such as the BBC can't be trusted because they all have hidden agendas,[7] that "objectivity is a myth that is proposed and imposed on us."[8] It's a far cry from Radio Moscow, with its commitment to upholding scientific, Marxist truth. And you can see the difference in the content. When, in the 1980s, Radio Moscow broadcast "active measures" claiming that the CIA had invented AIDS as a weapon against Africa, the lies were carefully curated over many years. They involved scientists in East Germany who had supposedly found the evidence. An effort was made to make the elaborate lie look real. Today the Russian media and officials push similar stories, claiming that American factories were pumping out the Zika virus in East Ukraine to poison ethnic Russians, that the US is harvesting Russian DNA to create gene weapons,[9] that the US is encircling Russia with secret biological warfare labs. But these claims are just thrown online or spewed out on TV shows, more to confuse than to convince, or to buttress the phobias of audiences predisposed to seeing US plots all around them.

In America, impartiality and objectivity are under attack as well. Ted Koppel was one of America's most famous news broadcasters during the Cold War, "objectivity" personified. In the 1980s, he hosted *Nightline,* on which he interviewed presidents and prime ministers, and *Viewpoint,* where audiences could complain about perceived bias in network news.

In March 2017, on his CBS morning show, Koppel accused hyper-partisan cable news channels on the left and right of being "bad for America." They undermined reasonableness, debate, and democracy. Koppel was placing himself above the fray, implicitly making the case that balance and objectivity were still possible: after all, there has to be a position from which you can gauge partisanship.

One of his main targets was the Fox News prime time TV host Sean Hannity, as virulent a defender of Donald Trump as Russian state presenters are of Putin.

The typical Hannity monologue rises in a series of rhetorical questions until it topples over the edge of sense. On March 27, 2017, for example, in a two-minute series of questions, he attacked a rival network, CBS. CBS is the closest the US has to the BBC in its pretensions to impartiality, and Hannity was bringing its claims to objectivity into question, demanding if its presenters ever questioned their criticism of George W. Bush, whether they spiked stories that made Obama look bad, whether they had investigated Obama's ties to a former terrorist, his commitment to supposedly America-hating black liberation theology, or reported Obama's economic failings (here Hannity displayed a list of statistics on the screen, too rapidly to read fully). Had CBS, he wondered, listed all the laws Hillary Clinton violated when she used a private email server as secretary of state? Exposed every one of her lies about the death of US diplomats in Benghazi? Explored how media colluded with the Clinton campaign? Questioned how much time they had given to the "conspiracy theory" that Trump's campaign colluded with Russia?

The effect of such a long list, where some of the charges are serious, others spurious, many debatable, and none explored, is to leave the mind exhausted and confused. The semantic patterns reinforce Hannity's main message: that we live in a world where there is no epistemological certainty.

In answer to Koppel's charges, Hannity argued that by attacking opinion shows, Koppel was actually just "giving his opinion." Hannity described himself as honest because he admits being an advocacy journalist whereas Koppel's façade of being impartial actually is fraudulent. All pretense at objectivity is just subjectivity.

With the possibility of balance, impartiality, and accuracy undermined, all that remains is to be more "genuine" than the other side—more emotional, more subjective, more heroic. Hannity's studio displays a superhero-style shield, reminiscent of Captain America's, with the stars and stripes and his name emblazoned on it. In the Hannity mythos, the Fox hero has to fight off the monsters of the "Alt-Left-Destroy-Trump-Media" that have declared "war on the American People." In Hannity's world, facts are far less important than sticking it to the enemy. And if that means showing that you don't give a damn about their facts, all the better.

When Hannity lands on a failing of other media, the way some channels, for example, spent quite so much airtime trying to detect direct, covert, criminal "collusion" between Trump and the Kremlin for instance, his response is not to try and restore impartiality, but to say it is impossible per se.

The irony is that the rejection of objectivity that the Kremlin and Fox News push plays on ideas that originally championed "liberal" causes, the Hannitys and Putins of this world officially oppose. "Objectivity is just male subjectivity," was a slogan of the feminist movement; the student protests of 1968 celebrated feelings as an antidote to corporate and bureaucratic rationality.

But now Fox and the Kremlin exploit the same ideas: If reality is malleable, why can't they introduce their own versions too? And if feelings are emancipatory, why can't they invoke their own? With the idea of objectivity discredited, the grounds on which one could argue against them rationally disappears.[10]

WITH THE REPUTATION FOR IMPARTIALITY OF A BBC OR CBS undermined, online fact-checking agencies have stepped into the fray. However, they, too, face a problem: the very environment they work in, social media, is where falsehoods spread faster than facts. It's become something of a ritual: hauling up representatives of tech companies to lambast them for normalizing lying.

Take the summer of 2018 in Rome, where I attended the annual event of the world's fact-checkers. "If this group can't help make the information disorder problem a little less terrible, if this group can't clean up this mess that we're in, who will? We are the wrinkly arbiters of a take-no-prisoners war for the future of the internet," announced Alexios Mantzarlis, developer of the Fact Checkers Code, which defines the Five Principles of Transparency and Methodology. The principles establish who is a real fact checker and who isn't. Alexios's code was often invoked in Rome. Prospective new fact-checkers are monitored over a year to ensure they live up to the Five Principles. Among the greatest dangers to the movement are the wrong kind of fact-checkers, who claim the status for themselves without following the principles. Perhaps it was the fact that we were in Rome, but I began to feel that there was something a touch religious about the fact-checkers. In a world where facts have become sullied, they wanted to make them sacred again.

In the cloister-like courtyard of St. Stephen's school, I met everyone from the guy in Los Angeles who monitors the accuracy of celebrity gossip to those for whom facts are matters of life and death. Fact-checkers from India, for example, told me about efforts to stop murder sprees by squads of cow vigilantes. Hindu nationalists spread surreptitious rumors on closed social media groups about Muslim butchers, falsely accusing them of slaughtering the Hindus' holy animal. Fanatics would then descend on innocent butchers and slaughter them instead.

In Myanmar and Sri Lanka, where Facebook has been used to incite ethnic cleansing, the situation was even worse.

Looking around the cloister, I could see editors from Rappler and Ukrainian, Mexican, and Western Balkan fact-checkers. When the representative from Facebook took the floor, she was pilloried for allowing blatantly untrue news stories to spread on the platform and for allowing it to be a conduit for threats against fact-checkers.

The insurmountable problem is that for all the technology companies' statements of concern about this problem, it's the way their platforms are designed and how they make money that create an environment in which accuracy, fairness, and impartiality are at best secondary.

Back in 2011 Guillaume Chaslot, an engineer at Google with a PhD in artificial intelligence, discovered that the way YouTube was designed meant that it served people ever more of the same content, creating and reinforcing one point of view—and not one necessarily based on its factuality. So if you were to watch one video full of inaccurate, often downright disinforming content, the algorithm would feed you ever more. YouTube didn't want to be the judge of what is true, but they wanted their algorithms to be the judge of what gets promoted. As a consequence, untrue content could get massively augmented.

Chaslot offered his bosses potential ways of fixing the problem. Couldn't one offer people more diverse content? He was told this was not the focus. YouTube was primarily interested in increasing the time that people spend watching it. It struck him as a terrible way to define desire: purely by how much time someone spent staring at a screen—a far cry from the patrician public service ethos of the BBC. It's also, Chaslot told me, easy to manipulate: if you have resources to hire huge numbers of people to watch certain videos and create tons of content on a specific subject, that would help promote those videos. Having many YouTube channels that work together was also a good way to get your content recommended. There was a reason, he argued, why the Russian state broadcaster RT had such an impressive array of YouTube channels.

In his study "Emotional Dynamics in the Age of Misinformation,"[11] Walter Quattrociocchi of the University of Venice analyzed fifty-four million comments over four years in various Facebook groups. He found that the longer a discussion continues in a Facebook group, the more extreme people's comments become: "Cognitive patterns in echo chambers tend towards polarization," he concluded. This, argues Quattrociocchi, shows up the emotional structure of social media. We go online looking for the emotional boost delivered by likes and retweets. Social media is a sort of mini-narcissism engine that can never be quite satisfied, leading us to take up more radical positions to get more attention. It really doesn't matter if stories are accurate or not, let alone impartial: you're not looking to win an argument in a public space with a neutral audience; you just want to get the most attention possible from like-minded people. "Online dynamics induce distortion," concludes Quattrociocchi. It's a lamentable loop. Social media drives more polarized behavior, which leads to demands for more sensationalized content, or plain lies. "Fake news" is a symptom of the way social media is designed.

There's something even more insidious going on here. In his Cold War essays, Igor celebrated being as individualistic as possible as a way to resist oppression. Another exiled Soviet poet, the Nobel Prize winner Joseph Brodsky, who had emigrated in 1972, put it best in his commencement speech at Williams College in 1984: "The surest defense against evil is extreme individualism, originality of thinking, whimsicality, even—if you will—eccentricity. That is, something that can't be feigned, faked, imitated."

In the Cold War "extreme individualism" was interlinked with the struggle to receive and transmit accurate information, freedom of speech associated with freedom of artistic self-expression, both opposed by regimes that censored both facts and "whimsicality." Now social media offers limitless fields for a form of extreme individualism. Express yourself to your heart's content! But its very nature undermines factuality.

And then there's another twist. This self-expression is then transmuted into data: the frequency of certain words; times of postings and what that says about us; our movements and language all passed to forces that influence us with campaigns and ads we might not even be aware of. But if you were to look for your own data imprint among data brokers, in the hope of finding a reflection of your true self, you will be disappointed. Instead there are broken bits of information (something about health, something about shopping), jagged edges that can be added and stacked in different patterns according to various short-term purposes—little writhing squiggles of impulses and habits that can be impelled to vibrate for a few seconds to get me to buy something or vote for someone. Social media, that little narcissism machine, the easiest way we have ever had to place ourselves on a pedestal of vanity, also is the mechanism that most efficiently breaks you up.

That extreme individualism came with its own dangers is already there in Igor's early stories. Rereading them, I notice how often the impressionistic, self-obsessed narrator ends up subtly undermined. At the end of the story you realize they have been so caught up in themselves that they don't notice what is going on around them and are losing their touch with reality altogether.

WHY WE'RE POST-FACT

Social media technology combined with a worldview in which all information is part of war and impartiality impossible has helped to undermine the sacrosanctity of facts. But the more I thought about the issue, the more it seemed to me I was asking the wrong question. Instead of why had facts become irrelevant, why had they ever been relevant at all? And why were we seeing such similar phenomena from both of the Cold War superpowers? Facts, after all, are not always the most pleasant things—reminders, as I had discovered with my teacher Mrs. Stern, of our place and our limitations, our failures, and ultimately, our mortality. There is a sort of adolescent joy in throwing off their weight, of giving a big fuck-you to glum reality. The very pleasure of a Putin or a Trump is the release from constraint they offer.

But though facts can be unpleasant, they are useful. You need them, especially, if you are constructing something in the real world. There are no post-truth moments if you are building a bridge, for example. Facts are necessary to show what you are building, how it will work, why it won't collapse. In politics, facts are necessary to show you are pursuing some rational idea of progress: here are our aims, here is how we prove we are achieving them, this is how they improve your lives. The need for facts is predicated on the notion of an evidence-based future.

In the Cold War, both sides were engaged in what had begun as a debate about which system—democratic capitalism or communism— would deliver a rosier future for all mankind. The only way to prove you were achieving this future was to provide evidence. Communism, for all its many perversities and cruelties, was meant to be the ultimate, scientific, Enlightenment project. Those who lived under it knew it was a sham, but it was connected to a paradigm of Soviet economic growth based in Marxist-Leninist theory, whose objective laws of historical development supposedly were playing out as the theory maintained. Thus, it was also possible to catch the USSR out by exposing how it lied, by broadcasting accurate information, or by confronting its leaders with facts.

After the Cold War, there was only one political idea and one vision of the future left, of globalization fostered by the victory of "freedom": free markets, freedom of movement, freedom of speech, political freedoms. In democracies, political parties still had to prove that they could manage this process better than their rivals, though this was more a technocratic challenge than a battle of new ideas.

We can find many moments when that vision of the future crumpled.

The invasion of Iraq, called "Operation Enduring Freedom," undermined the idea that political freedom was a historical inevitability. When Saddam Hussein's statue was torn down in Baghdad in scenes reminiscent of the destruction of Lenin's statues in Eastern Europe, the visual imagery seemed to suggest a historical equivalence, a montage of shots signifying one great story. Great Cold War dissidents, including Václav Havel, backed the war, in terms that echoed their own battles against dictatorship.[12] Those who pursued the war invoked the struggle against the Soviet Union, posited it as part of one historical process:

"President Reagan said that the day of Soviet tyranny was passing, that freedom had a momentum that would not be halted," President

George W. Bush announced in 2003. "Iraqi democracy will succeed, and that success will send forth news, from Damascus to Tehran, that freedom can be the future of every nation."[13]

But instead of freedom and prosperity, the invasion brought war and hundreds of thousands of deaths. Words and images filled with potent meaning in East Berlin ended in Baghdad.

But we still lived in a world in which there was an idea of the future, at least an economic one of ever deeper and greater globalization. Then came the financial crash of 2008. The idea that free markets could deliver freedom from want for all suddenly seemed risible; the dream that Europe's carefully tended market was sheltered from vast economic shocks was shattered. With that the last of the old, Cold War–framed notions of a universal future fell away for many. Elsewhere, from Mexico City to Manila, it had already been dissolving gradually, like an old bar of soap coming apart in mushy flakes.

And if there is no future that your facts are there to prove you are achieving, then what is the appeal of facts? Why would you want facts if they tell you that your children would be poorer than you? That all versions of the future were unpromising? And why should you trust the purveyors of facts, the media and academics, think tanks, statesmen?

So, the politician who makes a big show of rejecting facts, who validates the pleasure of spouting nonsense, who indulges in a full, anarchic liberation from coherence, from glum reality, becomes attractive. That enough Americans could elect someone like Donald Trump with so little regard for making sense, whose many contradictory messages never add up to any stable meaning, was partly possible because enough voters felt they weren't invested in any larger evidence-based future. Indeed, in his very incoherence lies the pleasure. All the madness you feel, you can now let it out and it's okay. The joy of Trump is to validate the pleasure of spouting shit, the joy of pure emotion, often anger, without any sense. And it's no coincidence that so many of the current rulers are also nostalgists. Putin's internet troll armies sell dreams of a restored Russian Empire and Soviet Union; Trump tweets to "Make America Great Again"; Polish and Hungarian media lament lost nationhood.

"The twentieth century began with Utopia and ended with nostalgia. The twenty-first century is not characterized by the search for new-ness, but by the proliferation of nostalgias," wrote the late Russian-American philologist Svetlana Boym, who saw nostalgia as a way of escaping the strictures of rationally ordered time. She contrasted two types. One, which is healthy, she called "reflective nostalgia." This focuses on individual, often ironic stories, tries to narrate the difference between past, present, and future. The other, more harmful type she called "restorative nostalgia." This strives to rebuild the lost homeland with "paranoiac determination," poses as "truth and tradition," obsesses over grand symbols and "relinquish[es] critical thinking for emotional bonding. . . . Unreflective nostalgia can breed monsters."[14]

Restorative nostalgia has taken hold from Moscow to Budapest to Washington, DC. The last thing anyone who clings to these phantom, fabricated pasts wants is facts. But if in Europe and America this tendency manifests itself in eccentric politics, elsewhere the expression is deadlier.

IN ALEPPO

When the regime's rockets, shells, and bombs were being lobbed into eastern Aleppo, Khaled Khatib would grab a camera and record the destruction of his city. People would turn on him, screaming. "Aren't you ashamed to film us? Do you like to see our tears? We've lost everything."

He would try to explain that he was here to help, that if the whole world knew how innocent people were being targeted, then the world would have to do something. There were rules after all. Laws. You can't just bomb civilians, children, old people like this.

Dozens of young men and women were constantly scurrying around the city, shooting and uploading video of the damage at what they called the Aleppo Media Center. Some had travelled to Beirut for video training by humanitarian organizations. Capture the crimes and this will help stop the atrocities, they had been told. They were now "citizen journalists," "media activists." Assad's helicopters were circling over their town, hovering overhead, then dropping oil drums, fuel tanks, and gas cylinders filled with explosives and metal fragments on the city. The videographers were helpless beneath them. But they could record what was happening, and that, they felt and hoped, connected them to something greater and more powerful than the helicopters.

In 2011 several Syrian cities had risen up against the forty-year dictatorship of the Assad family, in the Syrian iteration of the Arab Spring. The protests had been sparked when the regime tortured teenagers who dared to graffiti anti-Assad slogans on a high school wall,[15] a subversive act under a system whose power was predicated on making people repeat its ridiculous slogans publicly as a sign of fealty, whether they believed in them or not: "This obedience makes people complicit, it entangles them in self-enforcing relations of domination,"[16] wrote the anthropologist Lisa Wedeen in her study of the Syrian regime, and which reminds me of Havel's interpretation of late communism. When I have talked to Syrians involved in those first demonstrations in 2011, they often come back to the intoxication they felt at finally saying, screaming, shouting, singing publicly what they thought about Assad.

Assad responded with bombs, rockets, snipers, chemical weapons, more executions, and more torture. In 2012, rebels took eastern Aleppo, and its bombardment by the regime began. A million people fled.[17] Khaled was sixteen. He wanted to do something that had meaning, to show the world what was happening in Aleppo.

The first people on the scene after an attack were the rescue services, led by former school teacher Ammar Al-Selmo, who pulled victims out of the rubble. When they arrived, they would ask everyone to be quiet, listen for the sound of sobbing under the stones, and then begin digging. Many of them had no background in rescue operations; they were taxi drivers, bakers, and primary school teachers. After 2013 they started to get money, training, and bulldozers from the UK, Dutch, and US governments. They became known as the White Helmets for their distinctive headwear. Khaled began to record their missions.

He spent days filming his first rescue operation after a barrel-bomb attack had flattened several houses at once. When you film, you have to focus on every detail. You focus so long it stays with you, and you remember the world as a sequence of close-ups: torn-off hands, screams, limbs, tears, everywhere dust, more dust, more hands, rubble. During that first rescue operation, Khaled's dreams became full of body parts. After he uploaded the footage at the media center he swore never to film again. Then he checked social media and saw his material going viral. He realized his efforts were worth it.

At first he hadn't told his parents about his filming; they would have thought it dangerous. But when he came home one time caked in dust, after nearly being caught in a bomb attack, he couldn't hide it anymore. His father was furious initially. Then, when Khaled explained to him how they were pulling people out of the rubble, how his footage was appearing on international TV channels, relating Aleppo to the whole world, his father relented. Shots of children being pulled miraculously out of the wreckage were particularly popular (many more they couldn't save, but that footage didn't always go so viral).

His life in Aleppo was guided by sound: a hiss, a pause, and then a rumbling, expanding explosion that meant barrel bombs; a spluttering engine, rockets. He would listen for them in the background as he watched the 2014 World Cup finals. He wanted Germany to win. He would watch his favorite player, Mesut Özil, ghost into the penalty area, hear the hiss and splutter, and run out to film the damage. You always had to be careful for a "double tap": a helicopter drops one bomb, waits for a crowd to gather, then drops another.

The moment he would get out his camera some of the survivors would rush toward the lens, right up close, and start crying, "Why are they bombing us? There are no soldiers here" or demanding justice; or saying it was their neighbor's fault, the one who'd joined the revolution—"The bombs had been meant for him, not me!"

Khaled got used to the sight of slaughter. Filming was a way to bring order to everything around him. At first, much of what he shot was out of focus; he waved the camera around too much, chasing the action around him, when what you needed was to make a mental map of the surroundings first, then choose what to capture. You had to start breaking reality down into separate shots that together told a story: corpses in the rubble, craters, the remains of toys and clothes, photographs on the collapsed walls—any details that would prove that civilians had been bombed. The dust from the destroyed buildings was a permanent problem, misting over the lens, clogging up the mechanics.

In 2015, Russia entered the war on Bashar al-Assad's side. The Soviet Union had propped up his father, Hafez. Now Russia was rescuing his son. For the first time since the end of the Cold War, Russia was back on the biggest stage. Putin's domestic image is founded on the notion that there is no alternative to his rule, that he is immense. Now he was showing he was supreme not just at home but in the Middle East. When Russia intervened, Assad only controlled 20 percent of Syria. The stated aim of the campaign was to help defeat Islamist terrorists. Instead, the Russian air force turned, crushing any resistance to Assad's rule, and Aleppo in particular.

The siege intensified in April 2016.[18] Supplies to eastern Aleppo were cut off. Barrel bombs crashed down on bakeries, markets, schools. Over four thousand barrel bombs would fall in 2016.[19] The work of the White Helmets became ever more relentless. One morning they pulled a man out of the rubble of his home and took him to Al-Bayan hospital; when a bomb landed in the vicinity of the hospital it was evacuated, and the man was taken to a suburb that was subsequently bombed in the evening. The same rescuers who had pulled him out in the morning now came to rescue him again. He began screaming at them to go away—they brought him nothing but ill. He had lost his wife and child in the morning's bombing.

By the time the European Football Championships came around in the summer of 2016, Khaled was too busy to pay attention to how

Özil was doing. Hospitals were being targeted to break the will of the resistance; doctors had to operate underground, in semi-darkness. Fifty thousand people fled the city.

Increasingly people no longer shouted at Khaled. They just sighed and asked him what was the point of all his filming.

MARY ANA MCGLASSON WAS IN STARBUCKS. SHE WAS AN AMERICAN nurse providing medical humanitarian aid for Syria, based out of the Turkish border town of Gyazantip, a city of one million where an extra five hundred thousand Syrians had arrived as refugees. She had spent the previous five years coordinating the construction of hospitals—which would then be destroyed again—first at Relief International, then at Doctors Without Borders. She had just managed to get six months of medical supplies into Aleppo but it was already clear that was not going to be enough. As she sat in Starbucks, she was getting live text and WhatsApp messages from doctors in Aleppo.

"The bombings have started again . . . we are operating in the basement . . . the generator has gone. We are operating by the lights from our mobile phones."

As a humanitarian worker, she was supposed to be neutral: build hospitals, deliver supplies, report fatalities and war crimes. She relied on the existence of a system of institutions, ideals, accountability, and actions that would be taken if she provided the necessary evidence.

In 2015, as Russia began its bombings, Mary Ana and dozens of other humanitarian organizations compiled report after report showing that the attacks were aimed not, as the Russians claimed, at areas held by ISIS, but at Aleppo itself. She still assumed the weight of evidence would mean something. She wrote letters to Congress members and UN representatives. She had long given up thinking there would be military intervention, or even a safe zone. That moment had passed when the Russians began bombing, but at least more sanctions, an outcry, last ditch negotiations . . . or, more important, millions in the streets, protests. But where were they? She knew that the politicians would only react if there was popular outrage. Did it not matter anymore if a regime gassed its own people? Did that just elicit a shrug?

The WhatsApp messages from Aleppo kept on coming through: "We have run out of gauze and bandages. The bombs are getting closer."

She struggled to look Syrians in the eye. They kept coming to her, thinking she had some sort of influence, planting hard drives of evidence in her hands. We have been killed by barrel bombs, they told her, we have been killed by sarin gas and by Sukhoi rockets. But what is killing us now is the silence. Then, in May 2016, there was hope: the UN Security Council, including the representative of the Russian Federation, passed Resolution 2286, strongly condemning attacks against medical facilities and personnel. It seemed, suddenly, that all their report writing might not have been entirely in vain.

The resolution passed on May 3[20]—but in the following months, attacks on medical facilities in Syria increased by 89 percent, to 172 attacks between June and December, one every 29 hours.[21]

The medics' messages from Aleppo flashed on her phone: "Pediatric hospital was targeted today by aircraft. Many fatalities and injuries."

As the fall of Aleppo became inevitable, Mary Ana's Syrian employees started asking for a month's pay in advance. She knew what that meant: they had given up any hope of ever going home and were prepared to risk everything on a boat to take them across the Mediterranean to Greece, and from there on to the long march through the Balkans to Western Europe. There were different prices. If you had $10,000, smugglers could take you in a luxury yacht that dropped you on a pleasant beach in the Peloponnese. A few hundred could get you on an overcrowded dingy.

The Syrians she knew in Gyazantip always had believed that they would go home. There was the doctor who walked around Gyazantip with the keys to his Aleppo apartment in his pocket—though he had been away for years—as if expecting to return there any moment. Other refugees in Gyazantip lived in squalor: middle-class families squatting in empty shipping containers, eking out a living cutting shoe leather for local factories. But even they had not moved on from the border town, hoping their time away from home was temporary. Now, with the final bombardment, they were abandoning all hope for home.

Since 2015, TV news had been full of stories of boats with refugees capsizing, the bloated corpses of toddlers washing up near sunbathing tourists on the beaches of Greek islands. So refugee families sent their strongest sons, used their last money to get them on the best boats possible, arming them with mobile phones, the most important navigational aid for the journey.

When Mary Ana would speak to her parents in Arizona, they would ask her why these men weren't fighting. Why did they have mobile phones? Weren't they all terrorists? Her parents were deeply Christian and they watched Fox News. She could tell that they were torn between their concern for her and sympathy for her work and what they were being told on television. Shots of the exodus of refugees walking across Europe were being used to fuel fear of being overrun by foreigners. "Breaking Point" went a poster advocating for Britain leaving the EU.

On September 23, the Russian and Syrian air forces launched forty air strikes on eastern Aleppo to prepare the way for a ground assault.[22] Over the next month there was an average of one attack every hour, every day and night.[23] Whole parts of the city went up in flames. The UN Special Envoy to Syria described the use of incendiary bombs that "create fireballs of such intensity that they light up the pitch darkness in Aleppo as if it were daylight."[24] As the rebels tried to break the siege, they shelled government-held western Aleppo indiscriminately, too: the Syrian Observatory for Human Rights recorded seventy-four civilian deaths in October.[25]

Mary Ana kept writing reports that recited crimes against humanity, but these facts no longer seemed to have any power. On television,

Donald Trump was debating Hillary Clinton. He wanted to build a wall, he wanted to stop Muslims coming to America, he said Muslims were terrorists, and he made up numbers as he went along. He claimed that there were thirty million illegal immigrants in America and that Clinton would let in 650 million more.[26] No one took his chances seriously. Mary Ana knew different; many would vote for him back in Arizona. And if facts didn't matter in Aleppo, why would they in the United States?

The sitting US president, Barack Obama, had often talked about history having a "right side" and a "wrong side" (which he accused Russia of being on). Like Cold War leaders, he invoked that history had an "arc," a future.[27] But in Aleppo such lofty words looked meaningless; history's direction was being barrel bombed into nowhere. By November the siege was reaching its crescendo: the Russians seemed keen to finish it before a new US president came in. Schools, orphanages, and hospitals were relocated into cellars. Bunker-busting bombs, the kind usually used to destroy military installations, were used to reach them even there.[28]

"We have twenty-seven more casualties," went the messages on Mary Ana's phone. "About half of them children. Here are the photos . . . please tell people."

Mary Ana was in Washington, DC, the night of the election, November 8. She watched the results in a bar near the Capitol. Everyone was anticipating a Clinton victory. When the first states went to Trump, she sensed immediately that he would win. Two Republican campaign managers, already jolly, came up to her and told her she seemed to be the most distraught person in the bar. She walked out and grabbed a taxi back to her hotel. In the back seat, she sat and wept. The taxi driver tried to console her: don't worry, it will be OK. He sounded Middle Eastern. She asked where he was from. He said Afghanistan. She asked if he had immigration papers.

"No."

She told him she was weeping for him, not her. For the soon-to-be-enacted travel bans and Muslim bans, the turning of immigrants into undesirables, immigration into an evil.

Aleppo, the election—they felt like different expressions of one breakdown, where all the evidence-based rules and humanitarian norms Mary Ana had worked toward had become hollowed out. And in this new world the taxi driver would be the first victim.

In December 2016, Aleppo fell. Mary Ana helped organize the final evacuations from the city. The Violations Documentation Center in Syria estimates that thirty thousand died between 2012 and 2016 in Aleppo, the vast majority in opposition areas.[29] Over 70 percent of those killed were civilians. The Syrian Network for Human Rights (which discounts reports provided by the Syrian regime) puts the civilian death toll in the war at 207,000—94 percent at the hands of the Syrian government and Russian forces.[30] No numbers in this conflict are 100 percent reliable. The UN gave up counting casualties in 2014, when it put the overall death count in the war at four hundred thousand, give or take.[31]

Khaled had gotten out of Aleppo in August, when the rebels managed to open a road out of the town, his bag packed with video archive (a lot had been taken to Turkey previously). Some of the material he had shot in Aleppo went toward a short documentary film about the White Helmets that won an Academy Award in 2017.[32] He travelled to LA but sounded a touch awkward about it when we talked: Khaled was glad his footage had been seen by so many, but he hadn't filmed death and the destruction of his city in order to go to Hollywood parties.

We met in Istanbul and then Amsterdam for the interviews I have used in this book. Khaled, now twenty-one, wants to make films about the slivers of Syria that still remain free from Assad and radical Islamists. Facts didn't save Aleppo and now he thinks that telling stories is more powerful. He's trying to preserve his home on camera before what's left disappears, whether under continuous bombardment or under the deluge of disinformation. "They are trying to say that we are all terrorists. I need to tell the world what Syrians are really like."

At first, Mary Ana hadn't taken the disinformation very seriously. Then she began to look further and found that it was everywhere. Search for White Helmets in YouTube and you will find that it is full of media claims that the White Helmets were actually terrorists, or that they were actors and everything they did was staged, or that they were a secret service psy-op, or that they didn't actually exist at all. She has dedicated herself to establishing the truth about what has taken place in Syria.[33] The attacks on the White Helmets, she fears, are part of a larger effort to wipe out the facts of what happened in the country.

But here she encountered the great paradox of the Syrian slaughter. In all the other historical examples of crimes against humanity that Mary Ana had looked into, she found the excuse that the world wasn't aware of what was going on. The Holocaust? We didn't know (or pretended not to). The slaughter of Bosnian Muslims by Serbs in Srebrenica? Happened too quickly to react to. Genocide in Rwanda? Politicians claimed they hadn't known the extent of what was happening. And now? Now everyone knows everything all the time. There's an abundance of video and photo, eyewitness testimony, scientific analysis, SMSs, JPEGs, terabytes of data showing war crimes, communicated virtually in real time, all streamed on social media for everyone to see. And yet the reaction has been inversely proportional to the sheer mass of evidence.

But if everyone knows everything and still does nothing, and the truth about what happened isn't locked into what Mary Ana has taken to calling "the psyche of history," what does that lead to? That anyone can carry out mass murders and it's now seen as just OK? A globe lacerated with black holes where no known norms apply?

All sorts of black holes, great and small, seem to be opening up everywhere. "Maybe the world should be held responsible, because the world is a dangerous place," retorted the American president in late 2018, when confronted with mounting evidence that his ally, the crown prince of Saudi Arabia, had ordered the killing of a journalist inside a Saudi consulate in Turkey. The president's phrase encapsulated an attitude that no amount of proof leads to accountability.[34] And when one looks at the slaughter of civilians by all sorts of forces in the Middle East (Saudi- and US-led, Iraqi, Israeli, Iranian),[35,36] the social media–powered ethnic cleansings and mob violence in

Myanmar and Sri Lanka,[37] which one can see instigated live, online, in full view, it's hard not to feel Mary Ana's worst fears are coming true. And is disinformation just the excuse we use to let ourselves off the hook? "We didn't do anything 'because we were confused by a bot farm'"?

Meanwhile, 22 TB of video recorded by the White Helmets sits in safe houses across Europe. To that one can add 60 TB of videos, tweets, and Facebook posts held by the Syrian Archive; 800,000 documents and over 3,000 witness statements collected by the Commission for International Justice and Accountability that link crimes to Syrian officials.[38]

It is as much archive as we have ever had relating to torture, mass murder, war crimes. And it sits there, waiting for facts to be given meaning.

CHAPTER FIVE

POP-UP PEOPLE

"Excuse me—are you English?"

"What do you feel, English or Russian?"

The incessant questions of my childhood, pursuing me from the mouths of every curious parent of school friends, as they drove me beyond London on weekends to visit country houses full of second cousins, infinite uncles and great aunts, a rootedness so different from our wandering family. On those long rides in the back of other people's cars, I would stare transfixed at the borders between the fields. The hedgerows parceled the land so irregularly yet somehow coherently together, even the fields seemed to be involved in a conversation so intricate and so entrenched it could feel rude to interrupt. The English were defined so precisely by class, accent, schools, postcodes, counties, political parties, and sports teams that it could be hard to know, for an immigrant like myself, where to fit in.

One of the earliest things I worked out as an immigrant child is that you're not meant to rush into Englishness. You can do that in the US maybe, but it would be utterly un-English to try to quickly become English. The English respected difference.

"Your English is so perfect, one would never suspect you are a Russian," I would be told, and I felt that my English was some sort of deception. But what should I do? Fake a Russian accent to be more genuine?

To make matters more complicated, I couldn't simply answer "I'm from Russia." I had been born in Ukraine after all, albeit to Russian-speaking parents. What did that make me, Soviet? Russia and Ukraine were vast splotches on the map that hung in our kitchen, part of the even bigger splotch of the USSR, splattered with coffee and wine, a territory I could only populate with books that I had read. Is that where I came from, books?

The only point where my identity fused with England was through mass media, the television and radio synchronizing my attention and emotions with the nation. This could be surprisingly intimate: in the 1980s, Igor's stories were being translated and broadcast on BBC Radio, including "Reading Faulkner," which, narrated by an English actor, made Czernowitz sound somewhere near Suffolk.

"Better to try again, to describe Chernovtsy once more.

"My childhood smelt of grapes, greenery, and caraway. It passed under the watchful eyes of grandfathers (later I figured out: only one was my grandfather; all the rest were his brothers). Can't remember any winters in my childhood; perpetual July, the air flowing from the swelling apples and tickling so your head swam . . . "

In 1988, Igor moved from the BBC World Service to the London bureau of an American station that broadcast into the Communist bloc. Radio Free Europe had been set up in

1949 by American strategists in what they called a "citizens' adventure in the field of psychological warfare"[1] *in order to help exiles from states newly controlled by the USSR express a different political vision of their home countries. In 1953 Radio Liberty was added to broadcast into the USSR itself. Unlike the BBC, where British editors controlled all output, here the exiles had more control. In the first years, this caused chaos and disaster. During the Hungarian uprising of 1956 against Soviet occupation, when half the Hungarian population tuned into Radio Free Hungary, the Hungarian radio hosts began to give the freedom fighters tactical advice, implying Western military assistance was on its way. When the assistance did not arrive, Hungarian dissidents felt lethally betrayed.*

When Igor joined, such escapades had long been reined in and Radio Free Europe was bound to create news that was "accurate, objective, comprehensive." It had changed in other ways, too. At its inception, RFE was sponsored by the CIA, under the cover of private donations to a campaign called Crusade for Freedom. The CIA connection was revealed in 1967, and it subsequently was funded by Congress through a board of academics, media, and political grandees to safeguard its independence. But its mission remained different from a station like the BBC World Service, which existed to represent Britain in the world; the aim of Radio Free Europe, and its affiliate Radio Liberty, was to be a surrogate station that would represent an alternative vision of countries under Communism. To better understand its audience, RFE had an ingenious method of polling (which it shared with the BBC). Starting in the 1950s, sociologists would visit the bars in busy ports or international fairs in the West that Soviet sailors and delegations would be allowed to visit, strike up conversations, and ask them casually but systematically what sort *of radio programs they liked to listen to and why. By the late 1980s they felt confident enough to ask Soviet tourists to fill in more formal questionnaires. Despite the best efforts of Soviet signal jamming, some 5–10 percent of Soviet adults wiggled and waved their antennas to tune in to Radio Liberty between 1972 and 1988—the percentage was much higher among the well educated and in the big cities—rising to 15 percent after jamming was removed in 1988, when Igor joined.[2]*

He was now empowered to create his own worlds.

"I have no interest in describing culture. But to create and blow culture like glass is thrilling," he would write later.

His aim was to intermingle Russia and Ukraine with a greater Europe:

"I am not a cosmopolitan, I am a patriot. But I have a different patria. I feel a sense of home in Istanbul cemeteries, Rome, Chernivtsi, London, Sergeev Posad."

He made programs about prisons, glass, windows, colors—things that brought together different nationalities, junctures where they meet and mix. He would make programs where all the guests spoke Russian with a foreign accent, so that the language itself would be refreshed.

Igor's weekly program was called Across the Barriers, *and from 1989, real barriers were crashing down. It was a time of miracles on our Grundig television, with its four channels (two of which were BBC). Press the remote and there was Václav Havel, now free from prison and president of Czechoslovakia, waving from a balcony to a great swell of cheering crowds in Prague; press the remote again and statues of Stalin were being pulled down throughout Eastern Europe, suspended in mid-air like concrete trapeze artists; press once more and people were clambering over the Berlin Wall, feet dangling over an edge, which they would have been shot for a few weeks earlier, chipping away at the concrete with little hammers.*

His own writing moved away from first-person impressionism: it had begun to feel merely self-indulgent without the heavy breath of top-down authoritarianism bearing down on you. Instead, he drew on anthropology and zoology, mapping new territories. Viticulture, wine-making, became an incessant theme, a tradition that travelled and transformed across continents. A glass of wine had magical properties, it could transport you in time and space. In a story from July 1991, the first-person is almost entirely absent. The tale is based around a dictionary of winds. It's clear that he's talking about freedom, but there's little mention of the "I" at all—just detailed, meteorological descriptions of gales, breezes, gusts, breaths.

On August 21, 1991, Soviet citizens woke to find their two TV channels tuned to a ballet performance of Swan Lake playing on a loop. It was briefly interrupted by an announcement from the Kremlin: the head of the KGB, the army, the prime minister, and the deputy president announced a state of emergency. Gorbachev, they claimed, was too ill to serve the country any longer. He was unwell in his country house in the Crimea. They were taking power and planned to save the Soviet Union. The television then returned to ballet.

With the local TV off, millions turned to the foreign media and the independent Russian station Echo of Moscow, to find out what was going on. On Radio Liberty, Boris Yeltsin, the president of the largest Soviet republic, Russia, called the state of emergency a coup. He called for crowds to come to the center of Moscow, hundreds of thousands forming human shields to defend the Russian parliament from the tanks and KGB battalions that had pulled into the city.

In Crimea, Gorbachev, who wasn't sick at all, had been placed under house arrest by the coup plotters and had all his communications cut. The only thing he had left was a small, battery-powered Sony radio. Gorbachev and his staff gathered around it, wiggling the antenna to get good reception, tuning desperately in to the foreign media. On Radio Liberty, Margaret Thatcher exhorted her friend Mikhail to hold on. This was Igor's work. He had been trying to persuade Downing Street to let him interview the prime minister. They told him repeatedly that she didn't give interviews like this. Then he gambled: "This isn't about just politics," he argued. "Her personal friend Mikhail is in danger. He might be knocked off any moment. Has she nothing to say to him?" That worked.

The coup failed. Within the year, the Soviet Union itself was gone. The vocabulary of identity I had grown up with, "there," "here," "them," "us," was no longer making sense. The map on our kitchen wall began to change. Fifteen new countries were created in one go. The colors on the map I had grown up with, a globe shaded into two blocks, started to mix like a messy palette.

Our personal geography was shifting, too. In 1992, Radio Free Europe closed its London bureau and Igor was transferred to the central office in Munich. It was housed in a building that looked like a medieval fortress, with high, thick walls and even higher security, the legacy of an attempt to blow it up by the Stasi-sponsored Venezuelan terrorist Carlos the Jackal in 1981, and in whose corridors Igor was delighted to discover vast, forgotten cabinets with reels of the great émigré writers who had worked at Radio Liberty over the past forty years. He was becoming ever more enamored of the power of radio to create new worlds, blend past and present, here and there into something strange and new:

"Drama, dramatic effect is born on radio when sounds collide, rub noses, give each other a slap. Radio language is wider, richer, more full-bodied than any spoken tongue. With it you can convey ageing, the approach of madness, dying."

He and his producers travelled everywhere with their audio recorders, picking up noises to be used in programs: the crunching of an apple made one think of snow in winter; a dingo howling in a zoo was yearning for love.

One is, perhaps, not very aware in childhood that one is part of vast experiments in the culture, the mindset, the language that make politics possible. While Igor worked for a station that symbolized American support of a Europe, as US president Bush called it in 1989, "whole and free," where countries were both independent and united by the vaunted Cold War values of the West, I was sent to a special school created by the founders of the European Union to change the political psychology of the continent.

Munich was home to one of nine "European Schools." Like all the others, it had, buried under its foundation stone, the mission statement set out by Jean Monnet, the creator of the European Economic Community, the forerunner to the EU:

"Without ceasing to look to their own lands with love and pride, they will become in mind Europeans, schooled and ready to complete and consolidate the work of their fathers before them, to bring into being a united and thriving Europe."

Intended initially for the children of the international bureaucrats, the European Schools were also meant to show how education might one day be conducted across the continent. "May the Europe of the European [S]chools definitively take the place of the Europe of the war cemeteries," René Mayer, the head of the ECSC, declared in 1957. By 1992, the schools were open to three categories of pupil: the children of bureaucrats; the children of employees of companies who had a relation to the EEC; and those like me, random ex-pats who got in through a lottery and an exam.

Every morning the headmaster, Herr Hoyem, a Danish former minister for Greenland, would greet us at the entrance of the school, built in the shape of a star, in honor of the stars of the European flag. The architects had forgotten fire escapes, and the building later was encased in a metal exoskeleton of stairs and walkways. At first glance, they looked like scaffolding, as if the school was under permanent construction. The European School was split into different language sections—English, French, German, Italian, and so on—with history and geography taught in a foreign language and from that country's point of view. English kids learned history and geography from a German or French point of view and in that language, German in French, and so on. When the first school opened barely a decade after the end of the Second World War, it must have been a stunning idea for French children to be taught history in German from a German perspective—and vice versa.

The kids in the English section had been in Germany so long their connection to the UK was tenuous. Fresh from London, I was in some ways the most English person there. This was novel. Back in London I had been known as "the Russian" though I had left the Soviet Union as a toddler and had no idea what being Russian really meant. Now, I was suddenly a representative of England.

Educated side by side, the children of the European School played up to caricatures of their homelands. The French were moody: the boys read graphic novels and girls *dressed in Chanel. The Italians were appalled by the food while the Germans were the beer-drinkers. We in the English section, the boys anyway, posed as eccentrics: we quoted Monty Python and made a point of eating Marmite. At play time we would teach cricket to our Italian counterparts. Not because we had any passion for it, but simply because as the "English" that's what we felt we ought to do to identify ourselves.*

I was taught history and geography in French. For me, this was less a case of sink or swim than simply sinking and having to survive by breathing underwater. Overwhelmed in my first months, I gradually began to grow linguistic gills and could make out the dim outlines of glowing underwater kingdoms: the St. Bartholomew's Day massacre, Versailles, Napoleon. But this Napoleon was different from the one I knew, a star of democracy promotion rather than a despot. I ended up with two Napoleons: one English and one underwater.

I became amphibian. I joined the other pupils in the Aula, where conversations would start in German and flow into French and then to English; or everyone would speak their own language but understand everyone else's. I remember once looking across the Aula at an English classmate and for a moment not recognizing him because, when speaking German, he shed his camp grimaces and laughed like a Bavarian, slow and macho. So, on the one hand, national traits were more pronounced as we defined ourselves against one another in playground rituals but they were also less fixed, something you could put on and take off again. It was an existence I found quietly ecstatic. After an immigrant, bilingual, awkward childhood—knowing I wasn't English like the majority around me but not quite sure what I was—here was a system that celebrated stepping outside and transcending one's identity, the one thing

I actually was quite good at. This was what "European" meant: not some superimposed identity, but the ability to wear identity lightly, to be able to wriggle outside of one and inside another.

As Igor and I tried to work out what being European meant, Lina was immersing herself in Russia. She had been the first of our family to return; since 1989, she had worked with documentary crews filming in the USSR and then in the newly independent states.

On first landing in Russia, she had the curious sensation that everything she saw was out of sync with what she heard, as if her hearing was straggling behind her sight. She saw the long queues of people all standing far too close to one another; the movements of the taxi driver's mouth, but would hear them moments later.

When sound and vision synched, she found herself in a country whose stomach had been ripped out, the intestines of its tragedies and traumas everywhere. Some of her earliest films were about the street children of St. Petersburg. There were whole colonies of them, sleeping underground alongside warm gas pipes, living in networks of dark, wet, bare-walled cellars where they mimicked normal apartment life by bringing in settees and watercolor paintings they found in dumps. Many of the children spoke an educated Russian but had run away from homes where their parents had become drunk, deranged as all sense of normality, family, sanity collapsed. All social roles were being overturned. Prostitution, previously taboo, seemed suddenly acceptable. Students would support their parents, answering ads for work as secretaries with "no complexes"—a euphemism for being prepared to sleep with the boss.

Political language, too, was in utter chaos. In 1994, Lina worked on a documentary about a popular new politician, Vladimir Zhirinovsky, sailing with him down the River Volga as he, dressed in a flamboyant all-white suit, gave speeches from his ship to excited crowds gathered along the banks. Zhirinovsky was the head of the Liberal Democrat party, but he was neither a liberal nor a democrat in the way the words previously had been used in Russia to signify something tolerant, well-spoken, pro-Western. Indeed, it was hard to pin down what he was. His speeches seemed stream-of-consciousness, yet somehow, he unerringly picked up his audiences' desires. It was impossible to tell when he was joking and when serious. He promised he would end poverty and homelessness within a few months of coming into power and that Germany would pay for it as they owed Russia World War II reparations. He railed against the US with its "Pepsi-Cola dollars," which, under his rule, would no longer be able to undercut the glorious Russian "golden ruble." He claimed that Russia would control the entire territory from the Pacific to the Mediterranean; annex Alaska. But he also told crowds that they lived in penury because of Lenin and his communist economics, that he, Zhirinovsky, would make them more like successful Westerners, they would own their own homes, have new cars and wide-screen televisions. He also promised the bands of Cossacks, who stood on the shore in their uniforms, that he would empower them to go and fight against the "enemy to the south." "We will give you weapons. Take your whips and ramrods, go to the regions where there is anarchy, disruption and anti-state activity and restore order."

Zhirinovsky meant the breakaway republic of Chechnya, where a year later Russia would be fighting a vicious war with little regard for civilian casualties and where a new type of Islamist terrorism was beginning to spread. Lina filmed up in the mountains of the Caucasus, with the Chechen separatists. They described their struggle as one of national liberation, but she also noted something new for Russia: Islamist preachers from the Gulf; women in chadors.

It was easy for Lina to film everyone from politicians to warlords in those years; just saying you were from British television made you a symbol of something better from "over there," an envoy from another world that still had a sense of norms, justice, stable social identities, where words meant something.

Away from her filming, Lina went to smoke-filled performances where the artists and poets of the 1990s tried to make sense of the all-pervasive uncertainty. Lev Rubinstein gave spoken-word performances standing with a stack of Soviet library catalogue cards, those little emblems of cultural order, on which he wrote cryptic stanzas, throwing them away as he read through them, symbolic of old meanings falling apart. Dmitry Prigov would howl and chant sound bites of Soviet agit-prop until they became shamanic dirges. Oleg Kulik threw language away altogether, transforming himself into a growling dog, down on all fours growling and snapping at visitors to his gallery: if words were meaningless all that was left was action.

"Soviet time has stopped," Zinovy Zinik wrote, "while the universe it rules disintegrates."[3] The art critic Boris Groys described the moment as the Big Tsimtsum, a term borrowed from the Jewish mystical tradition of the Kabbalah, an alternative version of creation where God first brings the world into being and then retreats from it. "The withdrawal of Soviet power, or the Tsimtsum of Communism, created the infinite space of signs emptied of sense: the world became devoid of meaning."[4]

In 2001, after university, I followed Lina's trail: moving to Russia to eventually work in television. "Moscow," I would write later, "seemed a city living in fast-forward, changing so fast it breaks all sense of reality. Russia had seen so many worlds flick through in such rapid progression—from communism to perestroika to shock therapy to

penury to oligarchy to mafia state to mega-rich—that its
new heroes were left with the sense that life is just one glit-
tering masquerade, where every role and any position or
belief is mutable."

THIRTY YEARS LATER, IT IS NOT ONLY RUSSIA WHERE SIGNS ARE "emptied of sense" and the world is "devoid of meaning." The Big Tsimtsum feels relevant among the victors of the Cold War, too, in countries where professional pollsters struggle to define models for our identities, where what was previously assumed as normal has dissolved, and there is a race to form new identities out of the flux.

OTHERING

As I was experiencing experiments with multilayered identity at the European School, Rashad Ali, also a child of first-generation immigrants, was going through a very different process in Sheffield, Yorkshire.

In 1996, Rashad was immediately impressed by the men from Hizb ut-Tahrir the first time they came to his school to give a talk on Islam. These were the days before September 11, before ISIS, when no one in the school's management thought anything bad could come of the well-dressed, erudite, young college lecturers in engineering and science who spoke so engagingly about big ideas: whether you could prove God exists, evolution, identity.

"What kind of Muslim are you?" they asked the pupils. "A Friday Muslim? A part-time Muslim? Can you be a complete Muslim?"

"Complete" sounded interesting to Rashad. What could that mean? He went to the Hizb study groups, held in an ordinary terraced house, among streets of similar, russet-bricked, terraced houses built for workers in Sheffield's once-mighty steel factories, rolling toward the green-sprouting hills of southern Yorkshire.

The recruiters explained that in Bosnia and Russia, Muslims had spent hundreds of years integrating with the locals: they drank, they smoked, they fornicated like secular Europeans. And what had happened? In Bosnia they were being slaughtered by their secular and Christian neighbors, armed and supported by Milosevic's government in Belgrade. In Chechnya, they were being bombed to bits by the Kremlin. What was the West doing to help these Muslims? Nothing. "Muslims in Bosnia are your brothers," said the recruiters. "They are your family, not the secular people around you, not the English."

Growing up, Rashad had always known that he was different. Rashad's father (who died when Rashad was eight) had come to England in the 1960s to work in the steel mills. He had done well, bought a house, opened a restaurant, wore a suit he had custom made from the tailors on the corner, watched the BBC News religiously twice every evening. But for all this apparent Englishness, both of Rashad's parents spoke with strong Bangladeshi accents. His home smelled differently from English homes. He was a different color.

And then there was the God thing. Rashad was religious in the way everyone in his community was religious: it was just something that was indelibly part of you like a limb, something most English just couldn't understand. But Rash had never defined himself as Muslim. In the early 1990s, all the talk was of Asian identity, or Asian-British, which encompassed Sikhs, Hindus, Indian Muslims, and Pakistani Shia. But what did these Asians really have in common? In their homelands they were at war with one another. Rashad had visited Bangladesh and knew he didn't belong in the home of his parents' past. He was aware he wasn't quite English, either. Now he was about to be offered a new home, a place where he would belong perfectly because it didn't yet exist, an Islamic state.

Each week Rashad and the other members of his study group would immerse themselves in Hizb's founding texts, which laid out in stunning detail every aspect of what the ideal Islamic state should look like. There were books on law, government, ethics, on how reality was shaped by a priori thoughts. Hizb had been founded in the

1950s by a Palestinian Islamic scholar, Taqi al-Din al-Nabhani, who had previously been a senior member of the Arab Socialist Ba'ath Party. For al-Nabhani, the creation of Israel was a sign that Muslims were weak, unable to stand up for each other, corrupted by Western notions such as "the nation," which had splintered them into different countries. It was the very language and concepts through which people saw the world that had to change.

At the foundation of Hizb's approach was the "Islamic personality."[5] This concept held that a person had natural instincts that had to be fulfilled, but training yourself to think in the correct way would channel those instincts into the "right" behavior. So, for example, man has a natural instinct for security, which was articulated in the search for acquiring things and property. Marxism suppressed that instinct and was therefore destined to failure. Capitalism, however, overindulged it and undermined another instinct, procreation, which expressed itself as the need to feel part of a community. Political Islam fulfilled both needs: it allowed you to satisfy the need for security by allowing a certain amount of private property, and procreation by defining your obligations to the greater community of Muslims.

Rashad asked his study group leader what was the methodology to bring about an Islamic state. The man invited him for a drive in his gold Honda Shuttle.

As they drove through Sheffield, he explained to Rashad that their plan was to convince the militaries of Jordan, Egypt, Iraq, and Syria to launch military coups, take power, and then unite into one super-Islamic state. For a moment Rashad paused: this sounded, even to his sixteen-year-old self, reckless. The group leader saw his reaction and continued.

"Remember what the prophet did at Mecca and Medina. He had no forces of his own, but he managed to persuade the tribal leaders to back him and be his army. It's the same with us."

That coming together of past and present, of holy books and current history, helped Rashad hurdle his initial doubt. And soon enough, it all was seeming less fantastical. The movement was growing stronger by the day. From 1996, when Rashad joined, to 2003, it grew from thirty to three thousand activists in the UK, hundreds of thousands globally. The Hizb leadership issued statements claiming that generals throughout the Middle East were turning in their favor. The leadership lived in such secrecy in Lebanon and Jordan that when they "spoke" at Hizb gatherings across the world it was only through an audio link-up: their voices were beamed in to thousands of followers in a hall but their faces were hidden.

By the late 1990s, Rashad was one of the leaders of Hizb in the UK. He would organize university debates about, for example, whether it is possible to be both Muslim and British simultaneously, arguing that the two were incompatible. In 2000, at the age of twenty, Rashad authored a core text of Hizb literature, a copy of which would later be found in the library of Osama bin Laden in his safe house of Abbottabad.[6] *The Method to Re-establish the Khilafah* (Caliphate) spends more than three hundred dense pages outlining Koranic arguments about how to correctly establish the Islamic state. The process starts with "culturing" (uniting drives, instincts, and ideas to form the "Islamic personality"). Then comes the "interactions" stage, the public outreach campaigns meant to convince populations in the Middle East that their interests are best served by military coups to overturn their corrupt governments, which were nothing but lackeys of Western colonialism.

"After this, the military would be capable of establishing the authority of Islam . . . and Jihad to the rest of the world."

One of Rashad's many responsibilities was to answer email questions from party members about the finer points of doctrine and liaise with the heard-but-not-seen leadership on the canonical response. He had now read enough religious commentary to know that some of the answers the leaders gave simply were wrong. When a member asked why the Prophet hadn't enforced all his decrees on his followers, the leadership answered that no scholar allowed any Muslim to follow the Prophet in this regard. Rashad knew that the leaders themselves were aware that this was false. Many scholars argued that it was acceptable to not enforce all decrees. The leadership were simply misusing people's ignorance to create a system of control. And now that he was more versed in Islamic ideas and history, he was discovering that many of the Hizb teachings were factually incorrect. There had never been a golden age caliphate under a single ruler: there had been many small and fractured treaties throughout Islam's history, a patchwork of jurisdictions. There was no original caliphate to restore.

There was no one moment when the scales finally fell from his eyes, but instead a process over many years. By 2004, Rashad began to notice how far Hizb was from fulfilling any of its promises. The leadership sent circulars that their plans for coup d'états were just around the corner but it was becoming obvious nothing of the sort was happening. And then there was the question of violence. Hizb officially opposed violent acts. However, it did not disapprove of others committing them under the right conditions. The 9/11 hijackers had been in the wrong, argued the Hizb leadership, because they had kidnapped planes belonging to a private company. If they had used Israeli ones, it would have been different. The contradictions seemed ridiculous to Rashad.

Slowly the idea that being Muslim was incompatible with being English fell away, as did the belief that he could be himself only in an Islamic state. He found he could be simultaneously Muslim and from Yorkshire, English and Asian, all held together with a vertebrae of belief in human rights, which he threw himself into, vehemently defending the rights of Palestinians in Gaza and criticizing anti-Semitism in British political parties.

In the summer of 2018, I took the train with Rash to towns in the north of England and the Midlands he grew up and preached in. On the way, as we rode past fields parceled as intricately together as I remembered from my childhood, Rash told me how he would practice recruitment techniques on strangers during train journeys, as lessons for younger Hizb disciples who would observe him. One time, on a train to Durham, he saw a woman reading a newspaper where there was a distressing report about how a ten-year-old boy had killed his baby brother when, for a laugh, he put him in a washing machine and then switched it on.

Rashad approached the woman and asked what she thought about the article. The woman told Rash the story angered her. She blamed the parents. They had gone to the pub that evening and left the children all alone. She was a nurse, and every day she saw how narcissism, irresponsibility, and negligence caused harm to others.

Rashad had his in. He asked the woman whether she thought that in a liberal, secular society where people were encouraged to think about nothing but their personal gain and pleasure, wasn't this sort of behavior inevitable? What we needed, argued Rashad, was a society where all the economic and social laws would encourage care for one another, where people would know good deeds brought high rewards. The woman nodded.

It may sound novel, Rashad said, but had she considered an Islamic state a way of establishing just such a society?

Rashad and his pupils got off soon after and we will never know what the nurse made of his proposal. But the essence of Hizb recruitment arguments was clear. Whatever issue a potential recruit cares about, your job is to connect it with the need for an Islamic state.

In Birmingham, Rashad and I walked through streets among the red housing complexes and low skies bustling with street vendors selling fruit and sandals, Mac Halals, Sudanese supermarkets selling brightly colored shawls, graffiti murals calling to Free Palestine, Somalis selling niqabs. But what struck me were the bookshops. I counted at least three large ones on one short stretch of street, with long rows of hardcover books of holy texts and commentary, garish soft covers on everything from polygamy to "God's Gentle Artistry," "Jihad," "Islam and Karma," and "The Prohibition of Homosexuality." All were sponsored by different Islamic movements and by different states, all tussling over the minds of English Muslims. At one point, Rashad and a friend drove out to a warehouse, where we were met by a man with a beard and a key who took us up an industrial elevator to a floor where books were piled in high towers, whole valleys and alleyways of spines with gold Arabic lettering, which Rashad clambered through excitedly. "I've found it!" he exclaimed. "Abu-Bakr Ibn Al-Araby. 'Commentary on the 99 Names of God'!"

It's his knowledge of Islamic law and recruitment techniques that makes Rashad so good at what he does today: extracting people from the sort of movements he was once a part of. He works at an organization blandly entitled the Institute for Strategic Dialogue, which tracks online extremist campaigns, and experiments with what it calls "counter-speech," reaching out to audiences coming under the sway of extremist movements. ISD defines extremism as "a system of belief that posits the superiority and dominance of one 'in-group' over all 'out-groups,' propagating a dehumanising 'othering' mind-set that is antithetical to the universal application of Human Rights." Sometimes they simply refer to it as "othering."

Across the ISD office there are dozens of people. There are teams looking at how hatreds are inflamed online in Kenya, where Islamist movements try to divide the country along religious categories, while political parties then try to redraw loyalty along tribal lines.

Others track neo-Nazis across online forums where awkward teens spend their days playing World War II games. Those who seem the angriest, most romantically frustrated, and loneliest, the neo-Nazis direct toward other chat rooms where they instruct the new recruits in digital marketing campaigns to promote far-right causes: which videos on YouTube to like or dislike, how to create swarms of automated accounts to boost far-right campaigns on social media. The recruits move from computer games to digital political campaigns, which feel like another sort of game, all the while never leaving their bedrooms, slipping from one virtual reality to another. On parts of Reddit and 4chan, anonymous administrators provide online crash courses in mass persuasion that in the Cold War would have been the provenance of secret services and their civilian psy-ops.

There is advice on how to use the values of your enemies against them. So, if you are attacking a leftist politician, you should create a fake online liberal persona and point out how politicians are part of the financial 1 percent, or how their white privilege has allowed them to rise to the top. There are instructions on how to control an internet forum, including tips on "consensus cracking": using a fake persona to express the ideas you oppose in such a weak and unconvincing manner that you can then use another fake persona to knock them down. "We are an anonymous swarm with a singular goal. We don't have to play fair," you will be advised on Advanced Meme Warfare: Successful Guerrilla PR. "We can say and spread whatever we want. We have to literally be the hate machine we're known as." Campaigns can come from anywhere. ISD once found a Russian bot-herder in Nizhny Novgorod promoting German far-right memes next to their other campaigns for escorts in Dubai, medical clinics in provincial Russia, and attacks on Russian opposition figures.

Yet other employees create educational videos for schools so teenagers learn how to recognize far-right and Islamist campaigns, which are becoming ever more difficult to discern. Jihadi recruiters, for instance, will first scan a potential target's social media profile, see what that person's favorite interests and hobbies are, and then try to engage with him or her. If they feel a young woman is interested in religion, romance, a family, they might strike up a conversation about the virtues of a Salafi husband. If a person doesn't respect God, they argue, how could he be expected to respect his wife?

The internet has made recruitment quicker and more dexterous than when Rashad was first pulled into Hizb but the underlying techniques of envelopment are similar. Today it is ISIS that is best known for propagating the need for an Islamic state, and though Hizb has officially condemned the movement, Rashad can see how it echoes Hizb's interlacing of feelings, concepts, language, and behavior.

"TELL THEM HOW MUCH YOU MISS THEM AND THAT TEARING YOUR-self away from family is *haram* [forbidden]."

Rashad direct-messages the parents of two teenage girls who have joined ISIS in the Middle East. The parents, in an English market town, are simultaneously talking to the girls somewhere in Iraq. They are asking their parents' permission to marry jihadi fighters. The girls write that they miss their parents, they're sorry, they don't want to cause them pain, but marriage is their duty to the soldiers of the caliphate. It is their contribution to a great cause.

The parents brought the girls up as conservative Muslims, sending them to study medicine in their hometown, Khartoum—and then found, to their horror, that the girls had turned toward a form of Islam so radical and political their parents barely could recognize it.

For Rashad, the fact that the girls are even writing to their parents for permission is a good sign: it means they still feel a bond to mum and dad. This is where the extremists' hold on them could be weakest.

The girls keep on asking for their parents' blessing. They explain it's only in the caliphate they can practice the pure version of the religion they believe in.

Rashad and the parents try to argue that the girls can practice Islam fully in England, that they don't give their blessing to this marriage, that their caliphate violates all Islamic ethics.

"ISIS is to Islam what adultery is to marriage," writes Rashad.

The girls don't immediately respond. Could they be thinking? After a while they come back with cut-and-paste quotations in medieval Arabic, misquoting arcane scholars in cut-out blocks of text. Clearly these aren't their words. Rashad can tell their ISIS handler has stepped in and is dictating their accounts. The conversation, for now, has become pointless.

Rashad opens up another window on his computer to reveal the Facebook wall of a young man in the Midlands. Photos of bungalows he rents out in his day job as an estate agent sit next to conspiracy videos supposedly proving that terrorist attacks in Europe actually were committed by the CIA; comments about how he prefers his new Samsung to his old iPhone intermingle with clips of preachers advocating killing gays. He writes how he feels sickened by the sight of drunks on a Friday night while British drones hit innocent Muslim children in the Middle East. "It's a duty to support the Khalifa [caliphate]," he declares. "The land of the Kuffar [non-Muslim] will never be a home for the believer!"

Rashad direct-messages him. He explains that he also was once part of a radical Islamist group but left. Does the young man in the Midlands want to talk?

At any one moment Rashad might be involved in dozens of such conversations online (for reasons of privacy, data protection, and security, the above extracts minimize, mix, and blur personal details of his interactions). If 5 percent answer when Rashad contacts them, that's already a success. His next task is to work out that person's motivations. Is he (let's say it's a he) driven by political passions, a radical who just happens to be Muslim? A telltale sign would be if they accuse Rashad of being an agent of Western imperialism. Or are they actually interested in religion? A personal grievance? Mental health issues? Or what combination of the above?

Then Rashad tries to parse the logic to which recruits have been subjected, to find the contradictions. When they argue it's a religious duty to unite in one state and impose Sharia, Rashad points out that since the time of the Prophet there always have been different Islamic empires and rulers; there's no one model. Or when they suggest cartoons of Mohammed should be banned in the West, Rashad asks them whether that means one should ban the Koran, too. Surely if one side has freedom of speech the other should?

And then he will zero in on one of their core false beliefs, let's say Holocaust denial, and then overpower them with so much evidence it becomes irrefutable. After all, Rashad argues, how do we know about the existence of the Prophet? Because authorities confirm it. We have historical evidence. Tradition. Conspiracy theories undermine the premises of Islam.

Rashad tries to help those to whom he talks understand how they have been manipulated, to break down the idea that one's Islamic identity is inherently exclusive from a British (or American or Danish) one.

But there's a problem. The types of thinking he looks to unwind, the belief in conspiracies, the "othering," is now becoming ever more pervasive. "Extremist" is not the same as fringe; an "extremist" movement can be one of the largest in a country. One of the barometers ISD looks at for their work is the "Positive Peace Index," which has an indicator called "The Acceptance of the Rights of Others"[7] that has plummeted in many Western countries, even as movements who push a line that "posits the superiority and dominance of my in-group over all other out-groups" surge.

Looking around, Rashad even sees politicians from long-established parties adopting a version of the approach popularized by organizations like the Hizb. One chooses a theme—religion, immigration, an economic principle—then builds it up so that it becomes the marker of who you are, not just a policy to be debated but a line on the other side of which everyone is deemed untouchable, lassoing the whole with the same mix of conspiracies dividing us from them.

"In religious terms we would call it sectarianism," says Rashad, "identity masquerading as ideology."

In a recent report ISD described the environment it works in as a "liquid society," invoking a world where old, more solid social roles have slipped the leash, where information moves so easily it fractures old notions of belonging, where a sense of uncertainty pervades everything, and where all sorts of forces can more easily reshape you.[8]

POP-UP PEOPLE

"All politics is now about creating identity"—that was the argument a spin doctor made to me as we sat in a bar in Mexico City so shaded by dense foliage it was darker on the street than in the Curaçao-blue sky above. He explained to me that the old notions of class and ideologies were dead. When he ran a campaign, he had to take disparate, discreet interests and unite them under a new notion of "the people."

The spin doctor wore a pinstriped shirt, his hair was slicked back, he looked quite the yuppie. "Populism is not an ideology, it is a strategy," he asserted, invoking two theoreticians from the University of Essex, Ernesto Laclau and Chantal Mouffe, who had first coined the notion—though they had meant it to advance a new socialism. I was surprised at his choice of favorite theorists—he didn't look like much of a socialist himself. He told me his personal preference was for the Left, but he would work with anyone who paid the rent.

The nature of social media encourages "populism as a strategy." Look at things from the point of view of the spin doctor. Social media users are organized through vastly different interests: animal rights and hospitals, guns and gardening, immigration and parenting and modern art. Some of these interests might be overtly political while others are personal. Your aim is to reach out to these different groups in different ways, tying the voting behavior you want to what they care about the most.

This sort of micro-targeting, where one set of voters doesn't necessarily know about the others, means you need some overarching identity to unite these different groups, something so broad voters can project themselves onto it—a category like "the people" or "the many." The "populism" thus created is not a sign of the people coming together in a great groundswell of unity but a consequence of "the people" being more fractured than ever, of their barely existing as one nation. When people have little in common, you have to reimagine a new version of the people.

Facts become secondary in this logic. You are not, after all, trying to win an evidence-driven debate about ideological concepts in a public sphere. Your aim is to seal in your audience behind a verbal wall. And it's the opposite of centrism, where you have to bring everyone together under one big tent, smoothing differences. Here the different voting groups don't even need to meet each other at all. To solidify this improvised identity one needs an enemy, the non-people. Best to keep it as abstract as possible so anyone can invent their own version of "the establishment," "elites," "the swamp." The spin doctor in Mexico sadly admitted that this could get nasty.

America serves as a good example. The Trump presidential campaign separately targeted free marketeers, American preservationists, and "anti-elites,"[9] and that doesn't even touch the multitude of microgroups targeted on social media. Some social media ads didn't even mention Donald Trump himself, avoiding showing the main man and focused instead on touchy-feely messages quite out of sync with Trump's vitriol.

Or one could look at Italy, where the Five Star Movement started as a series of Facebook blogs ranting at completely different grievances for different audiences, from ecology to immigration, potholes in roads to foreign policy, all laid at the door of the establishment, channeled through the manic energy of their anarchic, curly-haired, cursing leader of the time, the comedian-turned-politico Beppe Grillo.

And then there's England. I used to think the English were different, that if anyone in the world knew who they were it was them. But something has shifted. A sense of uncertainty underlies everything.

I'd first noticed something was changing in England while talking to one of the architects of the Brexit campaign, soon after his referendum victory, in a pub in London. He started by saying, "The problem for people like you is. . . ." I can't remember the rest of the sentence (it may have been something like "metropolitan liberals are so out of touch") because it made me feel so unexpectedly at home: I'd always been the Russian (or Soviet or Ukrainian?) immigrant!

But when that Brexiteer's sweeping statement included me, I was no longer being asked to play the part of the outsider. I was in. This made me feel warm. That happiness, however, was quickly followed by dismay. The only reason I was being included was to play the puppet, the "globalist" enemy. "People like you" was being invoked only to contrast us to the "real people."

I got a closer picture of the cultural logic and targeting tactics of the Vote Leave campaign when I met with its lead digital officer,

Thomas Borwick, who explained to me how the vote was won, reveling in the nerdy details of his craft. Borwick comes from a family of Tory grandees (mother an MP for Chelsea, father a baronet), and he approaches his work like a precocious schoolboy solving a puzzle or playing Risk.

Borwick's job as a digital campaign manager is first to gather as much data as he can about voters and try to calculate which ones are most likely to vote for his side. Over the decades, perceptions of the electorate have changed. During the Cold War, voters were defined by class and class politics: ideological left versus ideological right, *Guardian* readers and *Telegraph* readers. Then, during the 1990s and early 2000s, when politics was reduced to just another consumer product, pollsters would draw on the categories provided by marketing companies. Tony Blair's New Labour would target categories like "Ford Mondeo Man" (a person who was attracted to a certain kind of car), trying to satisfy their economic desires. Now that, too, seems outdated: people don't vote along simple categories of consumer choice. Nor do newspapers or parties necessarily represent clear social categories anymore. For several years in the early 2010s, it became fashionable to define the nation along psychological types, substituting economic class with "open" and "closed" psychology, based on the notion that your childhood experiences determine your political choices. There's even a psychological map of Britain that identifies each constituency in the country according to its psychological profile, which maps vaguely onto the Brexit vote (closed for Brexit, open for Remain), although it becomes frustratingly blurry in the swing areas that matter most.

Now social media groups can provide the most accurate reflection of the issues that could motivate different groups to vote: Was it animal rights or potholes? Gay marriage or the environment? A country of twenty million, Borwick estimates, needs seventy to eighty types of targeted messages. Borwick's job is to connect individual causes to his campaign, even if that connection might have felt somewhat tenuous at first.

In the case of Brexit, Borwick said that the most successful message in getting people out to vote had been about animal rights. Vote Leave argued that the EU was cruel to animals because, for example, it supported farmers in Spain who raise bulls for bullfighting. Even within the animal rights segment, Borwick could target even more narrowly, sending more graphic ads with photos of mutilated animals to one type of voter and gentler ads with pictures of cuddly sheep to others.

Animal rights supporters may actually have a very different stance on immigration—they may well be for it—than other Brexit voters, but that doesn't matter as you are sending different, targeted ads to various groups that the others never see. And of course, Borwick had a catchphrase, "take back control," so utterly spongy it could mean anything to anyone, with the EU being the enemy conspiring to undermine it:

"I believe that a well identified enemy is probably a 20 percent kicker to your vote," he told me, always keen to give a data point to any statement.

And the EU, distant and aloof, has made for an easy enemy. In February 2019, I went back to visit my old school in Munich. There was a new glass and steel cube next to the original star-shaped building. The school's student body increased from nine hundred to two thousand after EU enlargement. The Aula was now packed. There were so many people and so great a din that I couldn't make out any one language. The school had become so full of EU kids that it had stopped taking in any Category 3 students, that is, those whose parents weren't EU employees. The dream for the European Schools had been to be a model, to seep into the communities where they were located and transform them. Instead, the school in Munich, the new headmaster confessed, was disliked by locals. When I looked up the headmaster from my time there, Herr Hoyem, he was even more strident: "The schools were meant to be a pedagogical laboratory for Europe. Instead they are becoming isolated company schools." It felt like a metaphor for the European Union project, cocooned in its own utopia, unable to articulate why it was a vision for everyone.

THE BREXIT VOTE HAD BEEN ONE WAY OF RECONFIGURING IDENTITY—but it would be a mistake to think it was permanent or the only way to do so.

For the next general election, the Labour party quickly came up with its own formula. Their slogan became "For the Many, not the Few." "The Many" combined utterly different groups, from those in the north of the country who voted for Brexit, and resented well-heeled West Londoners; to well-heeled West Londoners who had voted to stay in the European Union and thought Labour would reverse the Brexit vote. Labour managed to gather enough votes to destroy the Conservative party's majority at the election. "The people" had been reconfigured into "the Many," the "enemies of the people" into "the Few." We are living in a time of pop-up populism, when the meaning of "the people" is in flux, we are constantly redefining who counts as an insider or an outsider, and what it means to belong is never certain, as political identities burst and then are remade as something else. And in this game, the one who wins will be the one who can be most supple, rearranging the iron filings of disparate interests around new magnets of meaning.

One person excited by Labor's rise was Chantal Mouffe, the theorist who first formulated the idea of "populism" as a strategy, and who wanted to reinvent the Left for an age where categories of economic class were no longer fixed. We met first in Vienna, and then in her flat full of plants and books in North West London. Despite living in the UK since 1972, Mouffe told me she had never felt English (it was the humor she couldn't understand), but she now saw a great change taking place in the country where she had lived so long.

In the decades since the 1980s—and the victory of capitalism over communism in the Cold War—we have lived, argues Mouffe, within a "normal" to which there had seemed no alternative. Terms that had been so important for those struggling under authoritarian rule

Mouffe saw as having been co-opted by economic interests. "Choice" had become a way to justify relinquishing public control of schools and hospitals. "Liberty" transmuted to selling off state assets:

"Thatcher managed to convince people that the state could only deliver benefits in a collectivist, oppressive way while privatization would bring you liberty," Mouffe told me in her highly accented English. "Liberal democracy," argued Mouffe, had been skewed too far in favor of the word "liberal," which had been used to give more freedom to financial powers, whereas what we needed was more "democracy," or what she termed "equality." It was as if she wanted to pry apart words that she felt had been soldered together poorly.

Since the financial crash in 2008, everything was up for grabs again. It was in the space where words, desires, meanings, and behaviors are put together and dissolved where the most important battles for power are played out similar to Hizb's process of "culturing." This is what defines "reality" and what becomes "normal." Mouffe used the term "meta-politics" to denote this process, coined by the Italian philosopher Antonio Gramsci.

Mouffe is much more than a theorist. She has worked closely with two left-wing political parties: Podemos in Spain; in France, La France Insoumise. She told me that new leftist politicians had gone to places in France that had voted for the anti-immigrant party of Marine Le Pen (formerly the National Front, now the National Rally) and tried to convince them that their actual enemy was not immigration but an economic system that kept them poor. She described how one could almost see the audience's perceptions changing during these conversations. "Identities are the result of political construction," she asserted.

But despite Mouffe's enthusiasm, I was worried. Hadn't some of the old freedoms, if one could still use that term, been there for good reason? Mouffe spoke about the need for a charismatic leader as an "articulating agent" who could bring together the very different causes and grievances of the newly created "people"; of the need for strong passions, the expressions of our deepest, unconscious drives, to bind them; how important it was to define the enemy.[10] She argued this could be done within democratic rules, but it wasn't hard to imagine how it could turn into something frightening.

Mouffe agreed it was a dangerous time.

"It can go into a more authoritarian direction . . . or it can go also towards a more democratic thing. The whole question is how you construct the 'us' and 'them.'

There was perhaps no one who understood the game better than Martin Sellner, the Identitarian leader whom we met in Chapter two, when he used the ideas of Srdja Popovic's protest tactics to pursue his vision of a culturally homogenous Europe.

"We don't want Mehmed and Mustafa to become Europeans," the Génération Identitaire manifesto declared. "Europe belongs to the Europeans alone. Because we are Generation Identity."

Sellner, like Mouffe, talked about metapolitics (and Antonio Gramsci). When I reached out to him again, this time for a BBC Radio documentary, he explained that "our job as the avant-garde from the Right is to show the people that the normality of tomorrow doesn't have to be what is considered normal today. Political normality is something very volatile, dynamic and relative."

He taps into the language of rights and freedoms—women's rights especially—and connects them to his aims. In one stunt, female Identitarians attended a meeting in support of women's rights in Germany, and then let off rape alarms to advertise cases of rape by Muslim migrants (of which there have been several, though the vast majority of sexual assaults are committed not by wandering migrants, but by people who know the victim well). In another stunt, Sellner put a burqa over the statue of the Austro-Hungarian empress Maria Theresa in Vienna. But instead of violence his language invokes freedom of speech, democracy, openness to new ideas. . . .

"The powerlessness of our enemies is that they are still trying to describe and fight us as if we were the old right-wing fringe group parties that they faced decades before," he said on the program I presented, while my producer and I worried that by interviewing him, we were helping to make him all the more mainstream, if such a concept even still existed.

THE FUTURE ARRIVED FIRST IN RUSSIA

As I wondered about these endless transformations of the many and the people, these desperate, fluctuating attempts to reinvent identity on the fly, I was struck by how I'd seen this all before, in Russia.

"I first invented the idea of the Putin majority," one of his first spin doctors, Gleb Pavlovsky, told me when I still lived in Moscow, "and then it appeared!"

I left Russia in 2010, after almost a decade living there, because I was exhausted by living in a system that, as I'd put it in a previous book, unconsciously invoked Hannah Arendt's aperçu that "nothing is true and everything is possible." Those were still relatively placid days in Moscow, before the invasion of Ukraine (though the invasion of Georgia and the carpet-bombing of Chechnya should have been premonitions), but it was already a world where spectacle had pushed out sense, leaving only gut feelings to guide one through the fog of disinformation. I returned to London because, in my naivete, I wanted to live in a world where "words have meaning," where every fact was not dismissed with triumphant cynicism as "just PR" or "information war."

Russia seemed unable to come to terms with itself since the loss of the Cold War, or with any of the traumas of the twentieth century. It was ultimately, I thought, a sideshow, a curio pickled in its own agonies.

Then came the revolutionary year of 2016 and things went a touch topsy-turvier. Suddenly, the Russia I had known seemed all around me: a radical relativism that implies truth is unknowable, the future dissolving into nasty nostalgia, conspiracy replacing ideology, facts equated to fibs, conversation collapsing into mutual accusations that every argument is just information warfare, and the sense that everything under one's feet is constantly moving, inherently unstable, liquid.

And not only were attitudes I witnessed in Russia uncannily prevalent, the country also was headlining the news all the time. Invading Ukraine, bombing Syria, hacking America, buying Europe. President Putin smirked at me from newsstands and from the top of the ten o'clock news: "You thought you could get away?" he seemed to be saying.

Despite all my efforts to escape Russia, it had followed me. What if I had been wrong during my years there? What if Russia was not a curio on a historical dead end? What if it had been a pre-echo of what was to come in the thing once known as the West?

With these questions in mind, I found myself turning back toward Russia, to the roots of the system I saw during my years in Moscow, when Lina had been making her films in Russia.

I got back in touch with Gleb Pavlovsky. He agreed to let me interview him over the phone, and as I sat in a BBC recording studio while he explained his tactics for creating the idea of the majority, the people in 1990s Russia, it all began to sound remarkably familiar.

"The Communist ideocracy was sluggish, but it was an ideological entity, nonetheless," he said, gently advising me to ask more precise questions. "Even up to the end people could at least argue over the positives and negatives of communism. Now a vacuum arose, requiring a new language. We were an absolutely blank canvas. We had, in a sense, to reinvent the principles of the political system as best as possible."

The vision of a pretty future of "freedom" had fallen apart in the devastations of the early 1990s. Instead the landscape was dotted with new micro-movements making up their own terminology as they went along: National Bolsheviks; Liberal Democrats who were actually conspiratorial nationalists; Communists who were Orthodox monarchists with social programs. When he polled the country, Pavlovsky found Russians believed in contradictions that didn't fit into any old conceptions of left and right. Most believed in a strong state as long as it didn't involve itself in their personal lives. Soviet demographic categories like "workers," "collective farmers," and "intelligentsia" were useless to win elections. Pavlovsky experimented with a different approach to assembling an electorate. Instead of focusing on ideological argument, he targeted different, often conflicting, social groups and began to collect them like a Russian doll. It didn't matter what their opinions were; he just needed to gather enough of them.

"You collect them for a short period, literally for a moment, but so that they all vote together for one person. To do this, you need to build a fairy tale that will be common to all of them."

That fairy tale couldn't be a political ideology: the great ideas that had powered collective notions of progress were dead. The disparate groups needed to be unified around a central emotion, a feeling powerful enough to unite them yet vague enough to mean anything to anyone. In 1996, the fairy tale that Pavlovsky wrote for the campaign of the ailing, unpopular President Yeltsin played on the fear the country might collapse into civil war if he didn't win. He cultivated the image of Yeltsin as someone so reckless and dangerous he would be prepared to plunge the country into war if he were to lose. Survival was the story; fear of losing everything, the feeling.

Pavlovsky's agency, the Fund for Effective Politics, went about smearing the opposition Communist Party in a preview of today's fake news and sock puppets. Pavlovsky created posters that purported to be from the Communist Party saying that the Communists would nationalize people's homes. He filmed actors posing as Communist Party members burning religious pamphlets. He hired astrologers who would go on TV and predict that electing the Communists would lead to nightmare scenarios such as war with Ukraine.

Yeltsin won an unlikely victory.

Pavlovsky had conjured up a new notion of the majority but, as this was nothing more than an emotional trick with little political content, it fell apart soon afterwards. Work on a new one began immediately. Pavlovsky polled incessantly, and when it became clear that the candidate people most respected would be an "intelligent spy," a James Bond, the Kremlin and its oligarchs began to search for potential successors from the former KGB. They landed on Vladimir Vladimirovich Putin.

This might seem a strange place for someone like Pavlovsky to end up. He had, after all, been a dissident. In a book of conversations with the Bulgarian political scientist Ivan Krastev, Pavlovsky recounts how as a student in 1960s Odessa he already was pulling pranks by sticking sheets of paper to teachers' backs that read, "I vote for John F. Kennedy"—quite an act of anti-Soviet rebellion.

As a young man, he circulated samizdat copies of Solzhenitsyn's *Gulag Archipelago*. When the KGB hauled him in in 1974, Pavlovsky, to his own amazement, panicked under pressure and gave the name of one of his friends. Pavlovsky would later recant his testimony, which meant that his friend had to serve only a brief stint in a psychiatric ward rather than a prison.

In the early 1980s, Pavlovsky went to Moscow, edited one of the main dissident journals, *Searches,* and was arrested again. This time he confessed that he was guilty of "slandering the Soviet Union." Such a confession was seen as shameful in a dissident culture that prized above all else the sovereignty of the individual in the face of state pressure. Pavlovsky spent the years in prison and internal exile after his arrest in 1982 writing letters to the KGB, saying it should work with dissidents for the good of the Soviet Union. He was released in 1986. During perestroika he continued to believe that a reformed, cosmopolitan USSR was a better vehicle for progress than a potentially racist Russian nationalism. The need for a strong, centralized state became his great concern.[11] By 1999 he was working to bring a KGB man to power.

For the 2000 presidential election Pavlovsky pulled together everyone who felt they had lost out during the Yeltsin years, the "left behind," and imbued them with the sense that this was their last chance to be winners. These were disparate segments of society that in Soviet times would have been on different sides of the barricades—teachers, secret service types, academics, soldiers—whom Pavlovsky would bundle together under the idea of the "Putin majority." As Thomas Borwick and others would discover decades later, in an age in which all the old ideologies have vanished and there is no competition over coherent political ideas, the aim becomes to lasso together disparate groups around a new notion of the people, an amorphous but powerful emotion that each can interpret in their own way, and then seal it by conjuring up phantom enemies who threaten to undermine it.

Putin won the election, the candidature of someone with a security-service background made all the more prescient as the news became filled with horrifying, panic-inducing footage of Islamist terrorists from Chechnya setting off one devastating bomb after another in Russian suburban apartment blocks, with hundreds killed under the rubble.

During Putin's almost two decades in power since Pavlovsky helped him become president, the idea of the people has been reorganized over and over while always managing to unite disparate groups around a rotating enemy: oligarchs at first, then metropolitan liberals, and more recently, the entire outside world. Like some Actionist performance artist, Putin poses in photo-ops of derring-do; instead of ideological coherence he offered the emotional highs of a version of make Russia great again: "Bring Russia off its knees."

In that time Pavlovsky has been busy. He helped found Nashi, the youth movement that launched the distributed denial of service attacks in Estonia and harasses dissidents and journalists, and whose name, which literally means "Ours," reduces politics to a series of pronouns: "them," "us," "ours," "theirs." According to Dr. Ilya Yablokov of Leeds University, an analyst of conspiracy theories in Russia, Pavlovsky's frequent media appearances in the first decade of the twenty-first century invoked an image of Russia besieged by enemies, with the West planning to turn Ukraine into a "huge testing area for anti-Russian technologies." The "Putin majority" that he helped create became a "truncheon to delegitimise its opponents, the division of society into Putin's majority and its enemies became a dominant political tactic."[12]

At one point, Pavlovsky got on the wrong side of the divides he himself created, arguing in 2011 that Putin might not need to return to the presidency after having served a term as prime minister. He was thrown out of the Kremlin. Having worked across such different shades of the Russian political spectrum, he remains an object of fascination and the subject of much comment, a sort of everyman popping up in Russia's many tales.

WHEN PAVLOVSKY LOOKS AT THE WEST TODAY, HE SEES IT GOING through the same changes Russia underwent in the 1990s. A delayed reaction to a similar crisis.

"The Cold War split global civilization into two alternative forms, both of which promised people a better future," he told me when I interviewed him from the BBC's studios. "The Soviet Union undoubtedly lost. But then, there appeared a strange Western utopia with no alternative. This utopia was ruled over by economic technocrats who could do no wrong. Then that collapsed."

In this identity and ideological flux, political campaigners in the West have ended up adopting strategies strikingly similar to Pavlovsky's, though enhanced by social media and big data.

"I think that Russia was the first to go this way, and the West is now catching up in this regard. In general, the West can be considered to follow a proto-Putinism of sorts," remarked Pavlovsky, wryly.

This is the great paradox of the end of the Cold War: the future, or rather the futureless present, arrived first in Russia. We in the West are just catching up. Maybe there's a simple cultural logic at work here. If our own ideological coherence was based partly on opposition to the Soviet Union's, when it collapsed, we inevitably would follow.

In his book of conversations with Krastev, Pavlovsky invokes his mentor, a Russian historian of the Holocaust called Mikhail Gefter, who argued already in the late Soviet era that mankind was running out of unifying, universal visions of historical development. In the

1990s, Gefter predicted that the end of the Cold War would usher in an era of "sovereign murderers." In the absence of norms we have vacuums in which chaos agents behave according to rules they make up for themselves as they go along, who murder people and indeed whole peoples according to their own "sovereign" logic. Pavlovsky sees this as prophetic, a vision from the early 1990s that anticipates 2019. "The image of a common mankind is impossible, and no alternative has emerged. Everyone invents their own 'normal' humanity, their own 'right' history."

The current Russian regime finds itself at ease in this environment because it has been finding ways to adapt to it for longer. There's nothing mystical at work in its all-pervasiveness; it simply has a slight head start.

And as our world becomes more uncertain and liquid in ways that echo the new Russia, the more one can be tempted to yearn for the seeming certainties of the Cold War: if the Kremlin is the great enemy again, then maybe we will rediscover our own, once-victorious meanings, a desire that in turn augments the current Kremlin's status, which is exactly what it wants.

If there was one overarching aim to all of Pavlovsky's "political technology," it was to resurrect the idea of the strong state when it had all but come apart. He'd figured out back in the 1990s that though the Kremlin might be weak, he could make it seem strong domestically by spreading it everywhere in the information flows and media landscapes of people's lives. Now Putin, Pavlovsky told Krastev, can simulate global influence by purposefully leaving the fingerprints of his hackers and information operations all over the world. "It's all just theatre for a world audience. *Theatrum mundi!*"

CHAPTER SIX

THE FUTURE STARTS HERE

CONCLUSIONS AND RECOMMENDATIONS

Before he came to meet me at South Kensington station, Nigel Oakes visited an exhibition at the Victoria and Albert Museum entitled "The Future Starts Here." While strolling through the exhibit, Oakes suddenly found himself freezing in front of a display that startled him so much that his heart rate shot up and he had to rush outside for air.

The display, *Can Democracy Survive the Internet?* was dedicated to a "global elections management" company called Cambridge Analytica. Cambridge Analytica claimed to have gathered five thousand data points on every American voter online. What you liked and what you shared on social media; how and where you shopped; who your friends were—Cambridge Analytica claimed to be able to take this imprint of your online self and then use it to understand you better than even your closest relatives could and then use that information to change not just what you think but how you act. The boast seemed backed up by success. Cambridge Analytica had worked on the presidential campaign of Donald Trump; it also ran successful campaigns for the US senator Ted Cruz (twice), and all across Africa, Asia, the Caribbean, and Latin America.

Oakes was so overwrought by this display because here, finally, was proof that he had been right all along. Cambridge Analytica was a spin-off from a company he created, Strategic Communication Laboratories, and it drew on his philosophy. All his adult life he had tried to prove that he had discovered what he proudly called the ultimate weapon of persuasion. At first, he had been laughed at, then criticized. But now his ideas were being presented as the future that "starts here," imitated by all, and displayed in an exhibit at the V and A.

When we met, he was wearing a gray suit and a cap with the Strategic Communication Laboratories logo on it, pulled low over cornflower-blue, intense eyes.

"The thing about most advertising and influence campaigns—they're absolute bollocks," he told me at the start of our conversation. His dream, he repeats several times, was to create the ultimate influence weapon. Like any weapon, argues Oakes, it could be used for good or ill. He readily calls himself amoral.

Oakes originally wanted to be a composer. But there were no courses for composers at the Royal College of Music and he wasn't good enough at playing any one instrument to get in. He worked for a while as a composer of theater scores but there was no money in that. He still composes organ pieces for weddings in the late baroque style. He smiles beatifically and hums when he recounts the joy of transfixing a crowd with music. But he still needed a career, so in 1988, he joined the advertising company Saatchi & Saatchi.

Oakes never went to university and at his famous, posh public school, Eton College, he always had felt less academic (and poorer) than the other boys. Perhaps it was the need to overcome that feeling of academic inferiority that drove him to adopt an academic approach at Saatchi. Could the agency actually prove, he asked his colleagues, that its ads and campaigns worked?

To his surprise he found there was nothing solid. Advertisers were good at getting information out about their products (agenda setting), at making shiny, pretty things that attracted attention. They could shift attitudes about an issue (framing), make salt, or a politician, or a country look more or less attractive. But could they actually change behavior? The example Oakes likes to give is about smoking. You can create a campaign saying that smoking kills, and people will agree that it's a bad thing while still continuing to smoke. You need to work out why someone smokes. Young women, as he found during one of his research projects, smoked because they thought it made them look attractive. So, you focus the campaign on how smoking makes your hair and breath stink, your skin sallow.

In 1989, Oakes created the Behavioural Dynamics Institute (BDI), whose mission was to collect historical research on which forms of persuasion work and which don't. Over the next four years, backed by investors from the advertising industry, he commissioned studies from dozens of academics who specialized in the history of mass influence, social psychology, and behavioral science. They wrote, to give but one example, about how Goebbels, Hitler's propaganda minister, promoted the use of the raised-arm Sieg Heil salute because he had worked out that the forceful double exhalation of breath and repeated, strenuous arm movements caused hyperventilation and exhaustion among Hitler's followers, putting them in a trance-like state and making them more susceptible to messaging.

The BDI developed new ways to define social groups. Descriptive categories (age, gender, social class) were of limited use as predictors of behavior. Oakes pioneered polling by teams of anthropology students, who, usually without revealing their mission, spend long periods penetrating a community, inquiring about whom people hated and trusted, what they most desired, which friends would influence them, what dictated how they behaved within a group.

One research trip, to Moscow in 1990, stunned Oakes. After he gave a three-day talk at the state energy company Gazprom about advertising and influence, he was offered a tour of the Science and

Mathematics Research Center of Service A at the KGB, as a sign of mutual respect and exchange of knowledge. These were the dying days of the Soviet Union, and mutual openness was welcome.

He wasn't taken through the main entrance of the KGB but instead through an annex. It was November and he was wrapped in a thick overcoat and hiking shoes, with dress shoes in his bag in case the KGB expected him to look more formal. The building wasn't heated and the academics, sitting in one large, open-plan office, with few computers, were wrapped in thick coats. Most seemed cautious about speaking with him. Then the chief scientist arrived and the mood changed. He was keen to tell Oakes all about his work. He had the freedom to conduct control tests on entire villages, to test hypotheses about communication and persuasion.

Oakes thought for a moment about the ethics of all this (could you kill someone to test a hypothesis?) but was too excited to dwell on it. Such research was impossible in the UK. Then they sat down to lunch and a watery soup was served: Nigel realized the chef had given him the portion with the bone and a little meat on it as a sign of hospitality. The research that Service A was conducting was epic in its sweep but the whole system was coming apart.

In 1993, Oakes's BDI collated its findings and Oakes created Strategic Communication Laboratories (SCL), expecting to be swamped with offers because, unlike anyone else in the industry, he could prove that his method worked. But instead of clients beating down his door at Lots Road, Chelsea, no one could understand what he was talking about. Why would you spend months penetrating a community to sell a chocolate bar? Then Oakes got a call. From South Africa. Apartheid was ending, black people were being given the vote for the first time. But would they go to the polling stations? Oakes was asked to conduct a "targeted audience analysis" to identify the "influencers" in each region whom locals would listen to when they encouraged them to vote. It worked. Oakes realized that elections, rather than chocolate bars, could be his game. More followed. In

1995, in Indonesia, he persuaded President Suharto, who was holding elections for the first time, to create completely separate political campaigns for the country's thousands of islands and across its population of 200 million. But though his client list began to grow, Oakes was never in the big leagues of PR companies. His methodology was slow and expensive. His clients could be the sort of rulers who might hire him, take his research and then refuse to pay; and as they were in countries where the courts were not exactly independent, there was little Oakes could do to get his money.

In 2008, another Etonian, Alexander Nix, joined SCL. Unlike Oakes he came from a fabulously wealthy background; he studied art history at university; his friends called him "Bertie," a nickname out of Edwardian England. Oakes says he wanted to drag research into the digital age. He wanted to make money. He was better with clients. In 2012, he took the elections component of the company and made it his own. Nix renamed SCL Elections Cambridge Analytica and energetically tested ways to replicate the behavioral change methodology by looking at social media usage. (A whistleblower would later claim that mentioning the prestigious university, with which the company had no official affiliation, impressed American clients.)

Cambridge Analytica explored the potential of psychographics: the idea that your social media preferences and language predict your personality. Consider if you were running a campaign to support the right to bear arms. If the campaign manager knew someone was an anxious person, then they could target them with messages which argued they needed guns to keep them safe.

This is the potential nightmare of the new media: the idea that our data might know more about us than we do, and that this is then being used to influence us without our knowledge. Not so much that "they" know something about me that I considered private, hidden— though that's unpleasant, it's also somehow comforting, reinforcing the idea that there's a stable "me" I am fully aware of, to protect me from them; more disconcerting is the idea that they know something about me that I hadn't realized myself, that I'm not who I think I am—one's complete dissipation into data that is now being manipulated by someone else.

Oakes, however, told me he was skeptical that Facebook "likes" and online product purchases could replicate months of in-depth, in-field research. He had refocused his own work onto Western militaries. (He called his part of the business SCL Defense.) The invasions of Iraq and Afghanistan had been disasters partly because no one had bothered to understand the local populations. "At least by the time we got out of Afghanistan we understood the locals: we left in a much more thought-through way than when we came in," says Oakes.

In 2018, Nix was recorded by journalists telling a prospective client from Kenya that Analytica could help him by setting up sexual honeytraps for his political rivals and had access to the data of eighty million Facebook users without their consent.[1] Cambridge Analytica was bankrupted by the ensuing scandal. At SCL Defense, Oakes's military clients all disappeared: no government would touch anyone remotely associated with Analytica. But Oakes doesn't sound bitter at Nix. They had been partners. Nix shared some of his profits with Oakes.

And though he's lost his business, Oakes feels that he has won the intellectual war. Everyone now agrees that influence means understanding your audience better and deeper than the next person, not by forcing themselves on you, but by tickling the "real you," fitting your message to them rather than pushing an ideology top-down.

"Isn't that democracy," asks Oakes rhetorically, "when you give people what they want?"

His former colleague Nix made a similar argument when testifying to the UK Digital, Culture, Media and Sport Committee, which I had been brought into as one of many "specialist advisors." "We are trying to make sure that voters receive messages on the issues and policies they care most about . . . that can only be good for democracy," Nix told the committee, utterly unrepentant about any of his actions.

By the time I joined, the committee had already been going for two years—and it had become obsessed with the question of what exactly was "good for democracy" in an age of "information abundance." It started by looking into "fake news," but then astounded members of Parliament heard testimony about how ethnic cleansing in Myanmar had been fueled on Facebook; about Kremlin interference in Europe and America; about how people's online information was used without their knowledge to target them in political campaigns. The committee's February 2019 report, "Disinformation and 'Fake News,'" stated that "our existing legal framework is no longer fit for purpose." The committee noted that "in this environment, people are able to accept and give credence to information that reinforces their views, no matter how distorted or inaccurate. This has a polarizing effect and reduces the common ground on which reasoned debate, based on objective facts, can take place . . . the very fabric of our democracy is threatened."

In February 2019, I sat in the back of a room in the UK Parliament as the committee, made up of MPs from all parties and their advisors, went through detailed edits of their conclusions and recommendations. This was just the start of a long process. Their report would then be submitted to the government, which was producing a white paper with its plans on the issue, which would be debated in Parliament. The committee's editing process was forensic to the point of being persnickety. Members of Parliament would question the meaning of each small phrase, the validity of each point of reference. It was slow going but I found it oddly reassuring. Many novels of the nineteenth and twentieth centuries satirized the fussy language of bureaucracy, policy, the law. But in an age of utterly unstable meaning, the slow, legalistic, evidence-scraping work of the committee seemed a touch heroic.

Behind the MPs hung a painting that depicted a scene from the House of Commons in the eighteenth century, with bewigged men making some sort of elegant argument while the other side listened politely and attentively. It was most likely not a realistic depiction, since the House of Commons has always been a rowdy place full of cads and liars. But it did, at least, envision an ideal, what I imagined the Digital, Culture, Media and Sport Committee meant by "reasoned debate" and "fabric of democracy." The room we sat in was oak-paneled; it also had thick, emerald-green wallpaper emblazoned with paisley prints. There were oil paintings of past prime ministers, their eyes brimming with arrogance and wit. The fireplace was engraved with wood carvings of heraldic signs. Sitting there one felt part of a tradition. But could it adapt to the present?

The committee began its report by stressing the need to have a common language to debate the problem. The committee originally described its concern with fake news, but then found the meaning of that term was morphing to denote any content someone didn't like. They tried, instead, to differentiate "disinformation" (content designed to mislead) and "misinformation" (content that misleads by accident). The committee recommended a system to define and monitor such content. But many of the most pernicious campaigns I'd seen didn't necessarily use disinformation. And even if disinformation is identified, would, or indeed should, that make it necessarily illegal?

What if one were to refocus disinformation from content to behavior: bots, cyborgs, and trolls that purposefully disguise their identity to confuse audiences; cyber-militias whose activity seems organic but who are actually part of coordinated campaigns full of fake accounts; the plethora of so-called news websites that look independent but are covertly run from one source, all pushing the same agenda? Shouldn't one have the right to know if what looks organic is actually orchestrated? How the reality one is interacting with is engineered?

Ultimately, what does it mean to be an empowered, democratic citizen, the kind that Srdja Popovic envisions, online? How can the digital world become the space where freedom, rights—all those big words that have been bled of their vitality—are regenerated and given meaning?

One part of this, as Camille Francois argues, is protection from coordinated campaigns of harassment and intimidation by the powerful. Such state-sponsored trolling should be instantly identified, taken down, and the instigators held accountable. Another part is protecting privacy: defining which bits of your online activity end up in whose hands and for what purpose.

Sitting in the committee room I began to imagine an online life where any person would be able to understand how the information meteorology around them is being shaped; why computer programs show you one piece of content and not another; why any ad, article, message, or image is being targeted specifically at you; which of your own data has been used to try and influence you and why; whether a piece of content is genuinely popular or just amplified. Maybe then we would become less like creatures acted upon by mysterious powers we cannot see, made to fear and tremble for reasons we cannot fathom, and instead would be able to engage with the information forces around us as equals. Could we even be empowered to have a stake in the decision-making process through which the information all around us becomes shaped, with public input into the internet companies who currently lord over how we perceive the world in darkness?

If one could instill these principles, then much of the framework of information war would fall away. The way to judge information would not be whether it came from "over there" or "over here," but whether the way it is offered allows you to engage with it on equal terms, rather than being belittled by some force that takes away your understanding of how you are being acted on.[2]

Sitting in that emerald-green room under the oil painting of an idealized parliamentary democracy, I considered the other ideas I'd come across to find "common ground on which reasoned debate, based on objective facts, can take place." In Denmark, I had first been told about "constructive news," a journalism that goes beyond merely balancing one set of opinions against another, but is always trying to find practical solutions to the challenges that face its audience, forcing politicians to make evidence-based proposals, which one could then evaluate over time, pegging their words back to reality, generating a conversation where facts become necessary again. This approach could help reinspire trust in journalism, because we trust those who work together with us for some greater goal. And by putting change back into our own hands, it can overcome the sense of helplessness that conspiracy-peddling politicians so like to push to make you feel that only they can guide you through a murky world of insurmountable and hidden powers.

The bell rang to signal a new vote in the House of Commons and I snapped back to the present. It was the middle of February 2019, and Parliament was in the midst of the struggle for how the UK should leave the European Union, as ordained by the Brexit vote Tom Borwick and his team had won two years earlier. Maybe, hopefully, by the time you read this, this question will have been happily resolved: political language will be clear again, political parties will represent clear interests, the future will be clear. But, in that moment, Parliament was somewhat different. Around the stone, curved, mock-gothic stairwells; through narrow, green and beige corridors; in crowded bars with barmen's faces like dried prunes, and on the terraces that seem to almost tumble into the Thames, you heard the same words repeated: "Brexit," "The People's Will," "Sovereignty," "No Deal." What any of them meant was moot. Borwick had won the vote by talking to so many audiences in different ways one couldn't really say what the will of the people really was. Had the country voted to stop immigration? To protect animal rights? "Brexit means Brexit," the prime minister had said, but what did "Brexit" mean? And were the people whose will it claimed to represent the same as the many, whom the Labour Party now claimed to champion vis-à-vis the few? But yet the few the Labour Party wanted to oppose were often the very ones who claimed to represent the people's will. And whom did these parties represent anyway, as in the middle of February 2019 they were all at war with each other, not only over leadership but about the meaning of themselves.

LEAPING THE WALL

Britain, Russia, the entity known as the West, and so many of the countries that had experienced "democratization" after the end of the Cold War, were in a swirling state where notions of progress, political and social identity and meaning were in flux. It would take more than a few regulations to fix that. But what about China? Was it on another trajectory, one that I perhaps might not like but which at least might have coherence, a concept of the future one could engage with, even if in opposition? Could I find the future in Beijing?

It was my first visit, and at Chinese passport control I had my fingerprints recorded and my photo taken to be fed into a system of web-cameras across the country that would instantly identify me wherever I might be. Indeed, the country can be viewed as a vast propaganda theme park offering every method of manipulation and coercion that I have touched on in this book, and more. In western China, there are labor camps right out of mid-twentieth-century totalitarian dictatorships, where entire communities of Muslim Uighurs are indiscriminately rounded up and hauled off for "re-education" because the government is worried that they might want independence. At other times, the situation can be more reminiscent of the 1970s.

China has a human rights movement called Charter 08 with a declaration of demands signed in the year 2008 that echo Charter 77, signed by Václav Havel and other Czechoslovak dissidents in 1977. As with Cold War dissidents, many of the Chinese signatories have been "disappeared," either imprisoned or under house arrest or marched on television to confess their so-called crimes against the people, or in the best-case scenario, exiled.

A more contemporary technique involves the legions of the Fifty Cent Army, named for the fifty cents they are paid to leave progovernment comments on Chinese social media. Researchers at Harvard University have established that these troll farms allow some criticism, but immediately censor any hints at protest. "The Chinese people are individually free but collectively in chains," concluded one study.[3]

China was also home to some of the more sophisticated "stateendorsed" campaigns Camille Francois researched for her study of state-sponsored trolling. A French journalist was forced out of China after online mobs had demanded her expulsion for daring to criticize

Chinese human rights abuses. The government said that it simply had to deport the journalist, as "the people" demanded it; indeed, they had to do so for her own safety. Yet all the while the Chinese government went out of its way to encourage the leaders of the online mob by honoring them with awards and banquets in Beijing. "How elegant," thought Francois. "One sends signals that encourage harassment, rewards those who practice it, and then claims one is merely following the will of the people in executing it."

Many Western websites are blocked in China behind the "Great Firewall," so one has to use internet services controlled by companies loyal to the regime. If any country would be first to perfect the use of data imprints to target people according to cognitive, psychographic and behavioral patterns, it would be China.

And then there's the "social credit score," still under development, which gathers information about your behavior, from how much money you spend on alcohol to your financial health to whether you visit your parents regularly, and then crunches it into a number that defines whether you can get a bank loan, a job, or are allowed to travel.

China also had a full suite of foreign-policy informational approaches. There's the international broadcaster CGTN; social media trolls who taunt politicians in neighboring Taiwan; pressure exerted on foreign academics who study China. A 2013 Pentagon paper about China's doctrine of three warfares (economic, media, and legal) concluded that "twenty-first-century warfare [is] guided by a new and vital dimension: namely the belief that whose story wins may be more important than whose army wins." China made this point in the South China Sea when it annexed vast maritime spaces by first building artificial islands and then claiming the surrounding waters as their own, all without firing a shot.[4]

But what, I thought as I moved through the immaculate, ambitious airport created as a symbol of China's emerging strength at the 2008 Olympics, were all these techniques meant to support?

2049. THE DATE IS REPEATED LIKE A MANTRA IN BEIJING, IN COM-munist Party speeches, on posters, newscasts, pop videos, social media posts, so that it seems the entire vast country is being concentrated into a single year. The party's politburo has declared 2049 as the year that the People's Republic of China finally will achieve "full modernization." It also coincides with the centennial of the founding of the People's Republic of China, still lead by a party created by Soviet agents in the 1920s to spread the revolution to the East, but which long ago outgrew its progenitor and became something far richer and stranger.

When I first landed in Beijing, this focus on 2049 intrigued me. Could it be that here, after futureless, flattened Moscow, London, and Washington, after all the nebulous nostalgias, I could find a hint of historical perspective?

The cityscape of Beijing reinforced the impression of progress, rising from the narrow alleys of the old town where workmen in white vests slept in dark doorways with steaming barrels of soup behind them, up through the smog-shrouded, endless cubist hills of apartment blocks that make Beijing often indistinguishable from Moscow, and then up to the boastful, bullying ambition of the central business area, with skyscrapers that manage to be both gargantuan and somehow squat, as if they are titans defecating in a line, leading to the mind-bending building that houses the headquarters of CGTN, China's international broadcaster, which promotes China across the world as something big, inevitable, immovable, intimidating. From a distance, the building looks like a giant pair of empty trousers striding across the skyline. But as you draw closer, you realize it's one continuous tube, with the two side towers joined at the top and bottom into what its designers call a "three-dimensional cranked loop structure," a vast glass and steel, jagged Ouroboros.

In the staff cafeteria of Tsinghua University, a university of immaculate lawns with its own opera house, I asked two academics about the future that 2049 was meant to designate. They immediately started disagreeing. One argued the official line: China was still on the path to communism, but that because the communist idea of objective history presupposed that communism had to proceed from capitalism, the Communist Party was fostering a Chinese capitalism to be able to surpass it with a true communism. The other academic thought China was using capitalism as a way to return to a previous model of Chinese greatness, to a Confucian empire that, she argued, had little notion of linear historical development. The year 2049 was meant to return China to a futureless past.

China was sounding more familiar.

The next day I met with Angela Wu, a media and communication scholar from Beijing who now taught at New York University and who had researched the formation of political identities on the Chinese internet. I wanted her to explain to me what being pro- or anti-regime really meant. As we walked along the side of a traffic-congealed motorway, we passed posters bearing the latest government slogans:

Community of Shared Future of Mankind!
Democracy! Liberty! Justice! Friendliness!

The slogans were in such contradiction with reality that their effect was to strip these pretty words of any meaning, so that they became codes that must be loyally repeated to signal fealty.

We were on our way to the school Angela attended as a child, where her own journey into investigating self-formation on the Chinese internet had begun. On the outer walls of the school were head shots of the latest, most successful graduates, printed on laminated posters to protect them from the rain, with the names of their destination universities. Most were heading to the United States.

Across from them were huge sports fields, where Wu's exploration of political identity first began, quite by accident. As a pupil she had never understood why she wasn't being allowed to join the Communist Youth League. She was marked down for "political performance," but she had never had any thoughts about politics at the time. Finally, a teacher told her the reason. Every morning the school had to gather in the playing fields for "radio calisthenics": mass warm-up exercises to music and instructions blared from a radio loudspeaker. Officially it was an exercise, but the teachers used it as a way to measure political appropriateness, in the sense of participating in collective activities. Wu thought herself too cool and too clever to dance with too much determination. She had not meant it as a form of political rebellion, but her teachers marked her down for it anyway.

Later, when she was studying at the Chinese University of Hong Kong, she began to ask more questions about what was considered normal. In the library, she discovered books with photos of Chinese murdered after the anti-regime demonstrations of 1989 in Tiananmen Square, which, unlike most uprisings across the world during the "first wave of democratization," had been crushed. On the mainland she had never seen images of those events and there was something visceral for her in seeing them for the first time, even though the books upheld a state-sanctioned version of the demonstrations. Instead of photos of civilians murdered by soldiers, there were photos of government soldiers purportedly murdered by the demonstrators. Next to the photos other readers had scribbled "lies!" The difference between Hong Kong and China, thought Wu, was that in Hong Kong there was a need to go so far as to create books that presented the official version of what happened in 1989, whereas on the mainland, the story was suppressed.

This was in 2008, when the Chinese blogosphere was blooming. But Wu was finding that the categories by which the government and dissidents defined people irked her. Political attitudes in China always had followed a binary, Cold War logic: right-wing critics were "pro-freedom," which bundled together everything from political freedoms to libertarian economics; the other position was described as left, which supported the Chinese government in everything apart from its opening up to Western companies and Western culture. Angela felt that both of these categories were artificial: what if one believed in human rights, for example, but wasn't so sure about the libertarian economics?[5]

When she moved on to a PhD program in Media, Technology, and Communication at Northwestern University in the United States, Wu found that American analysis of China could be informed by a banal conception of innately freedom-loving internet users silenced by an oppressive state and ready to jump into the arms of an American-like democracy the moment they could escape censorship.

She wanted to work out what really defined political identity in China. She started by analyzing the issues that defined groups on the Chinese internet. She found that economic issues, as the "left" versus "right" categories would imply, actually were not particularly divisive. Neither was criticism of censorship something that divided people: both pro- and anti-government voices could want less of it. Instead, the divide lay along what Wu calls "China as a superpower ideology": a militarist, territorially obsessed nationalism intent on dominating others. In this ideology, China was surrounded by enemies weaving conspiracies against her; it harped on the humiliations China suffered from European colonial powers in the nineteenth century, humiliations that the Communist Party claimed it could allay by restoring past greatness. Rather than offering an alternative, China seemed another variant of what I had encountered in America and Russia, here peddling a nostalgia for a greatness before the "century of humiliations," much like Putin promised to "bring Russia off its knees" and Trump to "Make America Great Again" (MAGA).

After she defined the party line, Wu wanted to understand more about those who opposed it. Her petri dish was a blogging site called Bullog, home to opposition writers, publicists, and poets. She spent years as a dedicated Bullog follower herself. She wanted to know more about the people who visited the site. What did they have in common? She travelled across the country, to towns and cities she'd never visited. Bullogers came from all sorts of backgrounds, from fastidious civil servants in the provinces to fashion-conscious students in the coastal mega-cities; from self-made business people to housewives. They did not share much of a coherent ideology, but after conducting twenty-seven interviews across the country Angela began to detect a pattern.

First, many Bullogers had been voracious readers from a young age. But it wasn't necessarily factual material that they consumed but fiction, novels, poetry. This fit with previous academic studies Angela had seen that found that reading was related to an ability to imagine a different social and political reality from the one around you.

As they grew up, her fellow Bullogers moved from books to other media, and they shared a deeply emotional bond with them. One man told how he cried when the first television had arrived in his rural village: it represented his first link to the larger world. Others talked about how they preferred the company of blogs and newspapers to their friends and family.

This intense relationship with media led to an awareness of the extent to which their worldviews and personalities were formed by it. Then came a moment when they realized how duplicitous Chinese state media was. For many, it was in the aftermath of national catastrophes, earthquakes or train crashes that the government had attempted to hush up. This provoked a sense that they had been brainwashed by the regime and needed to purge themselves of the information they had been consuming.

And so began a journey of what they called "leaping across the wall," a reference to the Great Firewall of China that censors material on the Chinese internet. Finding ways to leap across the wall through the use of various computer programs became a subculture, with its own manuals. When they leapt across the wall, however, the Bullogers did not feel that they had landed on reality or any stable ground. There were Chinese anti-regime sites, but they could indulge in their own disinformation. And beyond them the West hardly seemed driven by informed factuality. And so, they carried on further, always trying to outstrip their own identities, endlessly leaping over walls.

Angela told me she'd been unhappy with the results of her research; it had not brought her to solid ground the way she hoped it would. After she got her PhD, she moved to big-data analytics: at least they gave solid answers. It was, however, the very lack of a fixed end-point that drew me in. It reminded me of how, at the European School, being European did not mean a new, supra-identity but the ability to move between different ones and wear them lightly. Or of Rashad's work to encourage those drawn to extremism to unpick the patterns that had closed their attitudes, so they could be both Muslim and English, Asian and from Yorkshire.

For the Bullogers, it was their relationship with televisions, radios, books, blogs that allowed them to reimagine themselves over and over.

That sticky day in Beijing, stuck in traffic on a flyover with the cranked looped structure of the CGTN building in the distance, I found myself turning back to Igor's first novella, *Reading Faulkner*. It seemed oddly relevant again. It spoke to the present, not just to the Cold War—or rather, perhaps it was the Cold War that needed to be redefined.

In the novella, the author is constantly writing and rewriting his own life and his own town of Chernivtsi in different styles and genres influenced by his favorite author, William Faulkner. It was a novella in part about one's relationship with media, full of the sound of typewriters, radio, poetry. For my parents, shoeboxes of samizdat, radio broadcasts, poems had literally been the things on which their lives had turned.

Early in the story the author is trying to work out where his sense of self begins, referencing Faulkner's writing, which constantly explores where awareness emerges. Does identity, Igor asks, begin with politics?

I am in a room of music and smoke. My father's taut back. The awfulness of newspaper editorials; what ponderous words father has to juggle. Machine and Tractor Stations, Party Directive. . . . Did Faulkner begin with this? No.

Are religion and creed, then, where identity begins?

Midday, helmets of cupolas, steep steps, we're in T-shirts, six years old, in the cool close air of the church. From above a voice and a pock-marked face grunts: "Out, Jewish runt." Did Faulkner begin like this? No.

And so Igor reaches for somewhere beyond these, to a place where, if I understand him correctly, identity only appears when it recognizes the presence of someone else:

A girl, on the shore of you. How high the sky. How deep the kiss. We do not say "you" to each other but "I." I swim far out into you: past—buoys, past—horizons; glancing back could not see the rim of the shore and was glad. Remember how ten Julys ago you went into the breathtaking Black Sea and were a warm current in it? But does Faulkner have anything to do with this? He does. He does!

Lines that I find impossible to read without thinking that he would be arrested by the KGB when emerging from a real swim in the same sea soon after.

CHERNIVTSI/CZERNOWITZ

During his decades away from Czernowitz Igor had learned to see his hometown afresh.

    Growing up, he had been dimly aware that it had once been a distant province of Austria-Hungary. He could tell it was an architectural, art nouveau dissident in the Soviet Empire, but he had no idea about the literary riches it had once yielded. It was only in Kiev, Vienna, and Cologne that he learned that it had once, before the Holocaust, World War II, and the arrival of the Soviet Army, been home to renowned German and Austrian poets and writers (Paul

Celan, Rose Ausländer, Gregor von Rezzori), legendary rabbis and Israeli novelists (Aharon Appelfeld), Romanian classics and all manner of great Austro-Hungarian tenors, economists, and biochemists who had emerged in one great burst of early twentieth-century energy and tragedy from this tiny town. Their memories had been ignored in the Soviet Union, and it was only when he arrived in the West that Igor would meet people who would suddenly become animated when he mentioned where he had been raised: "You are from Czernowitz? A city of geniuses!"

And before the Austro-Hungarian era the town had another life, as a distant outpost of the Ottoman Empire. This little place had so many histories, with little knowledge of each other: Turk and Viennese, Romanian, Soviet, Ukrainian. It had different names, too: Chernivtsy, Czernowitz, Черновцы, ernăuți, Czerniowce, Csernovic, Chern.

Away from the town he was even inspired by its prison. It had been built at the start of the nineteenth century. The square it stands on was called Criminal Square, then Soviet Square, now Cathedral Square. How many layers of curses, verses, promises were scratched onto the walls of its cells in how many languages, enraged at how many different overlords?

For decades Igor had tried to construct a world in the airwaves and with words that would combine different cultures and could thus be home, when all the time he had the material of Czernowitz to work with, a whole lost history to surface, like the computer scientists who raise unknown interconnections from the dark pools of data.

"Growing up," Igor wrote, "we were little barbarians, we couldn't feel solid ground under our feet. We had no idea what veins of gold we were trampling, what priceless ruins we walked over. We were not run-of-the-mill barbarians, of course. We had Russian, American, and French literature in *us, but barbarism is the absence of memory. It wasn't our fault. They had deprived us of memory."*

In 2009, Igor started going back to Czernowitz. He began to organize a poetry festival in the town. Poets came from across the world, drawn to see the forgotten home of their literary heroes, and the faded lecture halls, libraries and cafés—which had long forgotten their own polyphonic ancestry—were suddenly full of readings in German and Yiddish, Hebrew, Romanian, Ukrainian, Russian, Polish, as well as English, Flemish, French, and Spanish.

Igor's aim was to awaken the memory of the town, not because the past can be recoverable, but because it can give an impetus for how Chernivtsi and Ukraine can understand themselves tomorrow, beyond the dead ends of information war.

Igor and Lina currently live in Prague, the city that Soviet tanks entered in 1968 in an invasion that did so much to turn Igor against the Soviet regime. This is where Radio Free Europe is now based, invited in 1995 by then president Václav Havel as a sign of thanks for the support of the Western media in the Cold War. Havel is now dead, those who still trumpet his ideals of "living in truth" often scorned as naive Haveloids. RFE lives in a strange limbo, still dedicated to a set of ideals that it is unclear whether the US will continue to even pretend to support in the future. Indeed, calling it radio is already a misnomer, as it tries to straddle television, podcasts, texts. Europe is barely the right word either: most of the language sections are now from Central Asia and the Middle East. The majority of the Central and Eastern European services were disbanded after those countries began to enter the EU. Since then Hungary and Poland have slipped back into flirtations with authoritarianism, led by nationalist politicians who *were once anti-Soviet dissidents, but for whom "national rights" turned out to be not the same as "human rights"; being "anti-Communist" turned out to be not much of a political identity in and of itself.*

Tomorrow morning Igor will head to work. He is the last veteran of the Cold War at the Radio. When students are brought around on tours, he is pointed out like some sort of museum piece. He still dreams of a radio of the future that can "fuse the soul of mankind," that can find the echoes and interconnections between stories in Manila and St. Petersburg, Mexico and Tallinn. In one of his later books Igor came up with a tragicomic alter ego who works at an international radio station and has become obsessed with the idea that he can resurrect people through the power of radio—a story that captures the strange mix of megalomania and actual power bestowed on those who work in media. The idea had first come to Igor when he recalled how when Cold War political prisoners managed to get information about their cases to Western broadcasters it felt as if they had secured a few minutes' liberty, or at least been given the possibility of exercising in the open air—a second life in the airwaves when the secret police had squeezed their first. Now his alter ego stretched that feeling further.

I have released thousands of voices into the cosmos.
According to the laws of physics,
these voices will live forever.
Who would have thought it: some drudge
goes to the office every day,
records somebody and then . . .
yes, then grants them immortality!

It is half-term and I am visiting my mother and father with my nine-year-old twin boys. They want to know if the world now was the same as in Lina's youth. She tries to explain Kiev in the 1970s. Much sounds wild to them ("Igor was arrested for reading books? How? Why?" they ask). Other things can sound familiar.

"I had the sense that all the big, official words around us didn't mean anything anymore," says Lina. "They were like old linen blowing in the wind, empty."

And then she quotes a line from a poem:

"Dead words smell foul."

I am surrounded by dead words. Or, to be more precise, the association of words and images, stories and meanings that I inherited have lost their power. The sight of a statue of a dictator being pulled down is still important to those people who lived under him, but I don't instantly connect to a story of ever greater freedom anymore. Millions of people out on the streets of a city à la 1989 don't immediately signify a happy future. Perhaps it's not a coincidence that social media's favorite genre is memes: pictures that can be defaced by people with new phrases that change the meaning of the image, symptoms of a time when sense is ceaselessly unstable. So that one might take a picture of a pipe and write beneath it: "This is not a pipe."

The old associations were imperfect, often false. But they also held within them the memory of why they had mattered in the first place. Certain images and language were taboo because they acted like little knots tying in a notion of the unacceptable. Now these little knots are coming loose. In 2018, in Hungary, you could see government posters accusing Jewish financiers of undermining the nation, in visual motifs reminiscent of the 1930s, but that didn't stop an ever closer alliance between the Hungarian president and Israeli prime minister at the time, as if the latter no longer cared whether he's friends with someone who draws on Nazi codes. In America, when criticism of the president is labelled "McCarthyism," or Russia's trolls are compared to 9/11 or Pearl Harbor, the references are so shorn of context one imagines the wreckage from a plane crash in a desert, with commentators wandering around beating jet engines with wrenches to make a spectacular sound that has no relation to the thing they're beating; in Britain the best-selling newspaper accuses independent judges of being "enemies of the people," calls to "crush the saboteurs" who oppose the government, in language popularized in the Soviet Union to validate mass murder, and whose use today only serves to debase the memory of those misdeeds.

When I began working on the passages about my parents in this book, I started off looking at how much has changed between the centuries, how the calcified words "freedom," "democracy," "Europe," even whole genres of art have had their meaning stripped or hacked. Instead, I found myself awakening to the experiences that gave those words their power, which opens up the possibility for their regeneration in the future.

In a week's time we will be heading home to London, and I will be walking the boys up the hill to school. It's a Victorian pile, and when you walk in there are flags of all the nationalities of the children who attend. It looks like the UN, and I don't know half the flags. What reconfigurations of identity will play on this? Will there be ever more intense iterations of people and non-people? I keep on waiting for the questions from the twins to start. Are we English or Russian? Jewish? European? Ukrainian? What do any of those words mean? Already I am worrying about what to answer.

"The real you will emerge in the collisions between them! Consider Chernivtsi!"

I wonder if they will understand if I quote Igor to them? Or has something been passed on already?

The other day the twins were in a playground in the local park. Another child came up to them and began asking, "What are you? Who are you? Tell me."

There was a pause. What would the twins answer? Which nation, creed, tribe, in- or out-group would they claim as theirs? What clue would it give us for the future?

The twins considered the question seriously. Then they turned and said, in unison, "I'm Superman."

The other boy answered, "And I'm Batman."

ACKNOWLEDGMENTS

THIS BOOK DRAWS ON ESSAYS PUBLISHED IN *GRANTA, THE GUARD-ian, American Interest*, and the *London Review of Books*. I would like to thank my editors there for giving me the opportunity to develop my ideas. None of this would be possible without the support and advice of Sigrid Rausing, Luke Neima, Pru Rowlandson, Jonathan Shainin, Damir Marusic, Daniel Soar, Mary-Kay Wilmers, Leonard Bernardo, Chris Walker, and Thomas Jones.

Zinovy Zinik, Frank Williams, Seva Novgorodtsev, Peter Udell, Masha Karp, and Diran Meghreblian provided extensive and insightful background on BBC Russian Service history; Sergey Danilochkin and Arch Puddington on Radio Free Europe. Martin Dewhurst has been a source of many gems over the years. Michael Zantovsky advised on Václav Havel; Mario Corti on the *Chronicle of Current Events*.

Chloe Colliver and Melanie Smith have been most kind in helping me understand the basics of data analysis and "the space." Nick Cull has been a fountain of knowledge about the history of propaganda.

Ant Adeane was my excellent producer for the BBC Radio 4 Analysis Programs mentioned: "British Politics, a Russian View" (broadcast July 9, 2018) and "The War for Normal" (broadcast January 28, 2019).

Anne Applebaum, Daniel Soar, Ant Adeane, and Ben Williams have provided vital editorial support. Carolina Stern has been a terrific colleague at the LSE, helping me with extensive translations.

My debt of gratitude to Paul Copeland and my parents for all their time, patience, multiple rereads, and improvements is inestimable. Thanks also to Aunt Sasha for her amazing support.

My wife and children have been exceedingly understanding.

NOTES

I have intentionally changed one name and omitted some surnames to protect the contributors to this book.

CHAPTER 1: CITIES OF TROLLS

1. Alfred McCoy, "Dark Legacy: Human Rights Under the Marcos Regime," September 20, 1999, World History Archives, www.hartford-hwp.com/archives/54a/062.html.

2. H. P. Beck, S. Levinson, and G. Irons, "Finding Little Albert: A Journey to John B. Watson's Infant Laboratory," *American Psychologist* 64, no. 7 (2009): 605–614, http://dx.doi.org/10.1037/a0017234.

3. Jonathan Corpus Ong and Jason Vincent A. Cabañes, *Architects of Networked Disinformation*, University of Leeds, 2018, https://newtontechfordev.com/wp-content/uploads/2018/02/ARCHITECTS-OF-NETWORKED-DISINFORMATION-FULL-REPORT.pdf.

4. Maria A. Ressa, *From Bin Laden to Facebook: 10 Days of Abduction, 10 Years of Terrorism* (London: Imperial College Press, 2013).

5. "Philippine President Duterte Calls God 'Stupid,'" BBC News, June 26, 2018, https://www.bbc.com/news/world-asia-44610872.

6. Adam Forrest, "Jair Bolsonaro: The Worst Quotes from Brazil's Far-Right Presidential Frontrunner," *Independent*, October 8, 2018, www.independent

.co.uk/news/world/americas/jair-bolsonaro-who-is-quotes-brazil-president
-election-run-off-latest-a8573901.html.

7. Tom Parfitt, "Putin Praises Sexual Prowess of Israeli President," *Guardian*,
October 20, 2006, www.theguardian.com/world/2006/oct/20/russia.tomparfitt;
"Czech Women's Lobby Wants Zeman to Apologize for Remarks About Rape,"
January 23, 2013, www.romea.cz/en/news/czech/czech-women-s-lobby-wants
-zeman-to-apologize-for-remarks-about-rape; "Prezident Zeman o Straně
zelených: Vypálit, počůrat, posolit," Zdroj, September 12, 2013, www.denik.cz/z
_domova/den-druhy-milos-zeman-dnes-navstivi-orlickoustecko-20130912.html.

8. Mikhail Mikhailovich Bakhtin, *Rabelais and His World* (Blooming-
ton: Indiana University Press, 1984).

9. Maria A. Ressa, "Propaganda War: Weaponizing the Internet," October 3, 2016, www.rappler.com/nation/148007-propaganda-war-weaponizing
-internet; Chay F. Hofileña, "Fake Accounts, Manufactured Reality on Social Media," October 9, 2016, updated February 6, 2019, www.rappler.com
/newsbreak/investigative/148347-fake-accounts-manufactured-reality
-social-media; Maria A. Ressa. "How Facebook Algorithms Impact Democracy," October 8, 2016, updated February 6, 2019, www.rappler.com
/newsbreak/148536-facebook-algorithms-impact-democracy.

10. Alfred W. McCoy, *A Question of Torture: CIA Interrogation, from
the Cold War to the War on Terror* (Ogden: Owl Books, 2006), 79–80.

11. Carlos H. Conde, "Aquino's Last Chance on Human Rights," Human
Rights Watch, July 27, 2015, www.hrw.org/news/2015/07/27/aquinos-last
-chance-human-rights; Seth Mydan, "Aquino Said to Condone Human Rights
Abuses," *New York Times*, June 18, 1988, www.nytimes.com/1988/06/18
/world/aquino-said-to-condone-human-rights-abuses.html.

12. Nataysha Gutierrez, "Bots, Assange, an Alliance: Has Russian
Propaganda Infiltrated the Philippines?" February 26, 2018, www.rappler
.com/newsbreak/in-depth/196576-russia-propaganda-influence-interference
-philippines.

13. Tim Lister, Jim Sciutto, and Mary Ilyushina, "Exclusive: Putin's
'Chef,' the Man Behind the Troll Factory," CNN, October 28, 2017, https://
edition.cnn.com/2017/10/17/politics/russian-oligarch-putin-chef-troll-factory
/index.html.

14. Boris Nemtsov, "My Father Was Killed by Russian Propaganda,
Says Nemtsov's Daughter," *Guardian*, June 19, 2015, www.theguardian.com
/world/2015/jun/19/russia-boris-nemtsov-zhanna-nemtsova.

15. Philip Howard et al. *The IRA, Social Media and Political Polarization in the United States, 2012–2018* (Oxford: University of Oxford, 2019),

https://comprop.oii.ox.ac.uk/wp-content/uploads/sites/93/2018/12/IRA
-Report.pdf.

16. Nick Fielding and Ian Bobain, "Revealed: US Spy Operation That
Manipulates Social Media," *Guardian*, March 17, 2011, www.theguardian
.com/technology/2011/mar/17/us-spy-operation-social-networks; Andrew Cave,
"Deal that Undid Bell Pottinger: Inside Story of the South Africa Scandal,"
Guardian, September 5, 2017, www.theguardian.com/media/2017/sep/05
/bell-pottingersouth-africa-pr-firm.

17. Nicholas Monaco and Carly Nyst, "State-Sponsored Trolling: How
Governments Are Deploying Disinformation as Part of Broader Digital Harassment Campaigns," Institute for the Future, 2018, www.iftf.org/fileadmin
/user_upload/images/DigIntel/IFTF_State_sponsored_trolling_report.pdf.

18. Tim Wu, "Is the First Amendment Obsolete?" Knight First Amendment Institute, Columbia University, September 2017, https://knightcolumbia
.org/content/tim-wu-first-amendment-obsolete.

19. Jodesz Gavilan, "Maria Ressa's Arrest Part of Broader Gov't Campaign, Say Rights Groups," Rappler.com, February 14, 2019, www.rappler
.com/nation/223457-human-rights-groups-statements-maria-ressa-arrest;
Lian Buan, "Tax Court Denies Maria Ressa Appeal, to Proceed with Trial,"
Rappler.com, February 15, 2019, www.rappler.com/nation/223549-court
-tax-appeals-denies-maria-ressa-appeal-trial-to-proceed.

20. "Maria Ressa Accepts the 2018 Knight International Journalism
Award," International Center for Journalists, www.icfj.org/maria-ressa
-accepts-2018-knight-international-journalism-award.

CHAPTER 2: DEMOCRACY AT SEA

1. www.alo.rs/vesti/aktuelno/srda-popovic-rusi-vlade/120133/vest. A
2013 Pentagon paper about China's doctrine of Three War Fares (economic,
media, and legal) concluded that "twenty-first-century warfare [is] guided by
a new and vital dimension: namely the belief that whose story wins may be
more important than whose army wins."

2. Srdja Popovic and Matthew Miller, *Blueprint for Revolution: How to
Use Rice Pudding, Lego Men, and Other Nonviolent Techniques to Galva-
nize Communities, Overthrow Dictators, or Simply Change the World* (New
York: Spiegel & Grau, 2015).

3. "Democracy Continues Its Disturbing Retreat," *The Economist,* January 31, 2018, www.economist.com/graphic-detail/2018/01/31/democracy
-continues-its-disturbing-retreat.

4. Matthew Karnitschnig, "Aleksandar Vučić: Let's Not Go Back to the '90s," POLITICO, April 14, 2016, www.politico.eu/article/aleksandar-vucic-interview-serbia-balkans-migration-kosovo-bosnia.

5. "Serbian Media Coalition Letter to the International Community," October 22, 2018, http://safejournalists.net/serbian-media-coalition-alerts-international-community; Matteo Trevisan, "How Media Freedom in Serbia Is Under Attack," EUobserver, November 2, 2018, https://euobserver.com/opinion/143268.

6. Matthew Karnitschnig, "Serbia's Latest Would-Be Savior Is a Modernizer, a Strongman—or Both," POLITICO, April 14, 2016, updated April 21, 2016, www.politico.eu/article/aleksandar-vucic-serbias-latest-savior-is-a-modernizer-or-strongman-or-both.

7. D. Mercea and M. T. Bastos, "Being a Serial Transnational Activist," *Journal of Computer-Mediated Communication* 21, no. 2 (2016): 140–155, http://openaccess.city.ac.uk/13151/7/Being%20a%20serial%20transnational%20activist_prepublication.pdf.

8. Klint Finley, "Pro-Government Twitter Bots Try to Hush Mexican Activists," *Wired,* August 23, 2015, www.wired.com/2015/08/pro-government-twitter-bots-try-hush-mexican-activists.

9. Dulce Olver, "El 81.3% de los ataques de bots en Edomex fueron contra Delfina, confirma otro análisis técnico," June 1, 2017, www.sinembargo.mx/01-06-2017/3230408; Erin Gallagher, "Manipulating Trends & Gaming Twitter," December 18, 2016, https://medium.com/@erin_gallagher/manipulating-trends-gaming-twitter-6fd31714c06c.

10. Samuel C. Woolley and Douglas R. Guilbeault, "Computational Propaganda in the United States of America: Manufacturing Consensus Online," Working Paper No. 2017.5, Project on Computational Propaganda, http://blogs.oii.ox.ac.uk/politicalbots/wp-content/uploads/sites/89/2017/06/Comprop-USA.pdf.

11. Em Griffin, *A First Look at Communication Theory,* 7th ed. (New York: McGraw-Hill, 2008), www.afirstlook.com/docs/spiral.pdf.

12. Elisabeth Noelle-Neumann, *The Spiral of Silence: Public Opinion—Our Social Skin,* 2nd ed. (Chicago: University of Chicago Press, 1993).

13. Ibid., 218.

14. Konstantin Kosachev, "Neftegazovaia Diplomatia kak Ugroza Marginalizatsii," Nezavisimaya Gazeta, December 28, 2004, www.ng.ru/world/2004-12-28/5_uspeh.html. Accessed July 7, 2009.

15. Damien McGuinness, "How a Cyber-Attack Transformed Estonia," BBC News, April 27, 2017, www.bbc.com/news/39655415.

16. For background see Gatis Pelnens, ed., "The Humanitarian Dimension of Russian Foreign Policy Toward Georgia, Moldova, Ukraine, and the Baltic States," Centre for East European Policy Studies, International Centre for Defence Studies, Centre for Geopolitical Studies, School for Policy Analysis at the National University of Kyiv-Mohyla Academy, Foreign Policy Association of Moldova, International Centre for Geopolitical Studies, 2010. The Security Police of the Republic of Estonia, *Annual Review 2003*, 12.

17. Estonia was accused of rehabilitating fascist and Nazi ideology, revering Nazi symbols, glorifying SS veterans, brutally discriminating against the Russian-speaking population, denying the Holocaust, and Hitlerism. After the riots of April 26–28, 2007, direct threats against Estonia and insults targeting Estonians became widespread in the Russian press. Distorted versions of the names of the state and nation (e.g., "eSStonia" and "eSStonians") appeared in the press, on the internet, and at demonstrations organized by pro-Kremlin forces. Some examples of typical accusations follow:

Interfax, April 26—Moscow mayor Yuri Luzhkov: "Estonian leaders have started to condone Fascism and to collaborate with Fascists. They have no right to rewrite history! They identify with the people against whom the entire Europe fought."

Interfax, April 26—Speaker of the State Duma, Boris Gryzlov: "What is happening in Estonia is pure madness. What the Nazis did not manage to do to the living, the Estonian government is now trying to do to the dead."

Ria Novosti, Oslo, April 26—Sergey Lavrov: "The situation surrounding the Bronze Soldier is despicable. It cannot be justified. It will have serious consequences for Russia-NATO and Russia-EU relations because these organizations have welcomed a new member state that has trampled on all the values that form the foundation of the EU, European culture, and democracy."

Interfax, April 26—Chairman of the State Duma Committee on Foreign Affairs, Konstantin Kosachev: "In essence, Estonian authorities have taken a stand against the international public—against everyone who still remembers the price that was paid for victory. The actions of the Estonian leadership stimulate neo-Nazi and revanchist attitudes. As a result, Estonia is in opposition to modern European civilization, to the entire civilized world. Estonia is undermining its relations with all the states that hold dear the memory of victory over Nazis."

April 27—Statement by the Russian Communist Party: "At a time when sixty years have passed since the end of the war, Fascism is reborn in Estonia! The removal of the memorial statue is a Fascist orgy. The first public battle with Fascism in the twenty-first century was held in Estonia."

Strana.ru, May 2—Russian representative Boris Malakhov's speech to the UN Committee on Information: "Why are memorial statues to Soviet liberators removed? This raises the issue of whether these acts constitute attempts to rehabilitate Nazi crimes. Neo-Nazism is on the rise all over the world, as is demonstrated by the removal of memorial statues dedicated to soldiers/liberators."

Interfax, May 8—Chairman of the Federation Council, Sergey Mironov: "What was done by the Estonian leadership shows that Fascism and Nazism are reborn in Estonia."

18. Renee DiResta et al., "The Tactics & Tropes of the Internet Research Agency," https://disinformationreport.blob.core.windows.net/disinformation -report/NewKnowledge-Disinformation-Report-Whitepaper.pdf.

19. Associated Press, "US Secretly Created 'Cuban Twitter' to Stir Unrest and Undermine Government," *Guardian*, April 3, 2014, www.theguardian .com/world/2014/apr/03/us-cuban-twitter-zunzuneo-stir-unrest.

20. Mark Hosenball, "British Authorities Ban Three Foreign Right-Wing Activists," Reuters, March 12, 2018, https://uk.reuters.com/article /uk-britain-security-deportations/british-authorities-ban-three-foreign-right -wing-activists-idUKKCN1GO2LO.

21. Julia Ebner and Jacob Davey, "The Fringe Insurgency: Connectivity and Convergence of the Extreme-Right," Institute for Strategic Dialogue, 2018, https://www.isdglobal.org/wp-content/uploads/2017/10/The-Fringe -Insurgency-221017.pdf.

CHAPTER 3: THE GREATEST INFORMATION BLITZKRIEG IN HISTORY

1. *New York Times*, January 29, 1977.

2. "What Price a Soviet Jew?" *New York Times*, February 22, 1981, www.nytimes.com/1981/02/22/opinion/what-price-a-soviet-jew.html.

3. Frances Stonor Saunders, *The Cultural Cold War: The CIA and the World of Arts and Letters* (New York: New Press, 2000).

4. Jean Seaton, *Pinkoes and Traitors: The BBC and the Nation, 1974–1987* (London: Profile Books, 2015).

5. "Ricin and the Umbrella Murder," CNN.com, October 23, 2003, http://edition.cnn.com/2003/WORLD/europe/01/07/terror.poison.bulgarian.

6. Igor Panarin, *The First Information World War: The Collapse of the USSR*, Piter, www.koob.ru/panarin_i_n/collapse_ussr_p; see also Ilya Yablokov, *Fortress Russia: Conspiracy Theories in the Post-Soviet World* (Cam-

bridge: Polity, 2018), chapter 3; Shelepin Lischkin, "The Third Information-Psychological World War." *Moskva*, 1999; and Sergey Rastorguev, "Information War," *Radio and Communications*, 1999.

7. Rossiijskaja Gazeta, "I Packed My Gun with Data," Interview with Igor Ashmanov, https://rg.ru/2013/05/23/ashmanov.html.

8. Ibid.

9. Speech to Federation Council, September 13, 2018, www.youtube.com/watch?v=fyRlnBuUmhE.

10. Talk on Freedom of Speech as an Instrument ("Свобода Слова как Инстрымент"), www.youtube.com/watch?v=cb6fqc02vt0.

11. Rossiijskaja Gazeta, "I Packed My Gun with Data," interview with Igor Ashmanov, https://rg.ru/2013/05/23/ashmanov.html.

12. Rosemary Foot, "The Cold War and Human Rights," in Melvyn P. Leffler and Odd Arne Westad, eds., *The Cambridge History of the Cold War, Vol. III* (Cambridge: Cambridge University Press, 2010), 445–448.

13. "Question That: RT's Military Mission," Medium, January 8, 2017, https://medium.com/dfrlab/question-that-rts-military-mission-4c4bd9f72c88.

14. Michael Kofman, "The Moscow School of Hard Knocks: Key Pillars of Russian Strategy," War on the Rocks, January 27, 2017, https://warontherocks.com/2017/01/the-moscow-school-of-hard-knocks-key-pillars-of-russian-strategy.

15. Janis Berzins, "Russia's New Generation Warfare in Ukraine: Implications for Latvian Defense Policy," National Defense Academy of Latvia, Center for Security and Strategic Research, 2014.

16. A good resource for Kremlin influence campaigns in Ukraine is www.stopfake.org/en/news.

17. "Disinfo News: The Kremlin's Many Versions of the MH17 Story," May 29, 2018, www.stopfake.org/en/disinfo-news-the-kremlin-s-many-versions-of-the-mh17-story.

18. Thomas M. Hill, "Is the U.S. Serious About Countering Russia's Information War on Democracies?" November 21, 2017, www.brookings.edu/blog/order-from-chaos/2017/11/21/is-the-u-s-serious-about-countering-russias-information-war-on-democracies.

19. Andrey Shtal, personal website, https://www.stihi.ru/avtor/shtal.

20. Howard Amos, "'There Was Heroism and Cruelty on Both Sides': The Truth Behind One of Ukraine's Deadliest Days," *Guardian*, April 30, 2015, www.theguardian.com/world/2015/apr/30/there-was-heroism-and-cruelty-on-both-sides-the-truth-behind-one-of-ukraines-deadliest-days.

CHAPTER 4: SOFT FACTS

1. Stephen Ennis, "Vladimir Danchev: The Broadcaster Who Defied Moscow," BBC Monitoring, March 8, 2014, www.bbc.co.uk/news/magazine-26472906.

2. "A Nuclear Disaster That Brought Down an Empire," *The Economist*, April 26, 2016, www.economist.com/europe/2016/04/26/a-nuclear-disaster-that-brought-down-an-empire.

3. Radio Interview for BBC Russian Service, Margaret Thatcher Foundation, July 11, 1988, www.margaretthatcher.org/document/107072.

4. Ibid.

5. PolitiFact, "Donald Trump's File," www.politifact.com/personalities/donald-trump, accessed July 20, 2016; PolitiFact, "Hillary Clinton's File," www.politifact.com/personalities/hillary-clinton, accessed July 20, 2016.

6. BBC Breadth of Opinion Review, http://downloads.bbc.co.uk/bbctrust/assets/files/pdf/our_work/breadth_opinion/content_analysis.pdf.

7. "Kremlin's Chief Propagandist Accuses Western Media of Bias," BBC News, June 23, 2016, www.bbc.co.uk/news/world-europe-36551391.

8. Joshua Yaffa, "Dmitry Kiselev Is Redefining the Art of Russian Propaganda," New Republic, July 1, 2014, https://newrepublic.com/article/118438/dmitry-kiselev-putins-favorite-tv-host-russias-top-propogandist.

9. Tom Balmforth, "Gene Warfare? Russia Raises Eyebrows," Radio Free Europe/Radio Liberty, November 3, 2017, www.rferl.org/a/russia-biological-warfare-accusations-raise-eyebrows-lawsuit/28834069.html; Giorgi Lomadze, "Does US Have a Secret Germ Warfare Lab on Russia's Doorstep?" Coda Story, April 19, 2018, https://codastory.com/disinformation/information-war/does-the-us-have-a-secret-germ-warfare-lab-on-russias-doorstep; see also EU Versus Disinfo website, which tracks disinformation and has an archive of stories: https://euvsdisinfo.eu; https://euvsdisinfo.eu/report/ukraine-asked-the-united-states-to-spread-the-ebola-virus; https://euvsdisinfo.eu/report/there-is-a-secret-laboratory-near-kharkiv-where-ukrainians-with.

10. Maurizio Ferraris, *Introduction to New Realism* (London: Bloomsbury Academic, 2014), ebook.

11. F. Zollo et al., "Emotional Dynamics in the Age of Misinformation," PLoS ONE 10, no. 9 (2015), https://doi.org/10.1371/journal.pone.0138740.

12. Tony Judt, "From Military Disaster to Moral High Ground," *New York Times*, October 7, 2007, www.nytimes.com/2007/10/07/opinion/07judt.html.

13. Brian C. Schmidt and Michael C. Williams, "The Bush Doctrine and the Iraq War: Neoconservatives Versus Realists," *Security Studies* 17, no. 2 (2008):

191–220, www.tandfonline.com/doi/full/10.1080/09636410802098990; "In Bush's Words: 'Iraqi Democracy Will Succeed,'" *New York Times*, November 6, 2003, www.nytimes.com/2003/11/06/politics/in-bushs-words-iraqi-democracy-will-succeed.html.

14. Svetlana Boym, "Nostalgia and Its Discontents," Agora8, https://agora8.org/SvetlanaBoym_Nostalgia.

15. Jamie Tarabay, "For Many Syrians, the Story of the War Began with Graffiti in Dara'a," CNN, March 15, 2018, https://edition.cnn.com/2018/03/15/middleeast/daraa-syria-seven-years-on-intl/index.html.

16. Lisa Wedeen, *Ambiguities of Domination: Politics, Rhetoric, and Symbols in Contemporary Syria* (Chicago: University of Chicago Press, 1999).

17. "A Look at Key Events in Syria's Aleppo since 2016," Associated Press, December 14, 2016, https://apnews.com/300da72a31284420810e1ba9ebef2052.

18. Somini Sengupta and Anne Barnard, "Syria, Russia Appear Ready to Scorch Aleppo," *New York Times*, September 25, 2016, www.nytimes.com/2016/09/26/world/middleeast/syria-un-security-council.html.

19. "Indiscriminate Aerial Attacks on Aleppo," Breaking Aleppo, Atlantic Council, www.publications.atlanticcouncil.org/breakingaleppo/attacks-overview.

20. "UN Security Council Calls for End to Attacks on Doctors, Hospitals," Physicians for Human Rights, May 3, 2016, https://phr.org/news/un-security-council-calls-for-end-to-attacks-on-doctors-hospitals.

21. *The Failure of UN Security Council Resolution 2286 in Preventing Attacks on Healthcare in Syria*, Report of Syrian American Medical Society, January 2017, https://www.sams-usa.net/wp-content/uploads/2017/03/UN-fail-report-07-3.pdf.

22. Bethan McKernan, "Aleppo Attack: Syrian Army to Invade City with Ground Troops," September 23, 2016, Independent, www.independent.co.uk/news/world/middle-east/aleppo-syria-war-assad-troops-to-invade-city-under-siege-rebels-a7326266.html.

23. "Indiscriminate Aerial Attacks on Aleppo," Breaking Aleppo, Atlantic Council, www.publications.atlanticcouncil.org/breakingaleppo/attacks-overview.

24. "Syria Conflict: US Accuses Russia of Barbarsim in Aleppo," BBC News, September 26, 2016, www.bbc.co.uk/news/world-middle-east-37468080.

25. Ibid.

26. Samuel Osborne, "Donald Trump Wins: All the Lies, Mistruths and Scare Stories He Told During the US Election Campaign," Independent, November 9, 2016, www.independent.co.uk/news/world/americas/donald-trump-president-lies-and-mistruths-during-us-election-campaign-a7406821.html.

27. David Graham, "The Wrong Side of the Right Side of History." *The Atlantic,* December 21, 2015, https://www.theatlantic.com/politics/archive/2015/12/obama-right-side-of-history/420462/.

28. Kareem Shaheen, "Hell Itself: Aleppo Reels from Alleged Use of Bunker-Buster Bombs," *Guardian*, September 26, 2016, www.theguardian.com/world/2016/sep/26/hell-itself-aleppo-reels-from-alleged-use-of-bunker-buster-bombs.

29. www.vdc-sy.info/index.php/en/martyrs/1/c29ydGJ5PWEua2lsbGVkX2RhdGV8c29ydGRpcj1ERVNDfGFwcHJvdmVkPXZpc2libGV8ZXh0cmFkaXNwbGF5PTB8cHJvdmluY2U9NnxzdGFydERhdERhdGU9MjAxMi0wNy0xOXxlbmREYXRlPTIwMTYtMTItMjJ8; see also Schluter, Guha-Sapir, et al., "Patterns of Civilian and Child Deaths Due to War-Related Violence in Syria," The Lancet, December 6, 2017, www.thelancet.com/journals/langlo/article/PIIS2214-109X(17)30469-2/fulltext.

30. Syrian Network for Human Rights, Interactive Charts of the Civilian Death Toll, http://sn4hr.org.

31. Megan Specia, "Death Toll in Syria: Numbers Blurred in Fog of War," *Irish Times,* April 14, 2018, www.irishtimes.com/news/world/middle-east/death-toll-in-syria-numbers-blurred-in-fog-of-war-1.3461102; Priyanka Boghani, "A Staggering New Death Toll for Syria's War—470,000," Frontline, www.pbs.org/wgbh/frontline/article/a-staggering-new-death-toll-for-syrias-war-470000; Anne Barnard, "Death Toll from War in Syria Now 470,000, Group Finds," *New York Times,* February 11, 2016, www.nytimes.com/2016/02/12/world/middleeast/death-toll-from-war-in-syria-now-470000-group-finds.html; "2015 Marks Worst Year for Attacks on Hospitals in Syria," Physicians for Human Rights, December 18, 2015, https://phr.org/news/2015-marks-worst-year-for-attacks-on-hospitals-in-syria.

32. Steve Dove, "The White Helmets Is the 2017 Oscar Winner for Documentary (Short Subject)," ABC, February 27, 2017, https://oscar.go.com/news/winners/the-white-helmets-is-the-2017-oscar-winner-for-documentary-short-subject.

33. Olivia Solon, "How Syria's White Helmets Became Victims of an Online Propaganda Machine," *Guardian*, December 18, 2017, www.theguardian.com/world/2017/dec/18/syria-white-helmets-conspiracy-theories.

34. Andrew Buncombe, "Trump Suggests 'Vicious World' Should Be Blamed for Khashoggi Murder While Disputing Saudi Responsibility," Independent, November 22, 2018, www.independent.co.uk/news/world/americas/us-politics/trump-khashoggi-murder-blame-vicious-world-saudi-journalist-a8647701.html.

35. Amnesty International, "At Any Cost: The Civilian Catastrophe in West Mosul, Iraq," 2017, www.amnesty.org/download/Documents/MDE146610 2017ENGLISH.PDF; "A Spiralling Conflict," Amnesty International, Yemen War: No End in Sight, updated March 14, 2019, www.amnesty.org/en/latest/news/2015/09/yemen-the-forgotten-war; Micah Zenko, "America Is Committing War Crimes and Doesn't Even Know Why," Foreign Policy, August 15, 2018, https://foreignpolicy.com/2018/08/15/america-is-committing-awful-war-crimes-and-it-doesnt-even-know-why.

36. Michael Cruickshank, "A Saudi War-Crime in Yemen? Analysing the Dahyan Bombing," Bellingcat, August 18, 2018, www.bellingcat.com/news/mena/2018/08/18/19432.

37. Michael Safi, "Sri Lanka Blocks Social Media as Deadly Violence Continues," *Guardian*, March 7, 2018, www.theguardian.com/world/2018/mar/07/sri-lanka-blocks-social-media-as-deadly-violence-continues-buddhist-temple-anti-muslim-riots-kandy.

38. Eleanor Hall, "Syrian War Crimes Evidence Strongest Since Nuremberg Trials," ABC News, December 3, 2018, www.abc.net.au/radio/programs/worldtoday/these-are-crimes-the-world-wont-forget-stephen-rapp-on-syria/10577142.

CHAPTER 5: POP-UP PEOPLE

1. Arch Puddington, *Broadcasting Freedom: The Cold War Triumph of Radio Free Europe and Radio Liberty* (Lexington: University Press of Kentucky, 2015).

2. Eugene Parta, *Discovering the Hidden Listener, an Assessment of Radio Liberty and Western Broadcasting to the USSR in the Cold War* (Stanford: Hoover Institution Press, 2007).

3. Zinovy Zinik, *Soviet Paradise Lost: Carnegie International*, Vol. 1 (New York: Rizzoli, 1991).

4. Boris Groys, *History Becomes Form: Moscow Conceptualism* (Cambridge: MIT Press, 2010).

5. Sheikh Taqīuddīn An-Nabahānī, *The Islamic Personality*, Vol. 1., 2005, www.hizb-australia.org/wp-content/uploads/2012/03/Shakhsiyya-I.pdf.

6. Central Intelligence Agency, November 2017 release of Abbottabad Compound Material, www.cia.gov/library/abbottabad-compound/index.html.

7. Institute for Economics & Peace, "Positive Peace Report 2018: Analysing the Factors that Sustain Peace," October 2018, http://visionofhumanity.org/app/uploads/2018/11/Positive-Peace-Report-2018.pdf.

8. Amarnath Amarasingam and Lorne L. Dawson, "*I Left to Be Closer to Allah": Learning about Foreign Fighters from Family and Friends,* ISD Global, 2018, www.isdglobal.org/wp-content/uploads/2018/05/Families _Report.pdf.

9. "Study: No One Issue Clearly Unites 5 Groups of Trump Voters," National Public Radio, July 2, 2017, http://www.npr.org/2017/07/02 /535240706/study-no-one-issue-clearly-unites-5-groups-of-trump-voters; Karlyn Bowman, "Who Were Donald Trump's Voters? Now We Know," Forbes, June 23, 2017, www.forbes.com/sites/bowmanmarsico/2017/06/23 /who-were-donald-trumps-voters-now-we-know/#bdc19a138942.

10. Chantal Mouffe, "The Affects of Democracy," *Eurozine*, November 23, 2018, www.eurozine.com/the-affects-of-democracy.

11. Ivan Krastev, "Experimental Motherland. A Conversation with Gleb Pavlovsky," *Europa*, 2018.

12. Ilya Yablokov, *Fortress Russia: Conspiracy Theories in the Post-Soviet World* (Cambridge: Polity, 2018), 30.

CHAPTER 6: THE FUTURE STARTS HERE

1. Carole Cadwalladr, "Exposing Cambridge Analytica," *Guardian*, September 29, 2018; Channel 4 News, "Revealed: Trump's Election Consultants Filmed Saying they Use Bribes and Sex Workers to Entrap Politicians," March 19, 2018.

2. "Disinformation and 'Fake News': Final Report," Committee for Culture, Media and Sport, February 18, 2019, https://publications .parliament.uk/pa/cm201719/cmselect/cmcumeds/1791/179102.htm; Cathrine Gyldensted, *From Mirrors to Movers: Five Elements of Constructive Journalism* (G Group Publishers, 2015), Kindle edition; Dipayan Ghosh and Ben Scott, "The Technologies Behind Precision Propaganda on the Internet," New America, January 23, 2018, www.newamerica.org/public-interest -technology/policy-papers/digitaldeceit.

3. Gary King, Jennifer Pan, and Margaret E. Roberts, "How Censorship in China Allows Government Criticism but Silences Collective Expression,"

American Political Science Review 107, no. 2 (May 2013): 1–18, https://gking.harvard.edu/publications/how-censorship-china-allows-government-criticism-silences-collective-expression; Rebecca MacKinnon, "Liberation Technology: China's 'Networked Authoritarianism,'" *Journal of Democracy* 22, no. 2 (2011): 32–46, https://muse.jhu.edu.

4. Eleanor Roy, "I'm Being Watched: Anne-Mary Brady, the China Critic Living in Fear of Beijing," *Guardian*, January 23, 2019, www.theguardian.com/world/2019/jan/23/im-being-watched-anne-marie-brady-the-china-critic-living-in-fear-of-beijing.

5. Angela Wu, "Ideological Polarization over a China-as-Superpower Mindset: An Exploratory Charting of Belief Systems Among Chinese Internet Users, 2008–2011," *International Journal of Communication* 8 (2014): 2243–2272.

REFERENCES

IGOR POMERANTSEV EXTRACTS

"Reading Faulkner," translated by Frank Williams, with adaptations by Peter Pomerantsev

"KGB Lyrics," translated by Frank Williams

"Eye and a Tear," translated by Peter Pomerantsev (Syntaxis, 1979)

"Right to Read," translated by Marta Zakhaykevich (*Partisan Review* 49, no. 1, 1982)

"Radio Times," translated by Frank Williams

LINA POMERANTSEV DOCUMENTARY CREDITS

Tripping with Zhirinovsky, directed by Pawel Pawlikovsky, released 1995

The Betrayed, directed by Clive Gordon, released 1995

Mother Russia's Children, directed by Tom Roberts, released 1992

RADIO PROGRAM

"Reading Faulkner," narrated by Ronald Pickup, broadcast BBC Radio 3, August 2, 1984

INDEX

PHOTOGRAPH BY ELEANOR CROW

PETER POMERANTSEV is director of the Arena Initiative at the London School of Economics, a senior fellow at the SNF Agora Institute and Johns Hopkins University, as well as an author and TV producer. He studies propaganda and media development, and has testified on the challenges of information war to the US House Foreign Affairs Committee, US Senate Foreign Relations Committee, and the UK Parliament Defense Select Committee. He writes for publications including *Granta*, *The Atlantic*, *Financial Times*, *London Review of Books*, *Politico*, and many others. His first book, *Nothing Is True and Everything Is Possible*, won the 2016 Royal Society of Literature Ondaatje Prize, and was nominated for the Samuel Johnson, *Guardian* First Book, Pushkin House, and Gordon Burns Prizes. It has been translated into more than a dozen languages.

PublicAffairs is a publishing house founded in 1997. It is a tribute to the standards, values, and flair of three persons who have served as mentors to countless reporters, writers, editors, and book people of all kinds, including me.

I. F. STONE, proprietor of *I. F. Stone's Weekly*, combined a commitment to the First Amendment with entrepreneurial zeal and reporting skill and became one of the great independent journalists in American history. At the age of eighty, Izzy published *The Trial of Socrates*, which was a national bestseller. He wrote the book after he taught himself ancient Greek.

BENJAMIN C. BRADLEE was for nearly thirty years the charismatic editorial leader of *The Washington Post*. It was Ben who gave the *Post* the range and courage to pursue such historic issues as Watergate. He supported his reporters with a tenacity that made them fearless and it is no accident that so many became authors of influential, best-selling books.

ROBERT L. BERNSTEIN, the chief executive of Random House for more than a quarter century, guided one of the nation's premier publishing houses. Bob was personally responsible for many books of political dissent and argument that challenged tyranny around the globe. He is also the founder and longtime chair of Human Rights Watch, one of the most respected human rights organizations in the world.

· · ·

For fifty years, the banner of Public Affairs Press was carried by its owner Morris B. Schnapper, who published Gandhi, Nasser, Toynbee, Truman, and about 1,500 other authors. In 1983, Schnapper was described by *The Washington Post* as "a redoubtable gadfly." His legacy will endure in the books to come.

Peter Osnos, *Founder*